a dakini book

GODWIN KELLY
MANMADE THUNDER

a dakini book in
partnership with

Contents

1 **How NASCAR got here** 6
NASCAR timeline **40**

2 **Drivers get all the attention** 44
The first race **60**
Smoking the competition **64**

3 **Paying homage to "King Richard"** 68
Where this madness started **88**

4 **Man in black** 92
Mill town racer **110**
Racing bloodlines **114**

5 **Modern-day prototype** 118
Tug-of-war **134**
Multiheaded mania **138**
Ray Evernham *First person* **142**

6 **A caged personality** 144
The original three-peat **164**
One season of glory **168**
Jimmie Johnson *First person* **172**

7 **The driver you don't know** 174
February 18, 2001 **188**
NASCAR's rush to improve safety **194**
Dale Earnhardt Jr. *First person* **200**

8 **Smoke and fire** 202
The guiding force **220**
Custer's last stand **224**

9 **Gentleman racer** 228
Racing for wins **244**
The best that never was **248**
Mark Martin *Questions & Answers* **252**

10 **A call to duty** 254
Understanding drivers **268**
Richard Childress *First person* **272**

11 **Young and restless** 276
Number-nerd's hero **288**
Kyle Busch *First person* **292**

12 **Indianapolis importance** 294
Stealing talent **308**
All in the family **312**

Index **318**

How NASCAR got here

1

Previous page Almost 200,000 speed freaks pack the grandstands at Daytona International Speedway to watch the 51st running of the Daytona 500, the first and most prestigious event on the NASCAR Sprint Cup Series schedule.

This is a special moment, before every NASCAR Sprint Cup Series event, when the pit crews get in formation on pit road for the singing of the national anthem. This is where the color and pageantry of stock-car racing is seen and heard, before the roar of the engines drowns out every other sound around the spectators and competitors. NASCAR started this tradition of pit crews lining up for the anthem in the late 1990s to give its pre-race activity a more professional look. During the anthem, all the commotion along pit road comes to a complete halt to honor country and flag.

It is the damnedest sight in sports. It happens not once, but twice a year. Mass gatherings of humanity, drawn to two spectacular venues – somewhat alike yet very different – to experience the drama produced by speed. There is excitement and anticipation and eagerness swirling in the air as competitors rush through checklists and spectators scramble to find their seats.

The people swarming through the gates make these moments quite special in the sport of stock-car racing, which is relatively young compared to the timelines of baseball or prizefighting. But unlike most professional games, these followers not only have passion, but possession. There is a sense of belonging and community among these beer-toting, cooler-carrying, whooping, RPM revelers.

They have arrived for a celebration, a celebration of speed, where they openly discuss their favorite drivers on a first-name basis, as if the men behind the steering wheels are next-door neighbors, good friends or first cousins. In no other sport are the participants and spectators so closely linked, bound together on intimate and emotional levels.

It is an extraordinary, goose-bumps-on-the-neck view when loitering on pit road in those hectic moments leading to the start of the Daytona 500 or the Allstate 400 at the Brickyard. Before you are thousands, *hundreds of thousands*, of race fans, most in brightly colored attire representing their favorite driver. They are stuffed into every nook and cranny of these massive racing facilities.

Daytona International Speedway in Daytona Beach, hosts the "Super Bowl of stock-car racing" each February, while stately Indianapolis Motor Speedway, the compound that helped define racing in the United States, annually holds the second-most important NASCAR Sprint Cup Series event, in the middle of summer, in the hub of America's heartland.

Daytona and Indianapolis are very special places in the world of motorsports; each with racing roots that stretch back more than 100

Dover International Speedway has a unique walkover bridge from the grandstand to the infield. Here, the NASCAR Cup Series stock cars shoot under the bridge during the Dodge Dealers 400. NASCAR, as a rule, doesn't like these type of structures because they obscure the view of the track. There are only three tracks on the Sprint Cup Series where spectators can't see the entire course: Indianapolis Motor Speedway, and the road course layouts at Sonoma, California, and Watkins Glen, New York.

... one last chance to exhale before a deafening wave of man-made thunder sweeps over the massive racetracks.

years. On race days, they are simply stunning, awash in color, music, spirit and electricity. The pits are alive with activity as each race team's adrenaline-fueled crewmen test air guns, run to fill gas cans, prep tires and conduct radio checks over their not-so-private, two-way radio systems.

On race days at both venues, there is that tiny gap in the day's schedule, generally situated between the national anthem and the command to fire engines, which sends a chill through those who thrive on the smell of race-car exhaust with a tinge of burnt rubber. It's the last time during these awesome afternoons that you can hear normal conversation, or cell phones screaming to their owners, or children pleading for a souvenir.

The public address announcer implores those fortunate enough to have pre-race access to "PLEASE, clear pit road!" At Daytona, there's the Sprint Tower, which juts 10 stories high at the start-finish line. The primary grandstand stretches half a mile. At Indy, it is a mesmerizing canyon of humanity, grandstands on either side of the front straightaway.

During that moment of relative silence, you get one last chance to exhale before a deafening wave of man-made thunder – 43 cars outfitted with super-powered, V-8 engines – sweeps over the massive racetracks. These two tracks share only one measurement: both are 2.5 miles in length. These are astonishing places (national treasures, really) and these racers, in their fully enclosed, purpose-built, kick-ass sedans, with hues that range from black to red to pink, will run at full song for more than three hours.

Just before and during the race, the stock cars are the star of the show. In the days leading up to a race, or in the days after a Sprint Cup Series event, it is the drivers who get most of the spotlight – you know, *today's*

When it rains on a NASCAR Sprint Cup Series race day, the action comes to a grinding halt. Unlike other forms of motorsports, stock cars can't race in the wet because they compete on slick tires with no grooved tread. Here, the No. 1 Earnhardt-Ganassi Racing Chevrolet of Martin Truex Jr. is protected from the elements by a thick, plastic covering while it sits patiently on pit road at Daytona.

Cleanup time at Richmond International Raceway. Mass pit stops leave all sorts of debris on pit road, everything from lug nuts to brake powder. After each stop, members of each pit crew must sweep up their mess. A lug nut or other piece of metal left on the surface for one stop, could lead to a tire puncture on the next stop.

NASCAR. There's glitz and glamour, and the top drivers are treated like rock stars. In the garage area or along bustling pit road before a racing event, stock-car racing's marquee competitors are swarmed by adoring fans. These worshipers appear to be making it their life's mission to nab a five-second photo-op or an autograph on a collectible. Once accomplished, their life's mission quickly focuses on the next driver within reach.

As for their part in this ritual dance, the drivers follow two fundamentals: Never stop walking, and only look forward, toward the horizon. Usually accompanied by their team-appointed public-relations handler, a driver sticks to his age-old rules. He looks straight ahead, a blank look in his eyes – eye contact is avoided, since it can only invite further interaction and, therefore, delays in a race day that's scripted right down to fractions of minutes.

He keeps walking, only glancing down occasionally as he signs the next item and hands it back as he navigates toward his race car or garage stall or drivers meeting. As he moves closer to the safe-haven of an off-limits-to-fans zone, the pace quickens. The walking and autographing gains momentum. At that point, he looks like a comet rocketing through the heavens, but instead of leaving a trail of ice and rock debris, he sheds eager and squealing race fans along the way.

One glance at the logo-laced transporters in the garage tells you there is big money in this sport; gigantic corporations, which have directed millions of marketing dollars into racing, have their names splashed on the sides of these open-road behemoths. Almost every race car has 30 or more corporate stickers strategically placed from the front fenders to the rear bumper.

And there are those tremendous crowds at Daytona and Indy. Daytona gets about 200,000 for its big race date, while Indy, which has the largest grandstand of any sports complex in the world, tickles the 300,000 mark each season for the 400, which became an "instant classic" because of the track's long, prestigious history of racing.

The No. 20 Joe Gibbs Racing/Home Depot team does its Spiderman impression by climbing the catch-fence after driver Tony Stewart won the 2005 Allstate 400 at the Brickyard. Earlier that season, after winning the Pepsi 400 at Daytona International Speedway, Stewart climbed all the way to the flag stand to collect the checkered flag. IndyCar Series driver Helio Castroneves made the fence climb famous after winning the 2001 Indianapolis 500. Different drivers do different things to celebrate a win; Carl Edwards does a back flip off his car, Denny Hamlin likes to do a tire burnout with the nose of his car against the retaining wall, and Kurt Busch drives the length of the course in reverse.

How NASCAR got here 15

Left A skilled painter adds a few last-minute touches to A.J. Foyt's stock car in 1974. The NASCAR detail painter has gone the way of the dinosaur. Many of today's Sprint Cup Series cars are now "wrapped" in a plastic coating, which is applied with moderate heat. Some teams still spray paint the base colors then apply decals for the detail work.

Right Fireball Roberts, here wearing his car owner's distinctive cowboy hat, listens to what his No. 22 Pontiac is trying to tell him in 1961. From 1959 to the 1962 Daytona 500, Roberts drove for Smokey Yunick, winning many of NASCAR's biggest races. Roberts was NASCAR's first breakout personality. Roberts never ran a full Grand National Series schedule, but still finished top 10 in season-ending points six times, including a runner-up championship finish during his rookie season in 1950.

Daytona is the first race on the schedule, and thus gets first crack at a racing populous that has been devoid of speed for nearly 12 weeks and obviously famished for sheet-metal competition. And, Indy is Indy, which for decades did not welcome the stock-car faithful into its temple.

It seems ridiculous today, but NASCAR was not always embraced with open arms at Speedway, Indiana. As a matter of fact, in one ugly episode, NASCAR founder William H.G. France was literally tossed out of the Indy garage area by the track's "Safety Patrol."

NASCAR was shunned for decades by the track, which was quite comfortable behind the walls of its closed society. From 1911 until 1993, the only cars allowed to compete at this facility were open-wheel – as in no fenders – race cars, designed by the greatest engineering minds and wheeled by the bravest men on the planet. The objective was simple. Go fast, and build a car that could withstand the punishment of 200 high-speed laps over this mammoth rectangle.

Since this was a secluded pond, the Indy-type race car had its own evolution, one worthy of a Darwin study. As time marched on, most of those competing at this venue looked down their noses at other forms of motorized racing, including those dolled-up sedans known as stock cars – derisively called "taxicabs" by the Indy loyalists. Back in the day, a simple suggestion of stock cars competing at Indianapolis would produce a burst of laughter from an open-wheel purist.

Stock cars? At Indy? Please.

But France, with his wildly absurd dreams, who started adult life as a Washington, D.C., auto mechanic, along with his two sons, changed all that. It took almost 50 years, and two generations, but the goal to bust through the gates of famed "Gasoline Alley" in their stock cars was eventually realized.

Indianapolis Motor Speedway, built as an automobile test track in 1909, is hallowed ground to racing enthusiasts, who, for years, made the pilgrimage to the Indianapolis 500 every May and turned it into one of the

Most race fans say they go to races to watch racing. Many won't admit they get a thrill from a good crash. Racing and crashing go hand-in-hand during many NASCAR events. Before there were Steel and Foam Energy Reduction (SAFER) barriers lining racetracks, there were concrete walls. Before there were concrete walls, there was guardrail, which wasn't very effective when heavy stock cars hit it at speeds in excess of 120 mph. Here, Eddie Pagan busts through the guardrail at Darlington Raceway during the 1958 Southern 500. The crash looks nasty, but Pagan miraculously walked away with only minor scrapes.

world's great sporting spectacles. Up through the 1980s, the IndyCar Series drew more attention and had more name recognition among the motorhead population.

NASCAR has since developed into a sport with mass appeal. How does a sport know it has gained national attention? When the gossipy, American tabloids start reporting about the personal lives of drivers. They had a field day when Jeff Gordon's first wife, Brooke, filed for divorce. And there was that 2004 Spring Break episode in Panama City, Florida, when the *National Enquirer* reported on a group of young NASCAR drivers enjoying a booze-soaked weekend that included naked hot-tubbing on the pool deck of a private condo.

NASCAR competitors may have enjoyed clothes-optional parties in the early days, but nobody paid much attention, because performance, not personality, ruled the early years. From its start in 1948 through most of the 1970s, NASCAR racing was a regional sports oddity. Its fan base, mostly blue-collar, low-income, beer-guzzling males, was rooted in the Southeast. The most intense interest in this form of racing came from the Carolinas and Virginia, where France, known as "Big Bill" to competitors, scheduled a majority of events. He did all this conducting from his home base in Daytona Beach, which was another major incubation area for automobile development and, of course, speed. Indianapolis was built by man. Daytona got a big assist from nature, long before an asphalt course was imagined and put in place.

Daytona has a wide, hard-packed, pearly-white sand beach that stretches for more than 23 miles. When the automobile was born, it didn't take long for the smoke-belching mechanical beast to sniff out this patch of smooth sand, a drag strip and motorcar test facility crafted by the hands of Mother Nature. One speed-addicted competitor described the sand course as the perfect racetrack. "It's the only place in the world where it is possible to reach such a speed. No other straightaway speedway is long enough, or smooth and resilient enough."

18 Man-made Thunder

In recent years, Sprint Cup helmets have become a way for drivers to express themselves. The art form actually started in the ranks of motorcycle racers then jumped to stock cars, especially among younger drivers who have image-shaping sponsors. This helmet belongs to Dale Earnhardt Jr. The helmets, without a design, fetch a price near $1,000. No telling what the airbrush artist gets for a unique piece of work.

Some race fans will do anything to get into the Daytona 500 without a ticket! Actually, this was a pre-race, jet-pack demonstration before the 2004 Daytona 500 at Daytona International Speedway. This was a handmade contraption that was fueled by hydrogen peroxide.

The beach hosted its first "race" in 1903, and the area around Daytona Beach quickly morphed into the world's premier Land Speed Record site. This idea of performance-testing new automobile designs started in 1903 when Horace Thomas and Alexander Winton each bravely saddled aboard hand-crafted cars and charged down the beach in a spirited, side-by-side competition. Thomas was a driver-for-hire aboard a Ransom Olds design, the "Pirate," which was mounted on bicycle tires, while Winton was riding high aboard a car he built himself and dubbed "Bullet Number 1." They raced on the sand in Ormond Beach, Florida, just north of Daytona, in the inaugural Ormond Challenge Cup sprint race.

This was a full eight years before Ray Harroun crossed the finish line to win the inaugural Indianapolis 500. While reporting from the seaside resort was limited in those days, there were two consistencies about the first duel in the sand between Thomas and Winton. The two men reached a breakneck speed in excess of 50 mph, and at the finish line, Winton beat Thomas by one-fifth of a second. The speed revolution was about to take Daytona Beach by storm – a loud, fast-moving, dangerous sandstorm.

The contest between Thomas and Winton soon turned into an annual event, labeled by promoters as "Winter Speed Carnivals" and "International World's Championships." Along the way, Ormond Beach earned the nickname "Birthplace of Speed" as thrill-seeking men pushed the envelope of four-wheeled propulsion. Henry Flagler – railroad man, hotelier and promoter – catered to these men of derring-do by opening the Ormond Garage in 1904. The garage was nothing more than a barn-like structure built on a street that dead-ended at the beach, but the last names of the men who toiled in the facility are recognized to this day – Olds, Ford and Chevrolet.

In a handful of years, the 50-mph mark reached in 1903 looked laughable. A competitor's goal was simple enough: go faster than any human had traveled in the short history of mankind's motorized land travel. There were plenty of takers. The 120-mph mark had been achieved

Previous page Men of speed go where the speed is, which is why Bobby Isaac found himself on the Bonneville (Utah) Salt Flats in the late summer of 1971. His team dressed up his stock car for a straight-line pass through the Measured Mile. Isaac was clocked at 216.945 mph. More recently, Rusty Wallace made an "unrestricted" run – wheeling a stock car without a restrictor plate – at Talladega Superspeedway and topped the 230-mph mark.

Right The No. 24, leaves the competition in the dust during a classic NASCAR Grand National Series dirt race in the 1950s. Most NASCAR races were held on small, dirt ovals in the first 10 years of the racing series.

Next Page Dale Earnhardt Jr. gets his photo taken so often, he's oblivious to cameras. Here, he's leaning up against the pit box before the start of a practice session at Dover International Speedway in 2008.

in the first decade of racing on the beach. Starting in 1911, the goal of these daredevils and their designers was to top the magic 200-mph mark. In 1911, less than a decade after the first beach sprint, speed freaks were topping the 140-mph mark through the Measured Mile.

The rules for competing for the Land Speed Record are simple and exist to this day – make two timed runs in opposite directions through a Measured Mile within an hour. Cars get a long run-up to build momentum then blast through the mile course at full speed. Within 60 minutes, the car must reverse course and go back through the speed trap. The two speeds are then averaged together. Most of these speed runs in today happen on the Bonneville (Utah) Salt Flats and are sanctioned by the Southern California Timing Association. Renowned American racer Barney Oldfield, who cruised through Daytona's Measured Mile at over 130 mph in 1910, said roaring down the beach at that speed was like "the sensation of riding a rocket through space."

The 200-mph barrier was achieved in 1927, but the great gush to speed turned into a trickle by the end of the 1920s.

The 200-mph barrier was achieved in 1927, but the great gush to speed turned into a trickle by the end of the 1920s. In 1935, only one car and driver arrived to make a valiant charge down the beach. Sir Malcolm Campbell, an upright, chest-out, chin-up Englishman, arrived in Daytona to make one last attempt at the elusive 300-mph mark. To achieve this, he brought with him his famed "Bluebird," which weighed five tons and had a tail similar to an airplane's rudder. His massive machine was powered by a Rolls-Royce aircraft piston engine that produced more than 2,700 horsepower.

Campbell, they say, was possessed by speed. On March 7, 1935, he reached 330 mph on his first run, but the friction caused by the weight of the car and the blistering speeds shredded much of his tire tread. As a result,

NASCAR stock-car racing is pure American, a sport started in the South, which now has interest in all corners of the country. The Daytona 500 is the "Great American Race" while Texas Motor Speedway is the "Great American Track." Before every NASCAR race, a prayer is given and the national anthem is sung, usually by a famous entertainer.

Next page There is nothing in sports more exciting than watching a large pack of NASCAR stock cars thundering by at speeds approaching 200 mph. The action at Daytona International Speedway and Talladega Superspeedway are particularly enthralling because the stock cars race so close together for lap after lap. If you get up to the grandstand fence during a Sprint Cup Series race at Daytona, the wind wake caused by the cars moving in unison can blow a hat right off your head. It's so hypnotic that security must shoo away spectators for their own safety.

his return through the Measured Mile was more like a limp. Campbell's average speed of his two sprints was 276.820 mph – short of 300, but good enough for the world's Land Speed Record.

One of those curious people to see Campbell's strange-looking speed machine was "Big Bill" France, then a young, tall, lanky mechanic, who raced cars in his spare time. France had just moved to Daytona Beach with his wife Anne and their toddler son Bill Jr. from the Washington, D.C., area. The reason? France had had enough of the bitter cold and snowstorms that frequented the nation's capital. He wanted to grab a piece of paradise, so he loaded up his Hupmobile and rattled down to Florida with spouse and child in tow.

France was thinking he would settle in South Florida, but a stop along the highway changed that. Once he took a gander at the beach and other areas around Daytona, France decided to settle in the quiet Central Florida town, taking a job as a mechanic with a small car dealership. Within a year, he owned a gas station on Daytona's Main Street.

Meanwhile, the city fathers were fretting over the loss of the speed barons, whose well-publicized breakneck dashes helped fill motel rooms in the winter months. "Without racing, Daytona Beach would be like a prizefighter with a wooden leg," said one city official. The City of Daytona Beach wanted to continue its racing legacy, and it created a unique and enticing racecourse. Competitors would race north up the beach, make a hard left through an opening in the dunes that connected the beach to the A1A highway, then race south on the A1A blacktop before returning through another opening to the sand straightaway.

The city lost thousands of dollars on the 1936 project. The Elks Club tried its hand at the race in 1937, but forfeited most of its treasury. Enter France, who had some connections in racing and offered to test his race-promoting potential. He formed a partnership with restaurant owner Charlie Reese, who provided the front money for the project. With Reese's business savvy and France's young but apparent promoting skills, the two men made a profit. France had found his calling, and in

These race haulers, lined up in the garage area at Texas Motor Speedway, have little resemblance to stock-car haulers of NASCAR's past. Today's haulers are outfitted with all the tools necessary to maintain the cars and have several creature comforts, such as air-conditioned lounge areas and satellite TV.

Bobby Allison enjoys the last drops from a champagne bottle, the sweet taste of victory, after his triumph in 1981 at Alabama International Motor Speedway, now Talladega Superspeedway.

the mid-1940s he began scheduling events at little dirt tracks scattered throughout the South. Racing was a willy-nilly affair in those days. It had no direction and, much to the despair of the racers, very little conscience.

Unscrupulous promoters would set up an event, promise a big purse, then head out the back door with gate receipts while the cars were still turning laps. That made life tough on honest promoters, such as France, who made a living by matching venues with competitors. On December 14, 1947, France called a summit that included promoters, drivers, mechanics and car owners. They met inside the Ebony Lounge atop the Streamline Hotel in Daytona Beach, and as they filled ashtrays and emptied cocktail glasses, they hammered out the parameters of a national sanctioning body. They called it the National Association for Stock Car Auto Racing, or NASCAR, for short.

The "Strictly Stock" division soon became NASCAR's marquee racing division, attracting not only the interest of race fans, who could easily identify with the cars that looked like the vehicles parked in their garages,

> *... as they filled ashtrays and emptied cocktail glasses, they hammered out the parameters of a national sanctioning body.*

but car manufacturers, who saw this form of racing as a marketing tool to push product. It was either a stroke of genius or an obvious business model that had just been sitting there waiting for someone to take advantage of it.

The first Strictly Stock race (now known as the Sprint Cup Series) was held in Charlotte, North Carolina, where more than 10,000 spectators gathered to watch the historic race. That was a massive crowd in those early years of the sport trying to find its footing. No large transporters, either. The racers of the 1950s, and even into the '60s, showed up at the track towing a race car behind a pickup truck or a passenger car. The best drivers had a mechanic, but for the most part, relied on friends and volunteers to service the car during pit stops.

32 Man-made Thunder

LOOMIS
www.dupont.com
DUPONT
The miracles of science
EAGLE
BOSCH Spark Plugs
HAAS
UGS
sparco

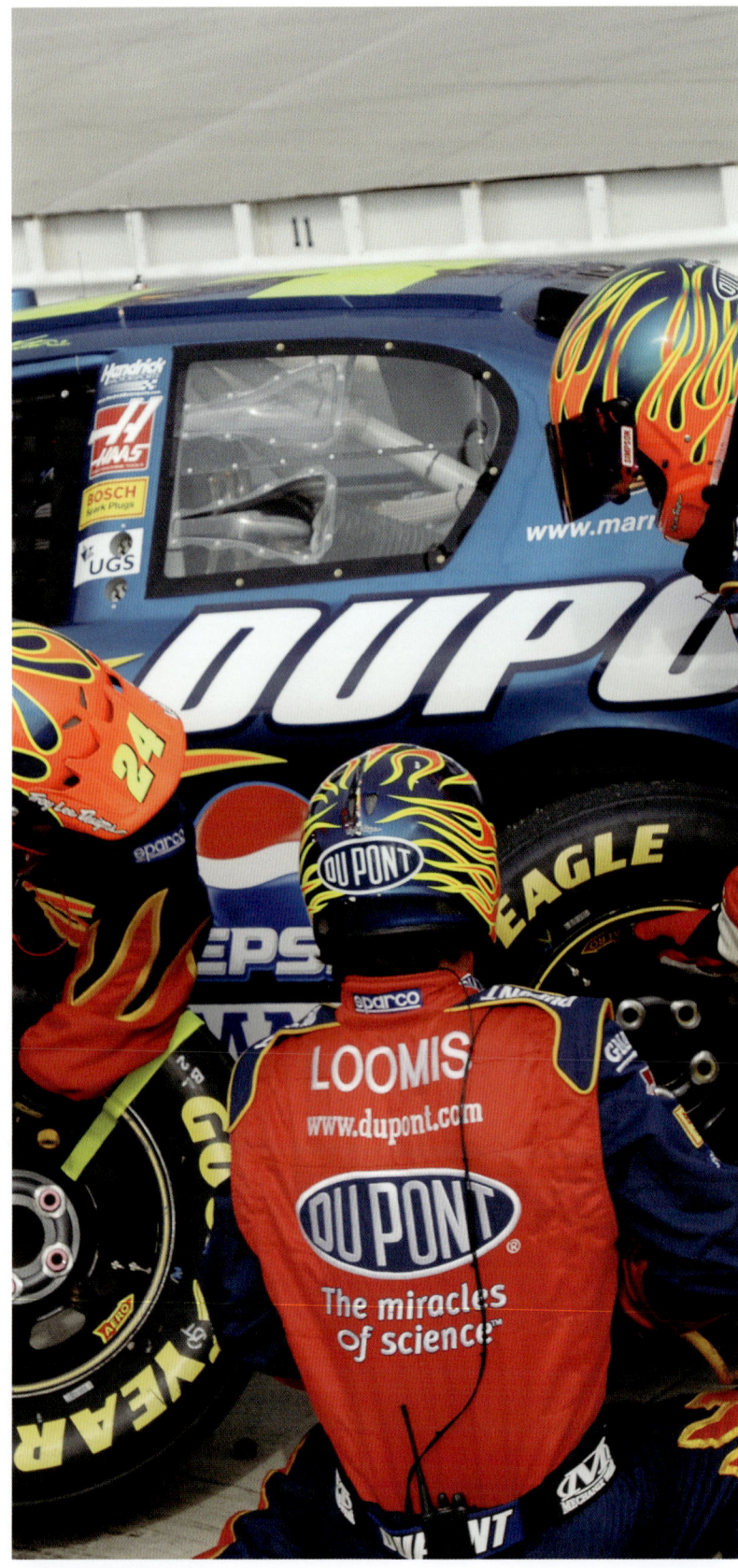

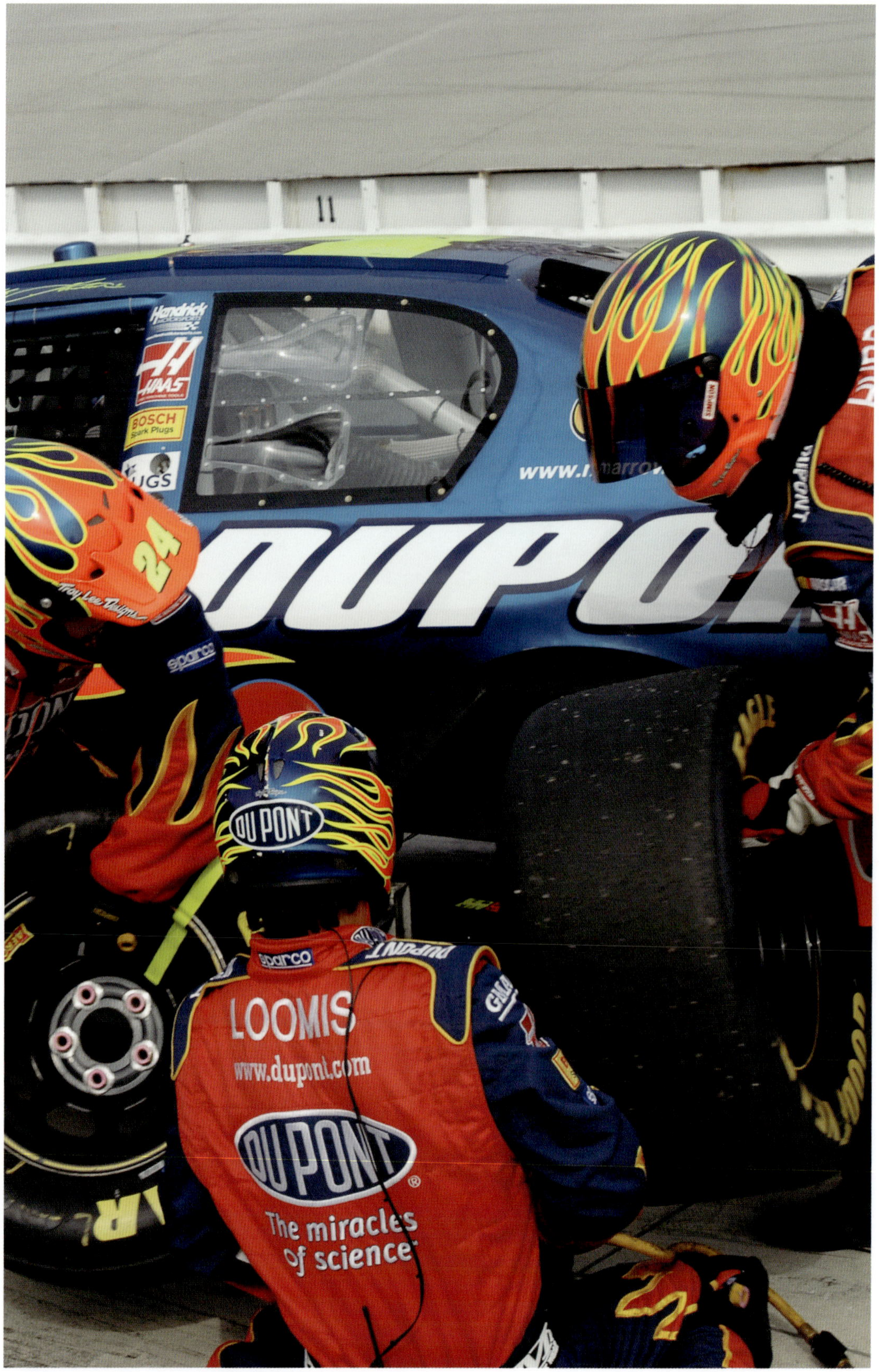
LOOMIS
www.dupont.com
DUPONT
The miracles of science
BOSCH Spark Plugs
HAAS
UGS
sparco

A Sprint Cup race team pit stop is like a choreographed dance. Seven people, mostly young, strong men, go over the wall to service the car. There are two tire changers, a jackman, two tire carriers, the gas man and the catch-can man. In this sequence of photos, you see Jeff Gordon's pit crew replacing the left-rear tire of the No. 24 Hendrick Motorsports Chevrolet. In the two photos at the left, the jackman and catch-can man assist the rear-tire changer with swapping out the tire. The tire changer's only concern should be removing then reapplying the five lug nuts on each wheel.

In the photo on the immediate left, the catch-can man heads to the pit wall rolling the left-rear tire with his left hand and carrying the catch-can can in the other. A pit crew member must "catch" any gas that comes through the overflow valve at the rear of the car. A four-tire stop averages under 15 seconds. Many elite teams have a pit-stop coach, who will video every stop then review performance the following week. Pit crews constantly practice at their racing facilities. Many shops have a practice area including a short, concrete wall simulating a pit wall. Many of these over-the-wall people have a rigorous workout routine to stay in peak physical condition.

How NASCAR got here 35

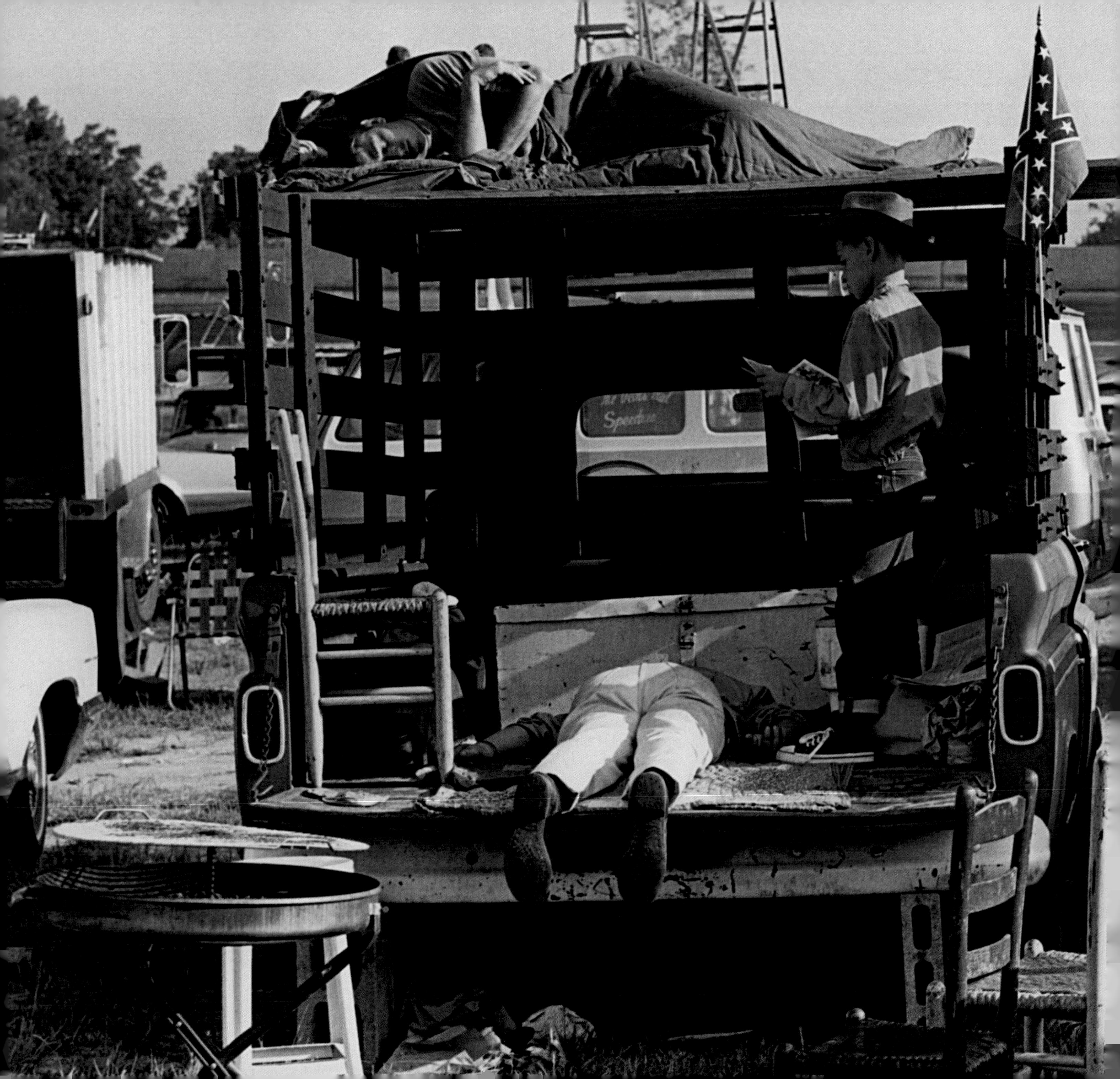

Just call it the "infield way" – those die-hard race fans who camp in the infield of their favorite racetrack for a NASCAR event. This photo is from the days leading up to the 1968 Southern 500 at Darlington Raceway. It looks like dad has passed out in the back of his truck while his son amuses himself with a good comic book. Today, fans are armed with RVs and the kids can play with their portable gaming devices.

Back in the day, before racetracks offered concerts or a midway area, race fans had to make their own fun at the facility. Here a group of young men have some fun with a barrel full of water, probably to beat the summer heat. If you look closely, there is somebody submerged in the barrel. To this day, there's always some sort of action going on in the infield.

Sponsors were practically nonexistent. Competitors were vagabonds going race-to-race and feeding off a limited pool of prize money. They were often shunned by the general populace, and categorized on the social scale somewhere between carnival folks and gypsies. They were, by nature, loud and somewhat crude, and after working on and under race cars all day, they looked dirty and smelled worse. Their dialogue was generally laced with profanities.

They lived on the edge and partied like there would be no tomorrow – for the men behind the wheel, sometimes there was no tomorrow. They played an extremely dangerous game and either genuinely needed to blow off that anxiety, or used that as a convenient excuse. Because of their death-defying work and mobile lifestyle, these early-day racers attracted their share of female fans. The James Dean–like "bad boy" effect was in full play.

No wonder stock-car racers weren't always received with open arms by the townspeople located near racetracks. In his autobiography, Smokey Yunick says, "I don't want to leave the impression that all racers were wild, drunk, womanizers – just 80 percent of us."

Those anything-goes days are all but gone, except the occasional Spring Break foray. Most drivers stay on the straight and narrow, because one ugly or unseemly incident could be a career stopper. There is too much corporate money – tens of millions of dollars per car – on the line for a driver to get their name in the headlines for all the wrong reasons.

How did the National Association for Stock Car Auto Racing get to this point? At first, it was strictly the cars, but now it's the drivers, their personalities, the way they drive, where they drive and their ongoing interactions. They generally all get along, but there is conflict, which creates a weekend-to-weekend soap opera–like storyline, which strings one race to the next.

As the personalities have grown, so has the sport. First, it was NASCAR leaving the dirt tracks in the dust, and then it was a calculated expansion to opulent racetracks near the nation's top urban areas. The interest

A pair of NASCAR Modifieds sit tangled and abandoned in this dirt track race from the early 1950s. In those days, if a race car was too badly damaged the owner would just leave it at the racetrack and let the promoter worry about it. The track owner could salvage parts or have it moved to the scrap yard. Most of these cars were towed to an event behind a passenger car. It would have been too costly to have them towed back to the owner's race shop.

Today's race fans not only enjoy the action on the track, but want to see their favorite drivers talk about the sport. There is always a mob at the SPEED Stage, which is present at every NASCAR Sprint Cup Series event. If fans can't be at the track, they watch Cup racing on TV. Sprint Cup races generally beat all other sports competitions broadcast during a weekend, and NASCAR is second only to the NFL in terms of TV ratings.

was fueled by television broadcasts of all events by the mid-1980s. The growing audience and TV ratings pulled in more corporate sponsorship dollars, and by the end of the 1990s, NASCAR was considered a major-league sport along with the likes of the NFL, MLB, NHL and NBA.

One of the first superspeedways (in NASCAR jargon, that means an oval-shaped track longer than a mile) to be built was the giant constructed by France and opened in 1959. France knew the romantic days of racing on Daytona's Beach & Road Course were numbered because of encroaching development, and he wanted to construct a stand-alone racetrack, one that would rival the great Indianapolis Motor Speedway in size and scope.

France started talking about the speedway project in the early 1950s, and by the end of the decade, after years of planning, sweat and extreme financial risk-taking, he opened Daytona International Speedway in 1959 at the cost of about $3 million. It was the same length as Indy, 2.5 miles, but roughly shaped like a "D." And its turns were sweeping and enormous, soaring three stories high and banked at 31 degrees.

It took several years to get the speedway in the black financially. Through the mid-1960s, "Big Bill" and his wife Anne would have to annually mortgage their house to have enough cash for front-money expenses to jump-start the Speedweeks program. Fast cars and a big pile of prize money were the keys to the success of Daytona International Speedway.

One of NASCAR's biggest coups was landing a race date at Indianapolis in 1994. It gave stock-car racing a new boost of self-esteem, while uniting two gigantic rivals in North American motorsports. The marriage of Daytona Beach–based NASCAR and Indianapolis was almost a half century in the making. Ironically, NASCAR would also displace Indy-style racing as the top form of motorsports in America and, eventually, run one of its most prestigious races in the heart of open-wheel racing country.

Stock cars at Indianapolis? No one is laughing now. ■

38 Man-made Thunder

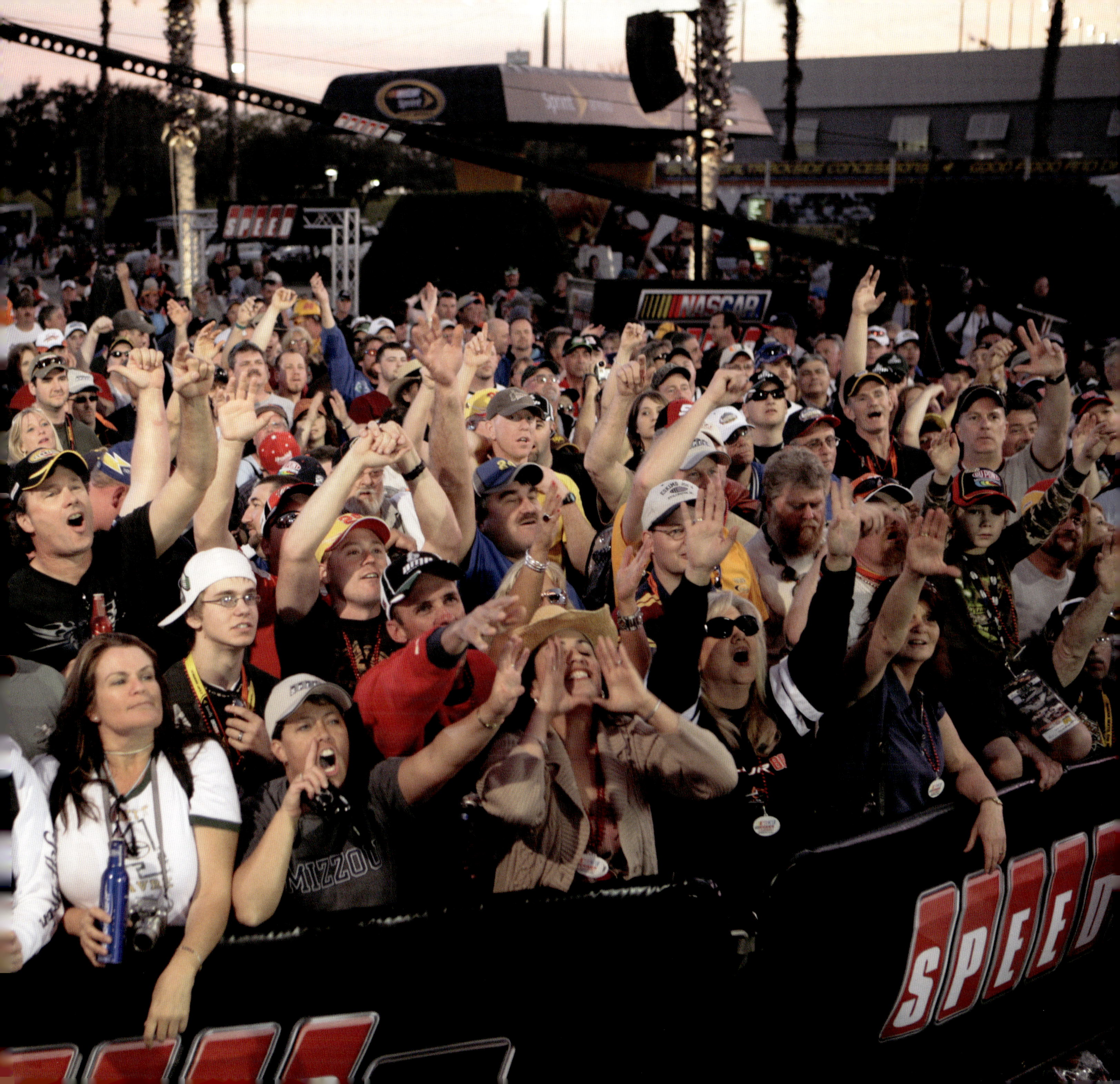
SPEED
NASCAR
MIZZOU
SPEED

William H.G. France brings together all significant players in the rogue world of stock-car racing for a conference at the Streamline Hotel in Daytona Beach, Florida, on December 14, 1947. From that gathering, France created NASCAR, officially incorporating the private company on February 21, 1948.

NASCAR adds the "Strictly Stock" series to its offerings in 1949. Today, that national tour is called the Sprint Cup Series. The series' name progression is as follows: Strictly Stock, 1949; Grand National, 1950–70; Winston Cup Grand National, 1971–85; Winston Cup, 1986–2003; Nextel Cup, 2004–07; Sprint Cup, 2008.

Jim Roper, from Halstead, Kansas, who read about the race in a nationally syndicated cartoon strip, won the inaugural Strictly Stock event at Charlotte Speedway, a three-quarter-mile dirt oval. The date of the race was June 19, 1949.

Red Byron, of Anniston, Alabama, captures the 1949 championship, winning two out of eight races.

In 1950, NASCAR stages its first 500-mile race on a superspeedway (paved ovals longer than one mile) at Darlington Raceway.

Larry Mann becomes the first NASCAR driver to die in a Grand National race, at Langhorne Speedway in Pennsylania, on September 14, 1952.

thrill 1947 1949

victory 1950 1952

NASCAR timeline

Since the National Association for Stock Car Auto Racing was formed in 1948, the sport of stock-car racing has seen many highs and lows, and either thrived on or recovered from numerous milestone experiences that helped shape the course of its manifestation from a rural Southern sport to a national pastime. This is a condensed timeline of events that will take you rapidly through NASCAR's history.

"It's the darndest thing you ever saw. It's the Hollywood of racing. For the man who really wants to race, this is it."
Buck Baker, Daytona International Speedway, 1959

tension stakes

1959
Daytona International Speedway, built by France on a shoestring budget, opens in 1959. The first Daytona 500 was staged on February 22, 1959, but after a photo finish, Lee Petty isn't declared the winner until three days later.

1960
Atlanta International Raceway and Charlotte Motor Speedway, both tracks over 1.5 miles long, open in 1960, ushering in a new age of high-speed competition.

1961
ABC Sports becomes the first network to broadcast a NASCAR race. ABC used snippets of Daytona's Firecracker 250 on its "Wide World of Sports" anthology show on July 16, 1961.

1964–65
NASCAR endures a troubling flurry of driver deaths – six of them during the 1964–65 seasons. The drivers who died were: Joe Weatherly, Glenn "Fireball" Roberts, Jimmy Pardue, Billy Wade, Buren Skeen and Harold Kite. Pardue and Wade died in tire tests at Charlotte and Daytona. Two important pieces of safety equipment emerged from the carnage: Goodyear developed the inner-liner – a tire within a tire – while Firestone created a rubber bladder to keep fuel from spilling from the gas tank in the event of a crash.

1969
Alabama International Speedway, built by France, opens in 1969. It is bigger and faster than Daytona. The Professional Drivers Association declines to compete in the first race, claiming it's too dangerous. France cobbles together a field of 36 cars and the win goes to Richard Brickhouse, his lone victory in 39 career NASCAR starts.

1971
R.J. Reynolds Tobacco Co., through its Winston brand of cigarette, signs on as sponsor of NASCAR's marquee series, a union that would last through 2003. RJR pumps millions of dollars into NASCAR and is largely credited with showing NASCAR how to promote the sport.

> "There will be a race tomorrow. If you don't want to be in it, pack up and leave."
> William H.G. France, Talladega boycott, 1969

> "He went beneath me and his car broke loose. I got into the wall and came off and hit him."
> David Pearson, Daytona 500, 1976

On January 11, 1972, Bill France hands the NASCAR office keys to his oldest son, William C. France ("Bill Jr."). Also in '72, NASCAR streamlines the Winston Cup Grand National Series to 31 events (from 48 the previous season), all now on paved racetracks.

CBS Sports is the first network to offer live, flag-to-flag coverage of the Daytona 500, in 1979. The race ends with a fight in the infield between Cale Yarborough and brothers Bobby and Donnie Allison. The race proves to be a TV ratings bonanza.

The "200-mph Club" opens for business when driver Benny Parsons tops the magic mark during qualifying for the 1982 Winston 500 at Talladega. His average speed over the 2.66-mile tri-oval was 200.176 mph.

Richard Petty wins his 200th Sprint Cup Series race at Daytona on July 4, 1984, the Firecracker 400, with President Ronald Reagan watching from a VIP suite.

Bill Elliott enjoys the season of a lifetime in 1985, winning 11 superspeedway races and earning a $1 million bonus for winning three of NASCAR's top four races. The feat lands Elliott on the cover of America's premier sporting magazine, *Sports Illustrated*.

Elliott records the fastest lap in NASCAR history when he tops 212 mph in qualifying for the 1987 Winston 500 at Talladega. A dramatic accident during the race ended the "200-mph Club" and ushered in the restrictor-plate era at Daytona and Talladega.

In 1989, every Winston Cup Series race is televised live.

spirit

magic

1972 1979 1982 1984 1985 1987 1989

"Why do these people hate me? I ain't never done anything to them."
Darrell Waltrip, Atlanta 500, 1980

"I said goodbye to my brothers, on pit road, because I didn't know if I would ever see them again."
Bill Elliott, Daytona 500 qualifying, 1987

42 Man-made thunder

Richard Petty retires as a driver after competing in the 1992 Hooters 500 at Atlanta International Raceway, while a hot prospect, young Jeff Gordon, makes his first start in NASCAR's top division.

The NASCAR Winston Cup Series is allowed to hold a 400-mile race at Indianapolis Motor Speedway, on August 6, 1994. Also in '94, Dale Earnhardt ties Richard Petty in career championships with seven.

NASCAR's groundbreaking $2.4 billion television contract is activated for Daytona Speedweeks in 2001 as Dodge returns to compete in the Sprint Cup Series after a two-decade hiatus.

Dale Earnhardt is killed on the last lap of the 2001 Daytona 500 – the fourth NASCAR driver to die in a 12-month period. NASCAR ramps up its safety program.

Bill France Jr., who is in failing health, turns control of NASCAR over to his son, Brian Z. France, who is given the titles of CEO and chairman of the private corporation in September 2003.

In 2004, Nextel, a wireless-phone company, is awarded naming rights to NASCAR's top series, replacing outgoing Winston (Nextel would later merge with Sprint and the series is renamed Sprint Cup Series in 2008). The '04 season also sees the introduction of the "Chase," a playoff-like format pitting the series' top 10 drivers in a 10-race championship battle.

NASCAR's "Car of Tomorrow" makes its debut at Bristol Motor Speedway on March 25, 2007. The COT was designed with eyes toward safety and cost management.

speed dreams

1992 **1994** **2001** **2003** **2004** **2007**

"When you beat Dale Earnhardt you know you've done a good day's work."
Dale Jarrett, Daytona 500, 1993

"You have to drive in like a gentleman and out like an animal."
Juan Pablo Montoya, describing Martinsville, 2008

How NASCAR got here   43

29
28
REFUEL
Office DEPOT
14
Old Spice
Office DEPOT
Budweiser
SHOOTOUT
AT DAYTONA
CHEVY
Budweiser
SHOOTOUT
NASCAR
Sprint
CUP SERIES

Drivers get all the attention

2

Previous page All the world's a stage, for NASCAR Sprint Cup Series drivers, who are constantly trotted out for public inspection. Here, the Chevrolet drivers are introduced like rock stars before the 2009 Budweiser Shootout at Daytona International Speedway.

Left The 1939 Ford Modified race car that took driver Red Byron to victory in the first NASCAR-sanctioned race on the Daytona Beach & Road Course on February 15, 1948. The car, owned by Raymond Parks, was on display in the Sprint FANZONE area at Daytona International Speedway in February, 2009. Byron and Parks would team up again in 1949 to capture NASCAR's "Strictly Stock" championship, a series featuring passenger car sedans. Today the series is known as the Sprint Cup Series.

Right NASCAR track owners would do about anything to sell tickets in the mid-1960s, such as have beautiful women wave checkered flags in front of stationary stock cars for a promotional photograph. In this case, the front row of the 1967 World 600 at Charlotte Motor Speedway, pole winner Darel Dieringer, left, and Cale Yarborough.

After a relatively easy birth in 1948, the father of NASCAR was tasked with keeping his infant sanctioning body alive. As any dad knows, conceiving the baby is the easy part, and so it was with NASCAR. William H.G. France threw a cocktail party with business acquaintances at a beachside bar in Daytona Beach, Florida. The gathering of stock-car stakeholders in the Ebony Lounge atop the Streamline Hotel wasn't akin to Thomas Jefferson and compatriots drafting the Declaration of Independence, but France was able to hammer out a standard set of rules to give stock-car racing some shape and form and boundaries. Staying in business, gaining acceptance, and growing the balance sheet of the private corporation would be the tricky part of this new venture. Anybody can develop a store that sells women's undergarments, but there's only one Victoria's Secret.

And so it was with France, who opened the NASCAR storefront and quickly needed to establish the sanctioning body's identity, intent and solvency. He had successfully initiated the enterprise, but needed customers – actually three types of patrons – to keep this operation in an upward and fiscally rewarding motion. First, he had to lure promoters with racetracks, then get enough cars and drivers to compete in a race, and finally he had to attract people willing to pay for the privilege of sitting in the bleachers to watch this motorized, dust-bowl madness. France didn't own racetracks, race cars or race drivers, per se. He was the ultimate middleman. He would establish a race date then woo race teams and spectators to the venue. Handbills and press releases, hand-delivered to local newspapers and radio stations, were the favored (and inexpensive) methods of advertising.

Crude billboards, announcing an upcoming race, were plastered on the sides and A-frame roofs of barns throughout the rural Southeast. In town, posters were nailed to utility poles. The participating track would pay NASCAR a sanctioning fee for its services – a business arrangement that still holds today. Once the competitors assembled, France's small team of officials made sure the cars conformed to NASCAR rules, then his

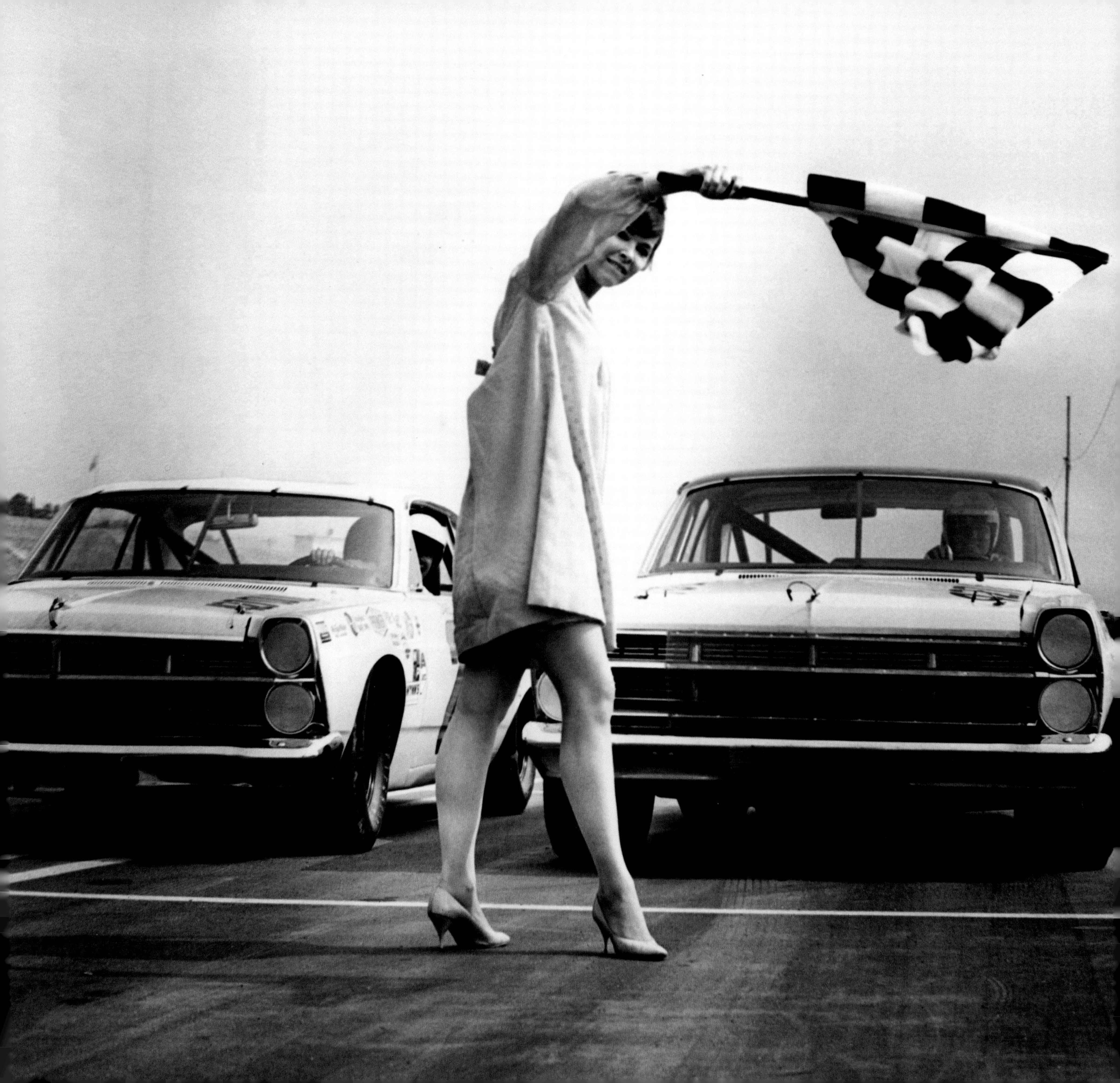

48   Man-made Thunder

There was no soft-wall technology for NASCAR Modifieds in the 1950s – unless you consider wood fencing soft. This safety crew looks a bit befuddled on what to do with this wrecked race car.

team timed and scored the event. When it was over, the stock-car circus would pack up and scurry on to the next racetrack and race date. The entire routine – from advertising to inspecting to dropping the checkered flag – would begin anew.

Back in NASCAR's formative years, France had the luxury of adjusting the season's race schedule on the fly, which is why the Sprint Cup Series schedule of yore had 40, 50 races – one time more than 60 – on the annual calendar. Nothing special happened that first year ('48) of racing, except that NASCAR distributed a year-ending points purse. NASCAR sanctioned 52 Modified races at dirt tracks across the South. Red Byron won NASCAR's first sanctioned race on the Daytona Beach & Road Course, then captured the Modified championship and $1,250 in first-place points money. No spark or drama to speak of, other than the July 25 death of W.R. "Slick" Davis, who lost his life after crashing in a race staged in Greensboro, North Carolina. He was the first driver to die in any form of NASCAR racing.

The game changer for France happened in NASCAR's second year. It was the "Strictly Stock" series concept – passenger cars rigged with modest safety features – that differentiated NASCAR from the competing sanctioning bodies that relied solely on Modifieds and Sportsman cars to fill fields. Many of those car bodies pre-dated World War II and did not reflect Detroit's contemporary designs. The Mods had body parts missing or altered to give the cars a sportier look and, in some cases, improve performance. The engines were unrestricted brutes that generated incredible horsepower numbers. They were ugly ducklings, but quick and noisy. Those kinds of cars raced from North Carolina to California, under the banners of different organizations.

France's reach was limited to the country's Southern territories. France's "Strictly Stock" idea was something entirely new and it quickly appealed to a greater pool of potential customers – generally speaking, anybody who had a Plymouth, Lincoln, Oldsmobile, Hudson or Studebaker tucked away in their garage and a love of driving in their heart. When the

Left These NASCAR Modified drivers of the 1950s were brave souls, here pictured in their race wear – everything from garage jumpsuits to white T-shirts.

Right Herb Nab, one of the greatest mechanics in NASCAR history, inspects the underside of a V-8 race engine at the Holman Moody race shop in Charlotte. Nab nabbed two Daytona 500 victories as a crew chief at Junior Johnson Racing.

series debuted midway through the 1949 racing season, it was an instant success. According to the race report from the inaugural Sprint Cup Series event at Charlotte Speedway on June 19, 33 cars competed, and 13,000 watched Kansas farmer Jim Roper become a footnote in NASCAR history.

Even if that attendance figure was inflated it was still a good crowd. Those were the kinds of numbers that made frugal promoters hum and whistle as they wrote their sanction-fee checks to NASCAR. France was no idiot.

He had stumbled upon a winning formula and quickly started to build image by changing the name of the series in 1950 from the mundane "Strictly Stock" to the more romantic "Grand National," a term with a strong association to prestigious horse racing. Hey, racing is racing. There were only eight races in that inaugural season. In 1950, under the new name, France scheduled 19 events, including a 500-mile, showcase spectacle at Darlington Raceway. Figuring you can't get enough of a good thing, the Grand National Series ballooned to 41 racing events in 1951. This

sedan racing caught fire in the '50s, as noted by Tom Wolfe in a piece he wrote for *Esquire* back in the mid-1960s. Wolfe observed: "Stock-car racing was building up a terrific following in the South during the early Fifties. Here was a sport not using any abstract devices, any bat and ball, but the same automobile that was changing a man's own life, his own symbol of liberation, and it didn't require size, strength and all that, all it required was a taste for speed, and the guts."

By now it wasn't just promoters, car owners/drivers and spectators taking an interest in this curious new form of racing. France and his teeny sanctioning body were catching the eye of Detroit, which was trying to sell domestic sedans after five years as the United States' primary war merchant. For instance, during World War II, General Motors transformed all of its auto plants – some 200 facilities – into factories that turned out everything from pistols to planes. Management scholar Peter Drucker once said, "General Motors won the war for America." Give an assist to Ford and Chrysler, too.

Drivers get all the attention   51

LEAKE'S AMOCO
860 N. LIBERTY
10
FRICTION PROOFING
H.HOLDER
ARNEY SHORE
97

It's hard enough to race a stock car, let alone try to peek around a popped-up hood. Driver Harry Leake makes the best of a bad situation during a NASCAR Convertible Series race in 1958, while Barney Shore tries to ease around the problem-plagued car. The Convertible Series seemed like a good idea, but lasted only four seasons, 1956–59.

Next page As the sun fades over Darlington Raceway, the action is heating up on the racetrack. Drivers say their stock cars handle better during night races because the track surface is cool and gives the tires more grip.

With the war over, those tax dollars stopped gushing in from Washington, D.C., so GM and its rivals had to go back to building and marketing cars for the public. In the late 1940s, when passenger-car production resumed, France appeared at America's automobile manufacturing doorstep, and to the Detroit barons, he must've looked like a street urchin with a tin can. At the start of the 1950s, boasting modest success with this newfangled racing idea, France was now getting some winks and grins from an industry eager to market its wares.

France wasn't PhD smart. He was street wise. He didn't have outstanding business acumen. His wife, Anne, handled the book work and balanced the numbers; but Big Bill was a marketing genius, and a showman, and a salesman, and not afraid of taking risk, not scared to push and prod and shake things up. His most important character trait may have been his strong gut. He was mentally tough, which some took as cold. The dean of auto-racing journalism, Chris Economaki, once joked that France "had the heart of a child – in a jar, on his desk." When you are building a sport or industry – not from the ground up, but from below sea level – there are bound to be casualties and hard feelings during the slog toward daylight. NASCAR was not a ground-floor operation, sometimes enlisting the services of men of ill repute who made and distributed moonshine, a potent alcohol distilled by rugged mountaineers and hill-dwellers in the so-called Bible Belt. Prohibition ended in 1933, but there were numerous "dry counties," where the sale of alcohol was not permitted.

These pockets of liquor-restricted areas were scattered throughout the Southeast. The moonshiners had a thriving backwoods business, which included a unique delivery system: young men in super-fast sedans, rumbling at high speed in the dark of night over treacherous, winding roadways. It was a necessary part of the business, since law-enforcement officers were duty-bound to hunt down those who would make and sell alcohol without the proper authority or, perhaps most importantly, without paying taxes on that product. Their intent

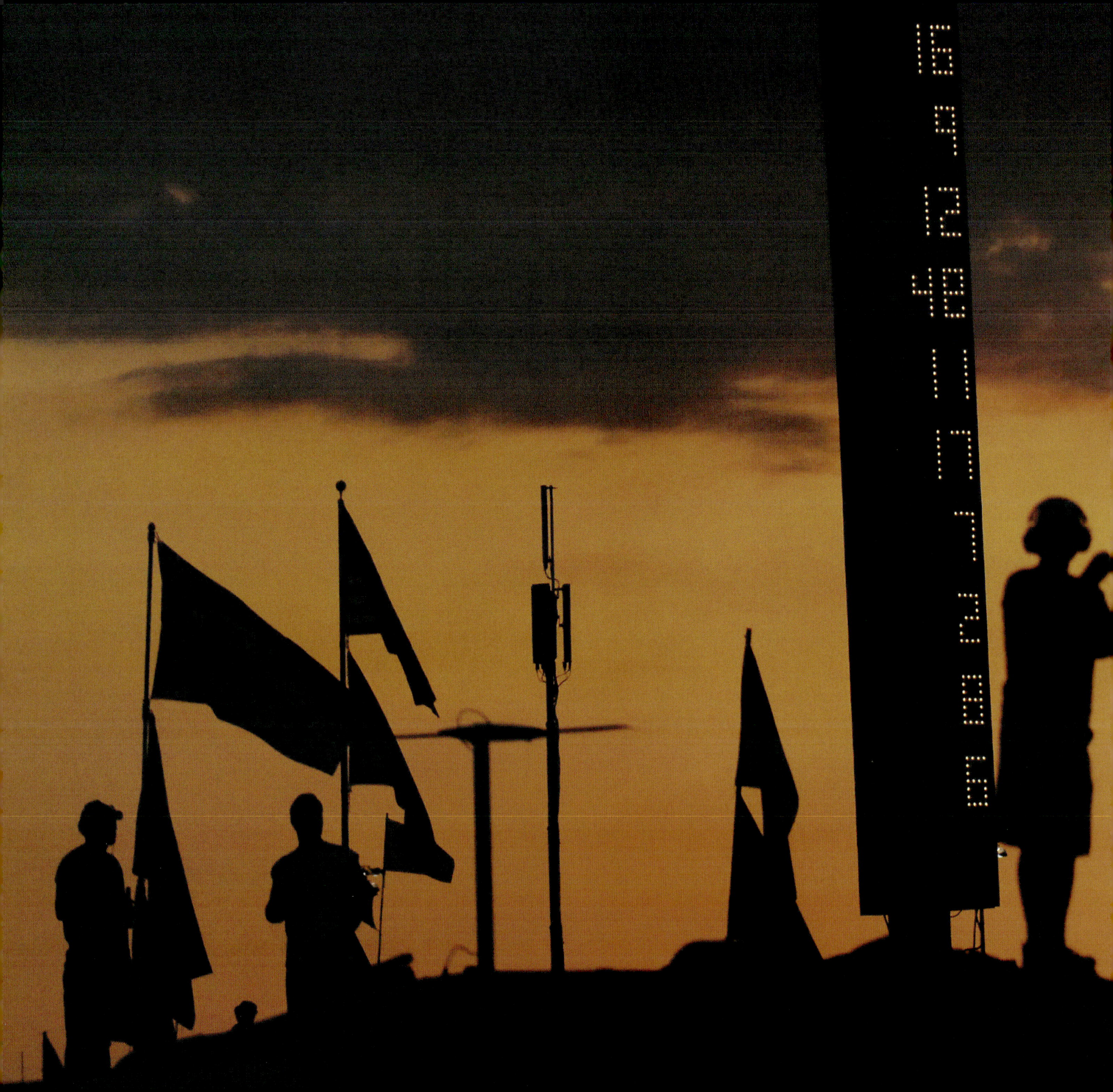

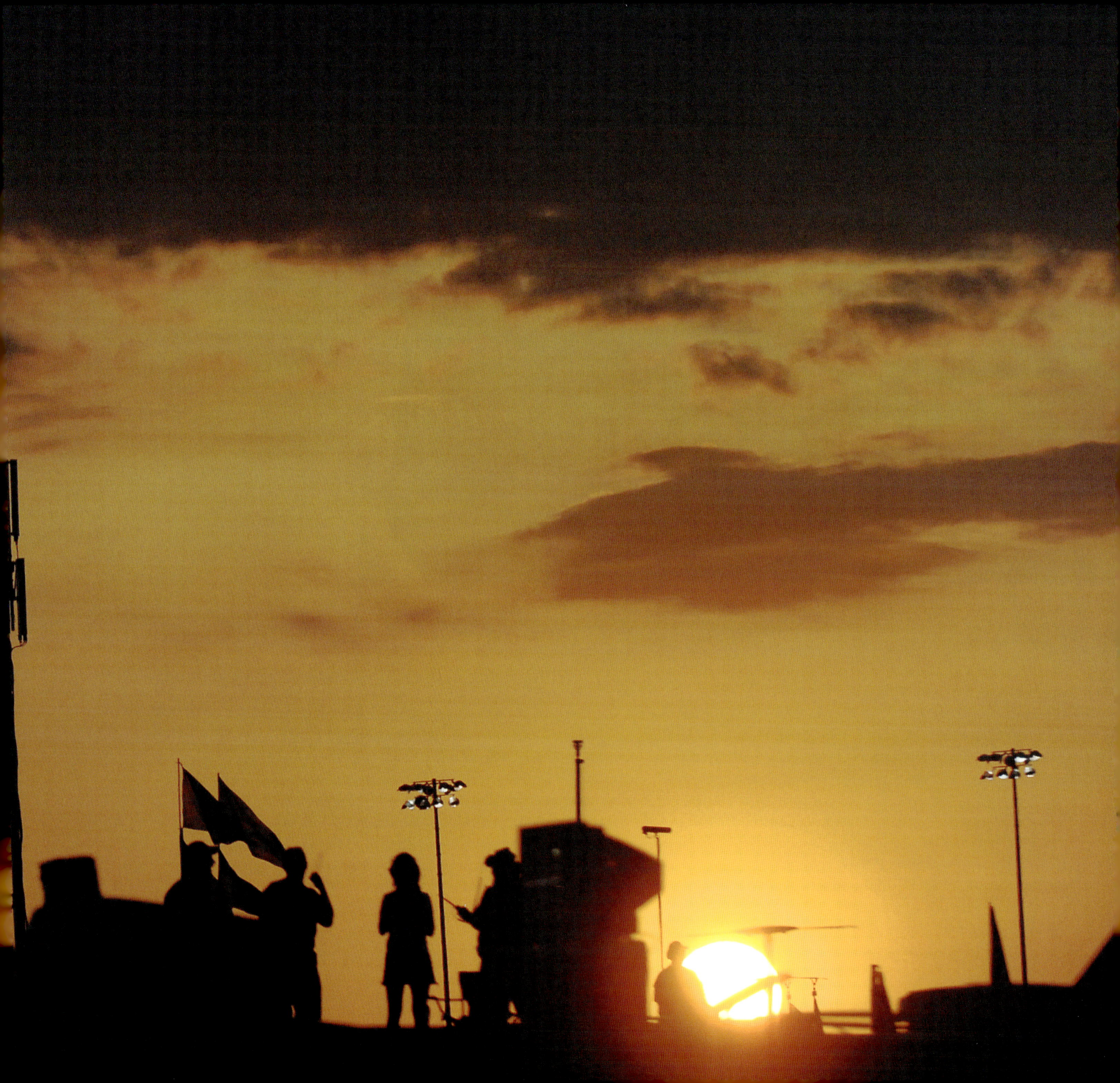

Racing is a dangerous and sometimes deadly game: Herb Thomas' No. 92 Pontiac, driven by Fonty Flock, following a nasty crash during the 1957 Southern 500 at Darlington Raceway. Flock was seriously injured and his driving career came to an end. Bobby Myers was killed in the same crash. According to reports from the race that day, Flock was fighting a bad-handling car and he lost control on Lap 28 going into Turn 3. Seconds later, Paul Goldsmith and Myers plowed into Flock's idle machine. Myers was killed instantly by the force of the impact.

This was a typical, old-style dirt "bull ring" that NASCAR raced on in the 1950s, with the No. 59 driven by Blackie Pitt crashing just feet from spectators protected by a chicken-wire fence at Asheville-Weaverville Speedway.

to collect government revenue earned them their common label: Revenuers. And the delivery men, when not outrunning the revenuers in a hell-bent-for-leather dash, would often race each other to see who had the fastest machines.

The rural areas proved fertile ground for NASCAR's earliest driving talent – young men like Junior Johnson. Racing seemed easy compared to a high-speed chase, on a skinny mountain road, involving U.S. Government agents or the local law. "I was good on the highway and good on the back roads, hills and small rural roads," Johnson told the *Daytona Beach News-Journal* in 2008. "The track was not quite as exciting as it was running from the revenuers. If you got caught, you knew you was going to jail." For the record, Robert Glen Johnson Jr. was never arrested on the open highways with a load of hooch. He did serve time in jail when federal agents found him working in the proximity of a still on his father's farm in Wilkes County, North Carolina, and took him into custody. The husky boy wasn't as swift afoot as he was with four wheels under him. Johnson says the fastest car he ever drove was a 1955 police-special Oldsmobile passenger car. He went to the factory in Lansing, Michigan, to pluck it off the assembly line, drove it home and reconfigured the engine block and added two superchargers. "Fastest car I ever run," Johnson drawled.

Yes, Johnson is one of a kind, but he was not unique in NASCAR's formative years. There were several other drivers with his moonshine-running credentials ready to go toe-to-toe, fender-to-fender on racetracks large and small. NASCAR had its share of garage characters in the 1950s, but unlike today, the cars were the stars. Detroit soon developed a stock-car mantra: "WIN ON SUNDAY, SELL ON MONDAY." By the end of its first decade, NASCAR's stomping grounds had become a fierce battleground for car manufacturers hoping to boost sales figures below the Mason-Dixon Line.

In 1949, only three carmakers won races. In 1956, six manufacturers went to Victory Lane. NASCAR racing had gone from an amusing skirmish into outright war as automobile companies funneled money, parts and

56 Man-made Thunder

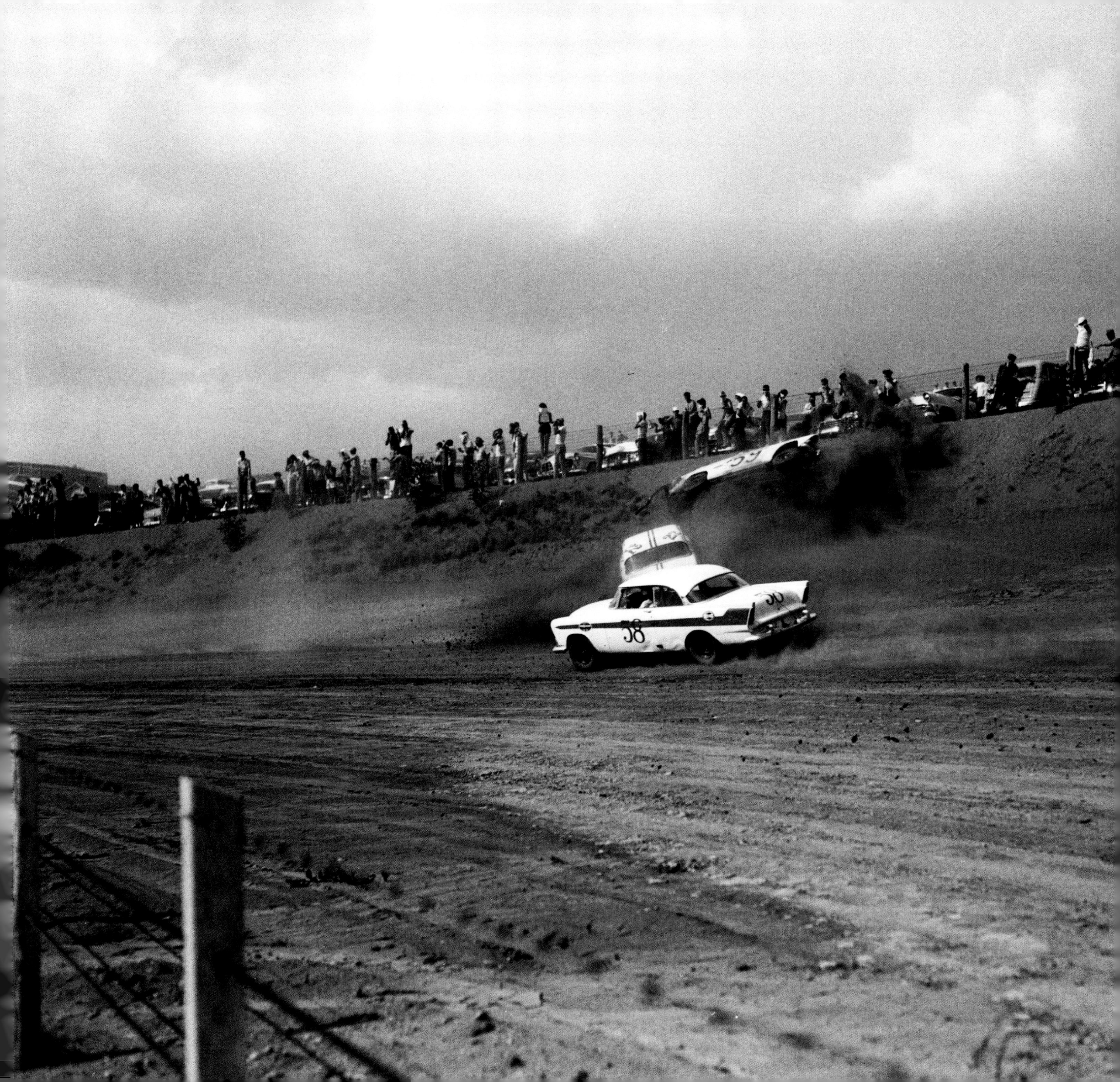
38

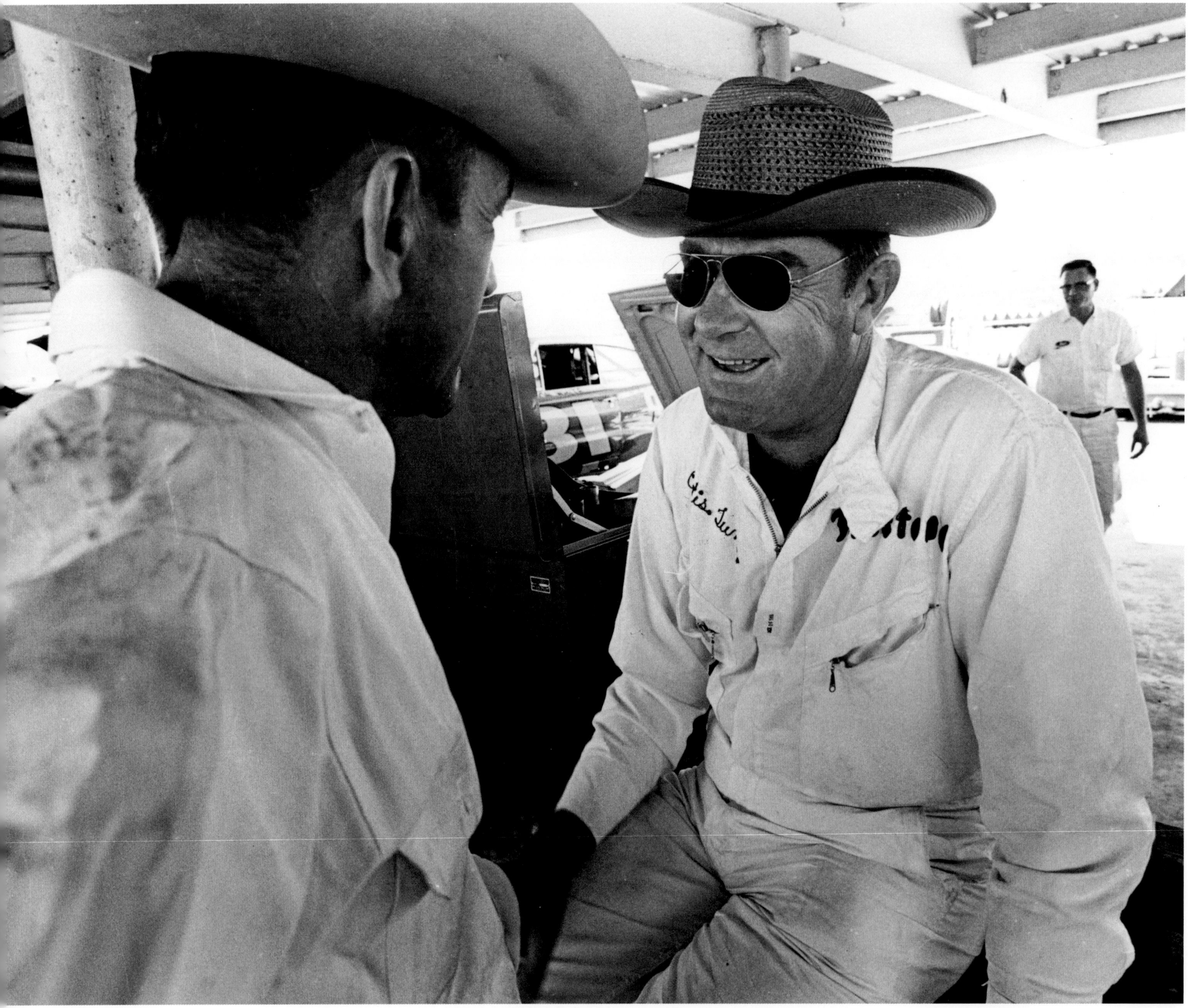

Two NASCAR Hall of Famers, mechanic/car owner Smokey Yunick, and driver Curtis Turner. They once landed a private plane on a city street to buy alcohol at a downtown package store.

engineering services to various car owners and innovative mechanics, such as Smokey Yunick, who sold trucks and owned a garage in Daytona. Deep inside the fenced compound of Yunick's "Best Damn Garage In Town" was an area devoted to race-car and engine development. It served as something of a research-and-development outpost for General Motors' Pontiac division, where young engineers were sent to test parts and pieces with the grand master of stock-car innovation. With car companies now showing a keen interest in NASCAR, they brought in the drum beaters to tout their products and, in a sign of things to come, their top drivers.

One of the first drivers to get a media blitz was Edward Glenn Roberts, better known to the world as "Fireball," a name he earned for the velocity of his fastball while playing baseball as a teenager. In 1957, Roberts won eight races and was named Florida's Professional Athlete of the Year by the Florida Sportswriters Association. Roberts called it his most important honor simply because he wasn't a stick-and-ball

"Men wanted to be like him; women wanted to be with him."
NASCAR's era of the racing star was about to unfold.

athlete. The mainstream media was starting to give NASCAR and its competitors some attention. Fireball Roberts, who grew up and lived in Daytona, would soon become stock-car racing's first star. He was good-looking, well-groomed, athletic, nicely spoken, educated and had a certain charisma about him – he was, to say the least, very different from most of his predecessors behind the wheel. As his fiancée once said, "Men wanted to be like him; women wanted to be with him."

NASCAR's era of the racing star was about to unfold. ■

The first race

When "Big Bill" France formed the National Association for Stock Car Auto Racing and began turning laps in 1948, there was organizational competition on all flanks.

Quaint little dirt tracks, such as the one at the right, eventually gave way to the behemoth superspeedways, which required industrial-sized equipment, left, to construct.

Right Marvin Panch, in the No. 98 entry, leads the pack to the green flag at Asheville-Weaverville Speedway, with Fireball Roberts, in the No. 22, by his side. Both Panch and Roberts called Daytona Beach, Florida, home. Ralph Earnhardt, father of seven-time NASCAR champion Dale Earnhardt, is wheeling the No. 188 entry. Buck Baker, driving the No. 87, won the race.

Rival sanctioning bodies raced under the acronyms of ASCRA, NARL and USCRA, but the one France feared the most was the National Stock Car Racing Association (NSCRA), founded and managed by Bruton Smith, based in Charlotte, North Carolina.

Smith proved to be a constant irritant to three generations of France leadership, first as a rival, then as an ingenious NASCAR "franchisee." Fueled by the imagination of his first lieutenant, H.A. "Humpy" Wheeler, Smith helped create today's modern NASCAR.

Some examples. Smith built condominiums in Turn 1 of his Charlotte Motor Speedway facility. His critics laughed. Most of the units sold out before the structure was completed.

Smith lighted CMS, now known as Lowe's Motor Speedway, and staged the first superspeedway race at night. It was one thing to light a half-mile track like Smith's Bristol Motor Speedway in Tennessee, but something else entirely to try lighting a track three times that length. Within a decade, night racing became quite in vogue because it boosts West Coast television ratings, and eventually even the France family decided to illuminate its monstrous Daytona track. When Smith wanted to raise cash, he created Speedway Motorsports Inc., and issued common stock on the New York Stock Exchange. He went on a racetrack-buying and building spree in the 1990s and at one time controlled more Sprint Cup race dates than the France family's International Speedway Corporation, a sister company to NASCAR.

The point is this: In 1948 and '49, France saw Smith, who was in his early 20s, as one of his most formidable opponents. When France decided to give the "Strictly Stock" division a whirl, it was no accident that the first race was held in Smith's backyard – practically between his grill and swimming pool. France wanted to leave his scent in Smith's briar patch. France scheduled the inaugural race at Charlotte Speedway, a three-quarter-mile oval with a corn-cob-rough dirt surface. Some of the great Modified drivers of the era, such as Curtis Turner, Red Byron, Herb Thomas and the Flock brothers (Fonty, Tim and Bob) filled out entry blanks for the 150-mile

Drivers get all the attention 61

Right The No. 22 sprints away from the troubles of the No. 86 driven by Neil Castles, who smashed the snout of his race car after making heavy contact with the outside wall during this Grand National/Convertible race in the late 1950s.

Right The No. 82 Red Bull Racing Toyota of rookie driver Scott Speed is measured by NASCAR's "claw" during tech inspection at Daytona, 2009.

Far right Petty Enterprises Inc. engine builder Maurice Petty, left, gets the restrictor-plate treatment from NASCAR official Bill Gazaway during pre-race tech at Alabama International Motor Speedway in 1970. Gazaway would later become Winston Cup Series director.

event. There was a lot of new blood in this race, including Lee Petty, from Level Cross, North Carolina, making his first-ever start in any kind of race, and a fellow by the name of Jim Roper, from Halstead, Kansas.

Roper, 32, learned of this race by reading the nationally syndicated comic strip "Smilin' Jack." Artist Zack Mosely was a race fan and slipped the date and place of NASCAR's new series offering into one of his cartoon panels. Roper wheeled a 1949 Lincoln from the Kansas plains, through the Ozarks and Smoky Mountains to the heart of North Carolina, just to compete in this start-up event. He qualified a surprising 12th in a 33-car field. "It was a new Lincoln," Roper told the media in 1998. But it didn't look new for long. "The track was very hot and very dusty because they didn't have the asphalt like they do today," he said.

The 35-year-old Lee Petty began his racing career in a manner that gave no hint whatsoever of what he'd become. The lanky legend-to-be wrecked on Lap 107 of the 200-lap run. His Buick Roadmaster tumbled through Turn 3. He exited the demolished car with a cut on his cheek and worry in his eyes. Later he explained to media why he emerged from the car and crouched on the crest of Turn 3, looking out over the countryside. "I was just sitting there thinking about having to go back home and explain to my wife where I'd been with the car," he said.

"It was a new Lincoln," Roper told the media in 1998. But it didn't look new for long.

Glenn Dunnaway took the checkered flag in a 1947 Ford owned by Hubert Westmoreland. It was Dunnaway in a runaway, and eyebrows were naturally raised. He beat second-place Roper on the track by three laps. As is custom, other drivers complained to France that Dunnaway's car was outfitted with cheater parts because it moved with ease through Charlotte's craggy, beaten turns. Remember, these were "Strictly Stock" cars that were allowed little leeway in modifications. NASCAR

62 Man-made Thunder

inspectors seized the No. 25 Ford and did a "tear down," or a detailed, post-race inspection. France's technical team found that Westmoreland's entry was a beefed-up, bootlegger car engineered to carry heavy loads of "white lightning" at a high rate of speed. Dunnaway was immediately disqualified. The win and $2,000 first-place prize money went to Roper, whose once-new Lincoln was barely running at the finish. Since he now had the winning car, Roper got the tear-down treatment by track officials. "We had to borrow a motor, because NASCAR took ours all apart, and gave it back to us in pieces," said Roper.

Roper, who passed away in 2000, made only one other "Strictly Stock" start in his career, a 15th-place finish at Occoneechee Speedway in Hillsboro, North Carolina. The bulk of his racing was done closer to home. "I got my share of wins over a period of time. The Charlotte win was the best win I ever had. If I had stayed with NASCAR, I might have wound up a little higher." His racing career ended after crashing a midget-class car in a race in Iowa. The wreck shattered his backbone in five places. The bones healed but the pain was more resilient. "After I healed up, I couldn't stand it," he said. "You took a pretty good beating in those cars, back in those days."

France's inaugural race, in the series known today as Sprint Cup, was a success, but didn't generate a whole lot of press clippings. Even the hometown paper to NASCAR headquarters in Daytona printed just a six-paragraph race report the next day. Still, this foray into Bruton Smith's North Carolina stomping grounds was a huge success for France and NASCAR. Not only did the event attract a solid field of cars, draw a nice crowd and give a swift, effective kick in the crotch to one of France's archrivals, but it established NASCAR's direction. In less than a year, the Modifieds were now the undercard to the newly christened Grand National Series. Broadway couldn't produce stars without its row of world-class theaters, and now France was building a stage like no other in the history of motorsports. ■

Smoking the competition

The NASCAR of today has a sophisticated and savvy in-house public relations/ marketing/broadcast/Internet machine in place to showcase the bright side of stock-car racing, but can react quickly and intelligently to a bad-news cycle.

Corporate money is the lifeblood of NASCAR and anything is game for signage, such as stock cars (left), scoreboards and people (right).

NASCAR is a private company and does not have to release financial reports, unlike its sister racing entity, International Speedway Corporation, which has sold shares since the late 1950s. NASCAR is rich in cash, thanks to a multi-billion-dollar television contract and a deep pool of corporate partners, who pay dearly for official status, such as the "Official Lug Nut of NASCAR" or "Official Panty hose of NASCAR." NASCAR's polished corporate image is a relatively recent phenomenon, engineered by Brian Z. France, the only son of Bill France Jr., who was named CEO and chairman of the family business in the fall of 2003.

When Bill Jr. handed the reins of NASCAR to Brian, the elder France waxed poetic to the

"Back in '48, my dad said, 'If we handle this right, it can become a national sport.'"

Daytona Beach News-Journal about how far the company had come from those early days when "Big Bill" worked out of his hat. "Back in '48, my dad said, 'If we handle this right, it can become a national sport.' If he could come back for about four days and hang around here to see what's going on, he'd be totally amazed." When William H.G. France started NASCAR, he didn't have much of a marketing/public relations budget. In those early days, he would hand-deliver a press release to

the newspapers and radio stations closest to the racetrack, and assign Bill Jr. to tack cardboard posters to trees and light poles in areas near the facility. That was about it. No television. No radio. Just a lot of legwork to get the word out about an upcoming race. "Money was tight," Bill Jr. said once of those early years.

Despite a grassroots and bare-bones marketing strategy, NASCAR continued to build a fan base, predominantly in the South, and relied heavily on the automakers to tout the success of their cars in the Grand National Series. That changed dramatically, thanks to the U.S. Government banning electronic advertising (no TV ads) by the

Drivers get all the attention 65

Posters and handbills were an inexpensive form of advertising for cash-strapped promoters. When a race was scheduled, posters such as these would be plastered all over neighboring towns.

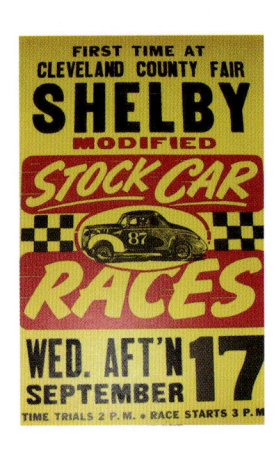

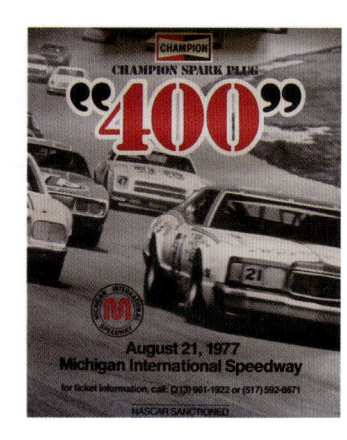

cigarette industry. The law went into effect on January 2, 1971. R.J. Reynolds Tobacco Company, based in Winston-Salem, North Carolina, suddenly had no national advertising outlet to tout its wares to the public. Enter Junior Johnson, one of North Carolina's favorite sons, who went from race driver to full-time car owner in 1967. Johnson smelled a cash cow in Winston-Salem and pitched the idea of sponsoring his race car to RJR's marketing department in 1970. Marketing director Ralph Seagraves declined the offer, but liked the idea of bonding the iconic Winston brand with NASCAR's Grand National Series. "He came to me about sponsoring his car," Seagraves

"I thought we should do something bigger ... sponsor a whole series."

told the *News-Journal* in 1997. "Back then it cost [practically nothing] to sponsor a car. I thought we should do something bigger, get more involved. We wanted to sponsor a whole series." In 1971, RJR became primary sponsor of NASCAR's marquee series. Each year, the company increased its stake in the sport, not only pumping money into the season-ending points fund, but assisting with marketing campaigns and offering its public relations expertise to NASCAR.

Bill Jr. rewarded RJR for its loyalty in 1986 by renaming the prominent national tour the Winston Cup Series. NASCAR and RJR shared the same bed from 1971 through 2003, and by joining forces, stock-car racing sprouted from its southern base to become a national sport with a rabid following.

Everyone within the sport benefited – from drivers to team owners to track operators like Bruton Smith. "That's the greatest thing that ever happened to the sport, when they came into it," Smith said of RJR. ∎

66   Man-made Thunder

Drivers get all the attention 67

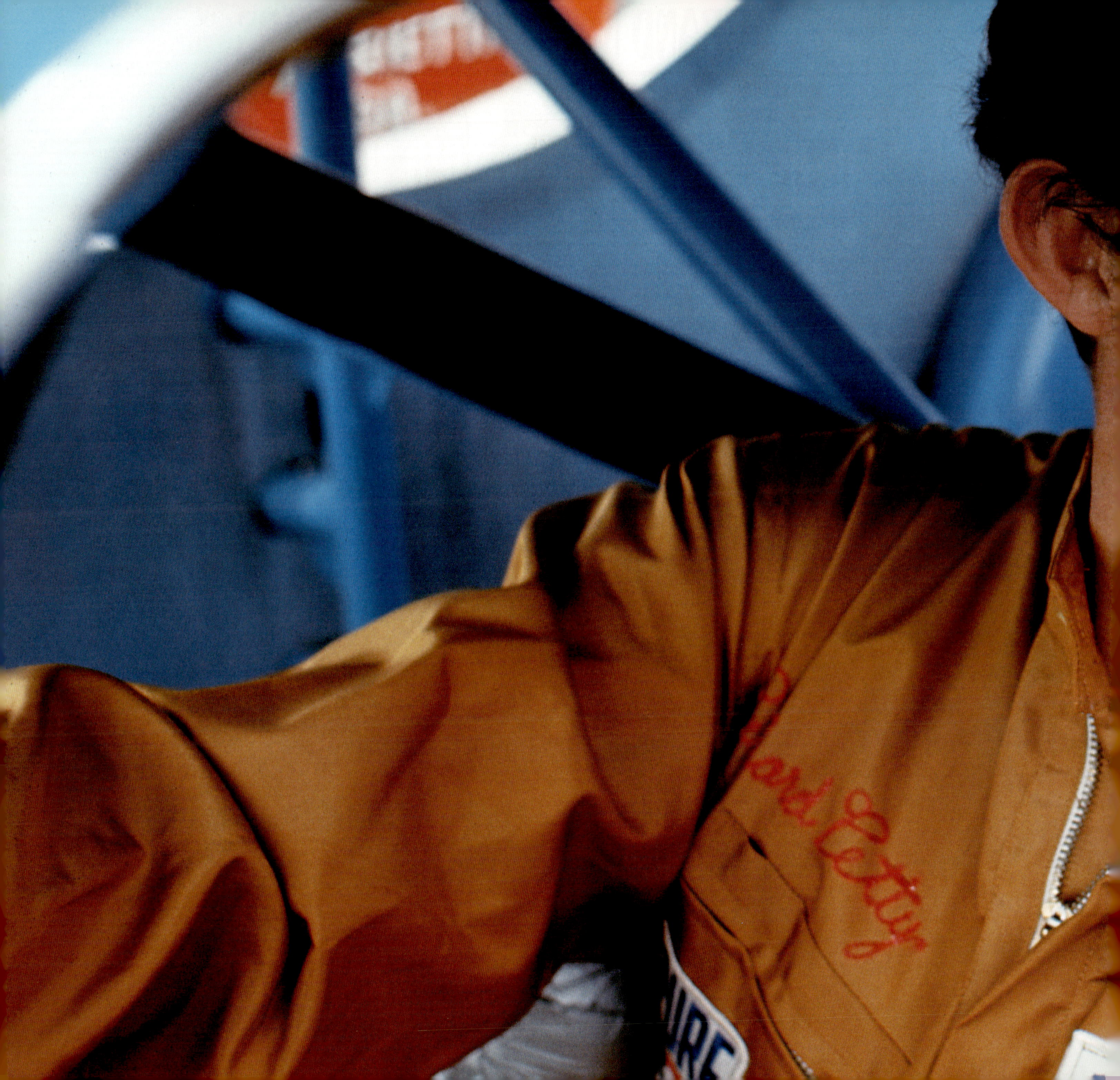

Paying homage to "King Richard"

3

Previous page Have you driven a Ford lately? Richard Petty did, in 1969. It was the only year Petty went an entire season racing for the "Blue Oval" company.

The front row of the 1960 World 600 at Charlotte Motor Speedway with pole-sitter Fireball Roberts, No. 22 Pontiac, far right, in Turn 4, leading the 60-car field to the green flag. Jack Smith is in the middle with CMS president Curtis Turner on the outside.

Richard Petty strikes a pensive pose as "his boys" work on the rear differential before the 1963 National 500 at Charlotte Motor Speedway.

The early 1960s was an exciting time for NASCAR. Fast, too. Ushered in was the era of the superspeedway – those mammoth, paved ovals longer than a mile, which pushed man and machine to new limits of propulsion and endurance. Daytona International Speedway, "Big Bill's" 2.5-mile dream course, opened for business in 1959. The 1960 Grand National Series season held inaugural races at Charlotte Motor Speedway and Atlanta International Motor Raceway, both 1.5-mile, high-banked brutes. Joined with the granddaddy of them all, Darlington Raceway (1.25 miles long at the time), there now existed a circuit of super-sized tracks outfitted with proportionate grandstand areas.

Some of NASCAR's top drivers didn't like racing on these Goliath courses; after all, they had been raised on much slower, half-mile dirt ovals. Others seemed to flourish on these long and banked rings of asphalt. Lee Petty, the guy who crashed out in NASCAR's first Sprint Cup race in 1949, was a spry 44 when he captured the 1959 Daytona 500. It was his only career victory on a superspeedway course. Petty's kid was in that first 500-mile run in Daytona. The sportswriters of that era referred to the 21-year-old driver, who was skinnier than a horsetail hair, as Dick Petty – he finished 57th in the 59-car field. He's better known today by his legal first name, Richard. He would have much better days at Daytona in the years to come.

One driver getting a lot of attention at Daytona in 1959 was the handsome, young, local driver named Fireball Roberts. Over the 1957–58 Grand National Series seasons, Roberts won 14 races and had gone from "up-and-comer" to near superstar status in the stock-car league. When he walked through the gates of Daytona's big track, he brought along a sense of excitement and anticipation. After the 1958 season, Roberts wandered over to Smokey Yunick's "Best Damn Garage In Town" to see if the Sultan of Speed would agree to take him on as a driver. It seemed like a natural union: NASCAR's top mechanic paired with one of the sport's most dynamic drivers, and they both lived in the same city. Yunick, a workaholic who chased speed theories into the wee hours of the morning

Man-made Thunder

Paying homage to "King Richard"   71

72 Man-made Thunder

Richard Petty, middle, would describe this as just a gathering of good ol' boys from Petty Enterprises Inc. On the far left is Petty's brother and engine builder Maurice. On the right is cousin and crew chief Dale Inman. This wasn't the PEI shop. This was a set-up shot for the cover of *Hot Rod* magazine in the early 1970s.

Next page Race tire management is extremely important in the NASCAR Sprint Cup Series. Goodyear makes tires specifically for the right and left side of the stock cars for every race. Air pressure adjustments can dramatically change the handling characteristics of the car during the race. Here, a tire man inspects and marks each tire before the 2008 Budweiser Shootout at Daytona International Speedway.

in the dimly lit bowels of his race shop, was not warm to the idea at first. Roberts had two reputations: That of a hard-charging driver whose win-or-break mentality was popular with the fans, and that of a slacker and party animal.

In his autobiography, Yunick wrote: "Even though we are kinda neighbors, and I consider him one of the four NASCAR driving aces, I'm hesitant to hook up with him. I know Fireball has two allergies – asthma and work . . ." Roberts persisted and finally got his handshake deal to run the bigger (and best-paying) races in 1959. They became the dynamic duo of NASCAR over the 1959–61 seasons, winning poles everywhere and enjoying uncanny success at Daytona and Atlanta. Roberts became so popular that in January, 1964, *Sports Illustrated* sent a female reporter down to Daytona Beach to see what the fuss was all about. The piece ran in February of that year. It was one of the first long feature-articles about a NASCAR driver in a national publication that served a general audience. *Esquire* published Tom Wolfe's groundbreaking profile of Junior Johnson in March, 1965. By the time Wolfe's article appeared, NASCAR was on something a downward slope because of a horrifying flurry of driver deaths the previous season. Joe Weatherly, a popular and fun-loving racer who won back-to-back Grand National titles in 1962–63, was killed in a gruesome accident at Riverside, California, in January, 1964. That summer, NASCAR's heart was further ripped apart when Fireball Roberts died a month after fire charred 80 percent of his body in a horrifying crash-and-burn at Charlotte. And Jimmy Pardue perished while testing tires at Charlotte in September. Billy Wade was killed in a tire-test crash in January, 1965, at Daytona.

NASCAR needed a new hero to help it escape this horror, and it found one in Richard Petty, who drove the No. 43 entry out of the Petty Enterprises Inc. race shop in Level Cross, North Carolina. Lee Petty's career – 54 wins and three championships included – came to a dramatic halt in February, 1961, when his stock car went flying over the fence during a Daytona qualifying race. His son then became Petty Enterprises'

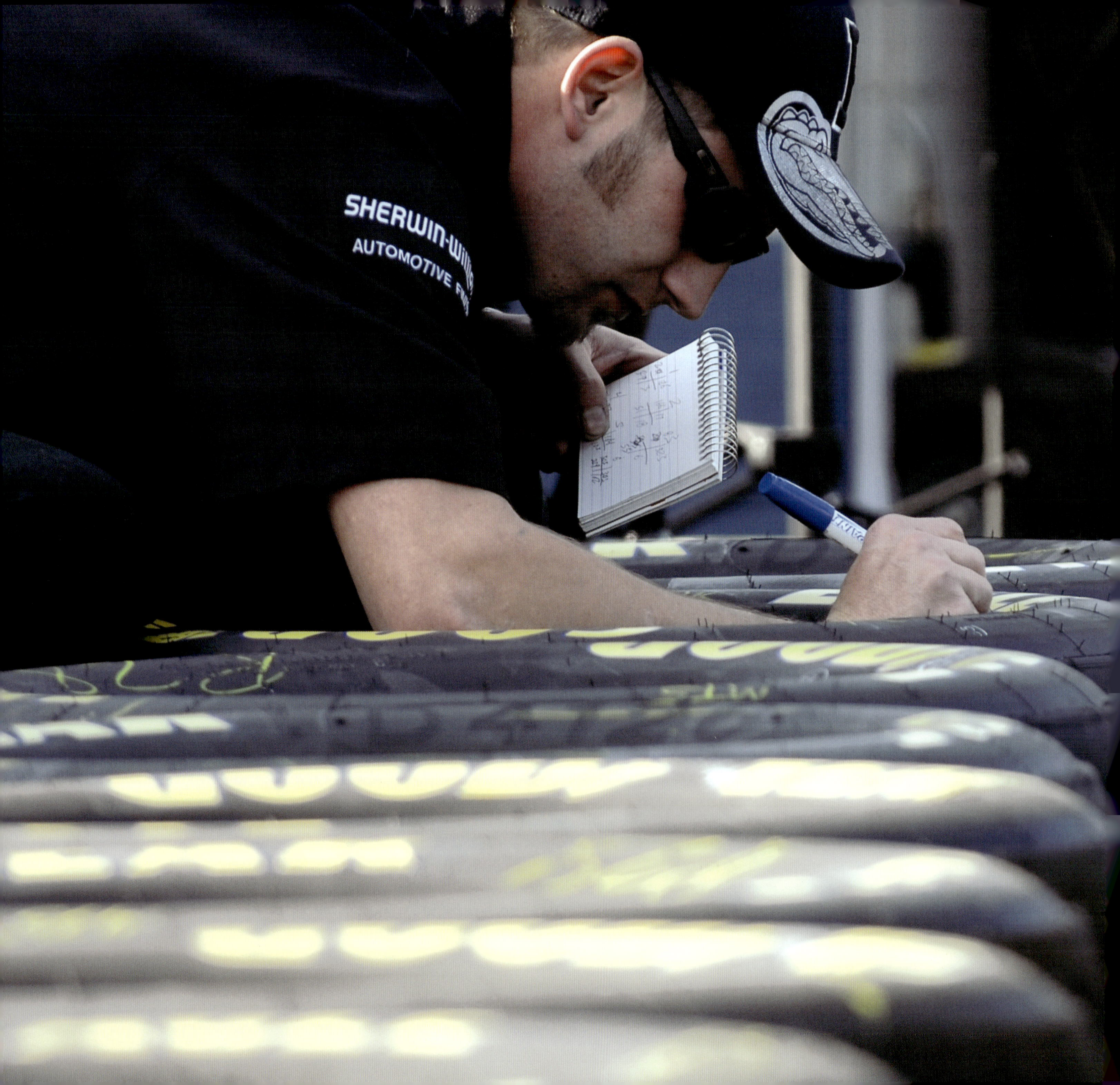

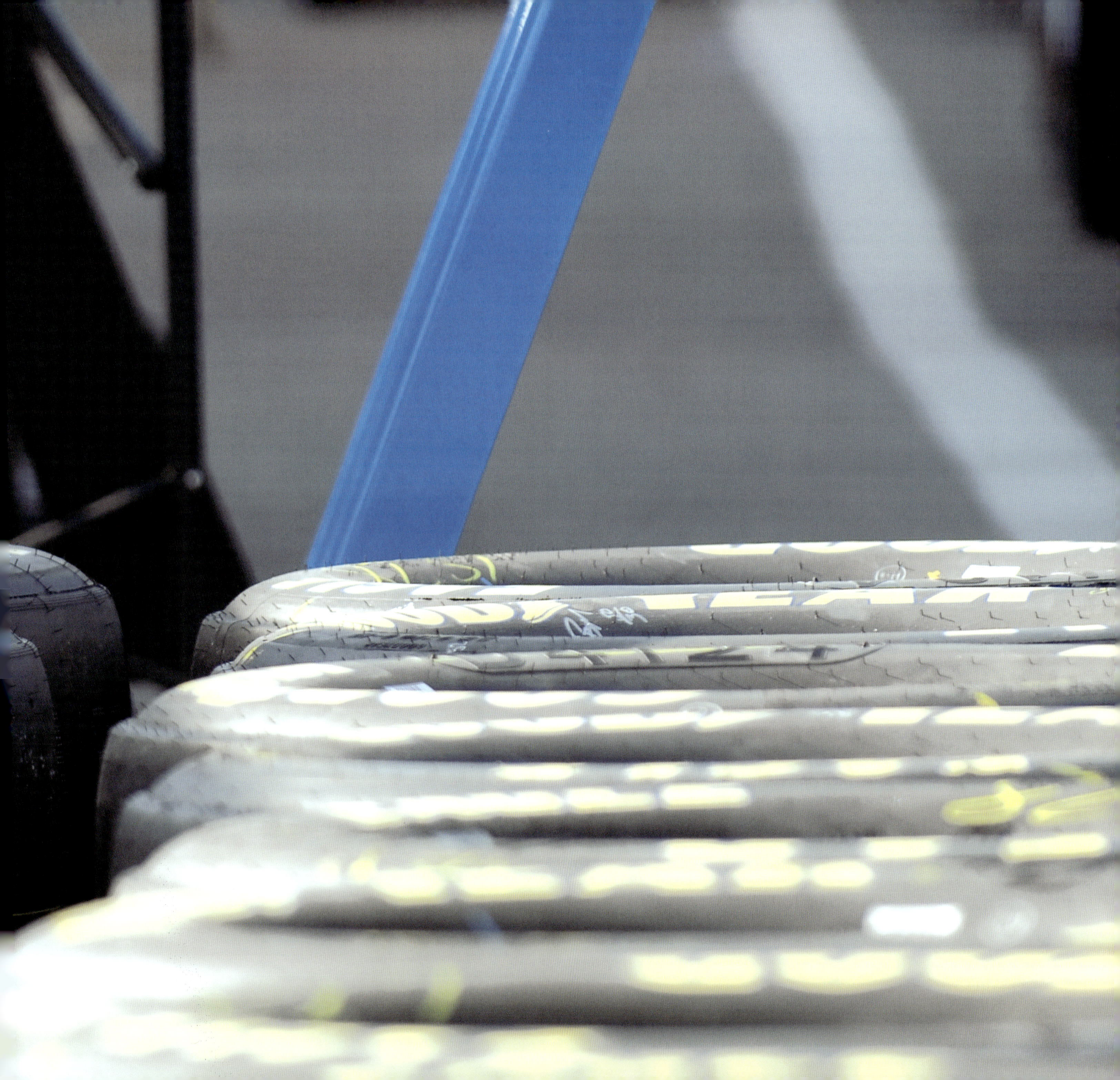

Richard Petty hits a pothole at Charlotte Motor Speedway during the 1960 World 600. The asphalt at CMS had not cured and was coming apart because of the weight of the stock cars and speeds they were going. It's a problem that plagues speedways to this day. Frustrated by its continuous asphalt problems, Dover International Speedway and Bristol Motor Speedway went to concrete surfaces. Problem solved.

bread-winning driver. In 1962 Richard busted out for eight wins. The next year, he had 14 victories in 55 starts. All the stars aligned in 1964 when he captured the Daytona 500 – leading 184 of 200 laps – and ended the season with his first Grand National championship. He accomplished all this in a Chrysler outfitted with something akin to a rocket under the hood: A bullish 426-cubic-inch V-8 engine. "The first time I cranked it," Petty told the *Atlanta Journal-Constitution* after winning the 1964 Daytona 500, "I thought it was gonna suck the hood into the engine." The No. 43 car became so synonymous with the driver and his family team, the car's familiar color became widely known as "Petty Blue."

Through genetic quirk, Richard Petty was on the opposite end of the personality spectrum from his father. Lee Petty was crude, cranky, foul-mouthed, ill-tempered, unruly and unkempt, and cared little about media opportunities. He focused on racing like a seamstress threading a needle. Richard was polite, polished, folksy, good-natured and went out of his way to please race fans and service the media. And so, as Petty

Paying homage to "King Richard" 77

78 Man-made Thunder

NASCAR folks love cars and many have a collection in their home garage. Here Richard Petty plays with one of his personal cars built in the 1930s.

piled up wins and championships, his popularity surged into the general population. He had name recognition, like other sports greats of the 1960s, such as Arnold Palmer (golf), Bart Starr (football) and Mickey Mantle (baseball). People might not have known all the details of Palmer's record in the major championships, but they knew he was one of golf's all-time great players. Petty, too, had that omnipresence. Over the 1967–71 racing seasons, Petty was an unstoppable force, winning 92 Grand National races and a pair of championships. In '67 he was practically invincible – at one point winning 10 consecutive events en route to a 27-win season. The always unassuming Petty claimed there was no rational explanation for his mastery of the series. "When you're on a roll, you just have to take advantage of it, because a lot of times you don't know why you're there," Petty said in 2008. With a humble attitude, wide smile and North Carolina twang, Petty had all the ingredients for a hyper-sized sports hero. He didn't run away from his fan base, as many stars do, but embraced it and waved the worshipers right into his inner sanctum.

Early in his driving career, a run that touched five decades, Petty figured out the big picture. Petty's logic went something like this: I drive a race car and make a good living. The people who come watch me race pay my salary. It would be in my best interest to cater to the people who pay my salary. Petty was ridiculously accessible, unlike today's driver, who surrounds himself with several layers of protection from fans and media. If a reporter wants to talk to a driver for a feature story, they must make contact with the marketing company that represents that driver and negotiate a day and time for a quick phone interview, which could happen over the next two or three weeks. Maybe. Back in the 1960s, if you called the Petty Enterprises shop number, there was a chance Richard Petty would answer the phone.

Petty was a real champion of the motorhead masses. Throughout his career, he would sign autographs along pit road or in the garage area following an event and stay until every racing patron left with his signature on whatever item they had clutched in their hands. Petty stayed many

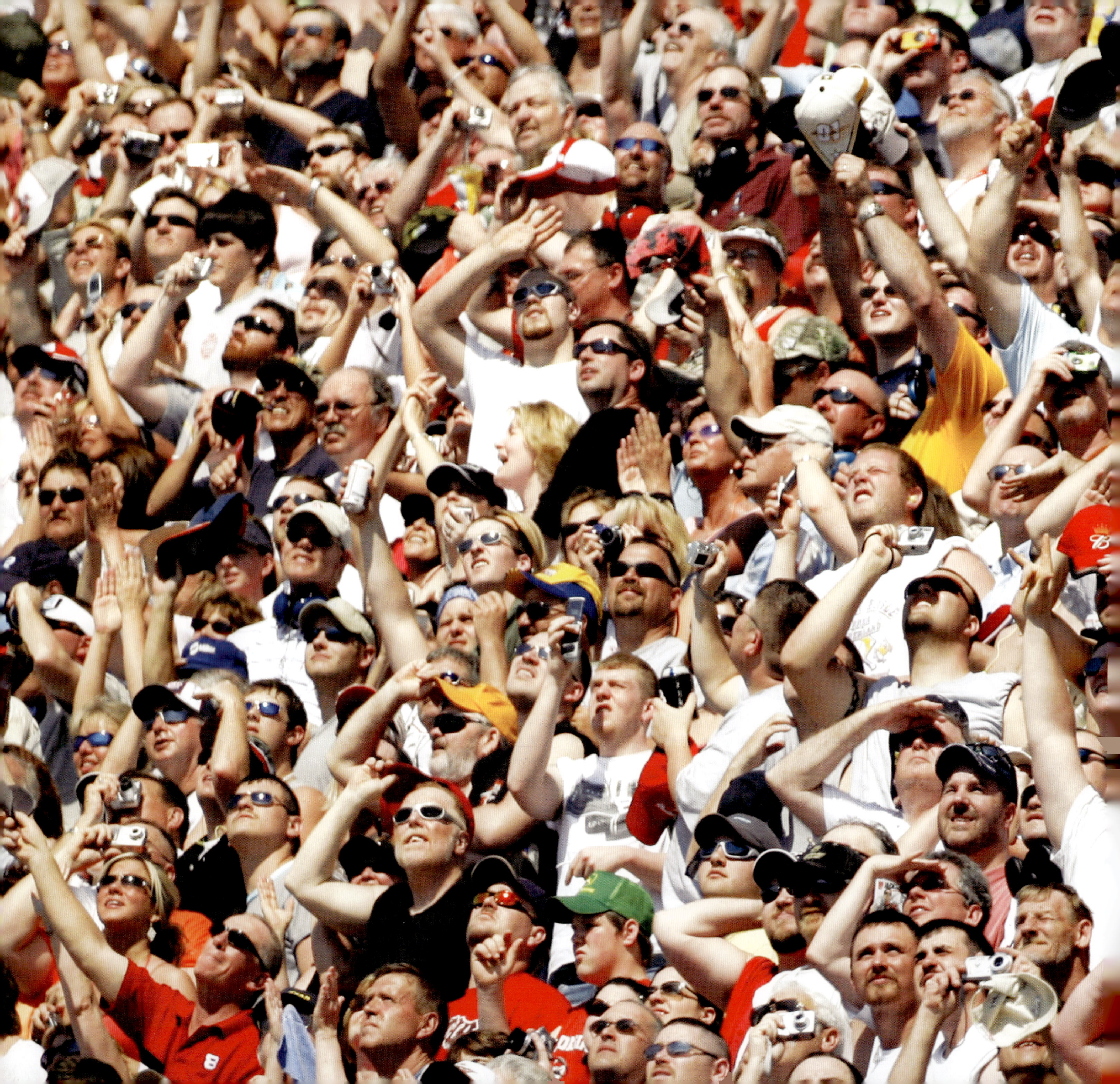

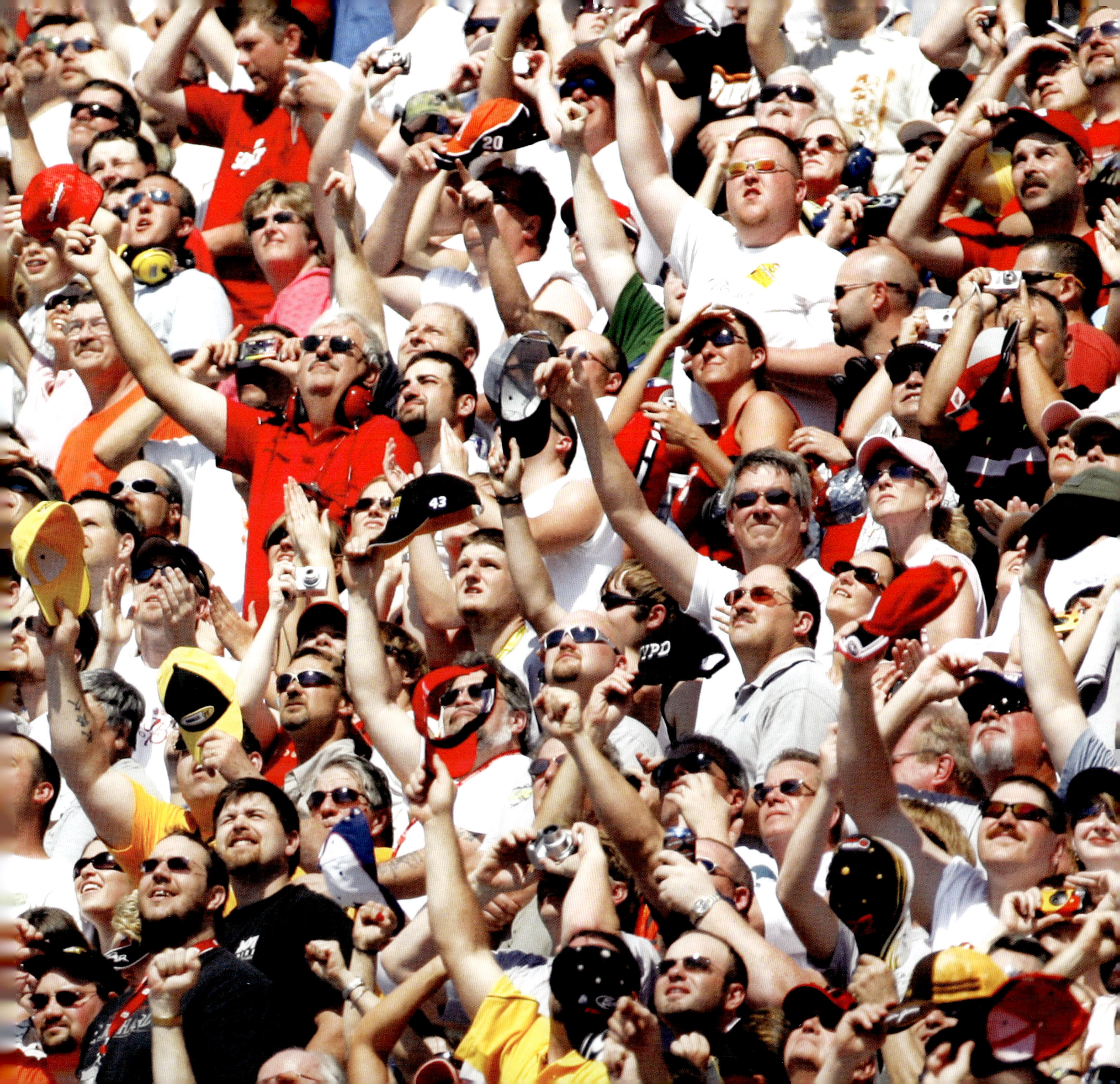
20
43

Previous page Fans cheer as jets fly over Bristol Motor Speedway before the start of a race. It is the only track on the Sprint Cup Series with grandstands that line the entire 0.533-mile course, giving it a stadium feel. Although "The Wave" has become an American tradition at arenas and sports stadiums around the country, this is not the case at NASCAR events – Bristol is the one exception.

Richard Petty in a tumbling crash exiting Turn 4 during the 1988 Daytona 500. Petty says he has been in far worse accident situations. "With the car turning over and over and parts and pieces coming off, that was absorbing all the energy of the crash," said Petty, who broke an ankle only after his car came to a near stop, then was hit by Brett Bodine.

times as the sun dropped out of sight on the horizon, as all his competitors were packing up and exiting the facility. There was no NASCAR mandate to be fan-friendly. Petty initiated that outreach program on his own, and by doing so, set a precedent that stock-car racing has grappled with since the mid-1990s. As the NASCAR fan base grew exponentially, drivers set up fan clubs and Internet sites as a way to connect to their followers. Petty didn't have that luxury – he didn't even have any professional public-relations assistance until 1972 when Petty Enterprises signed a sponsorship contract with oil-additive company STP.

Petty had the name recognition but he got there by battling the likes of Cale Yarborough, tenacious behind the wheel; David Pearson, generally considered the most naturally talented driver of his time, perhaps all time; and Bobby Allison. Petty and Allison had a long-running dislike of each other, which made for great newspaper copy. It was this supporting cast of characters, each with their own unique personality, always nipping at Petty's heels, which planted the seed of today's complicated and

There was no NASCAR mandate to be fan-friendly. Petty initiated that outreach program on his own . . .

sometimes robust storylines that helped create modern-day interest in drivers and their interaction on and off the racetrack. As Petty's triumphs mounted, the media crowned him the "king of stock-car racing," which led to him being called "King Richard," or simply "The King." Even his son Kyle, himself a longtime racer, refers to his dad as "The King" in casual conversation.

When asked in 2008 what it was like being Richard Petty and having people call him "The King," Petty said – in his own brand of the English language – the title simply came with his success in the sport. "I ain't never been nothin' else," Petty replied. "And what was fortunate from my standpoint, the times I came along, the personalities I was around, the

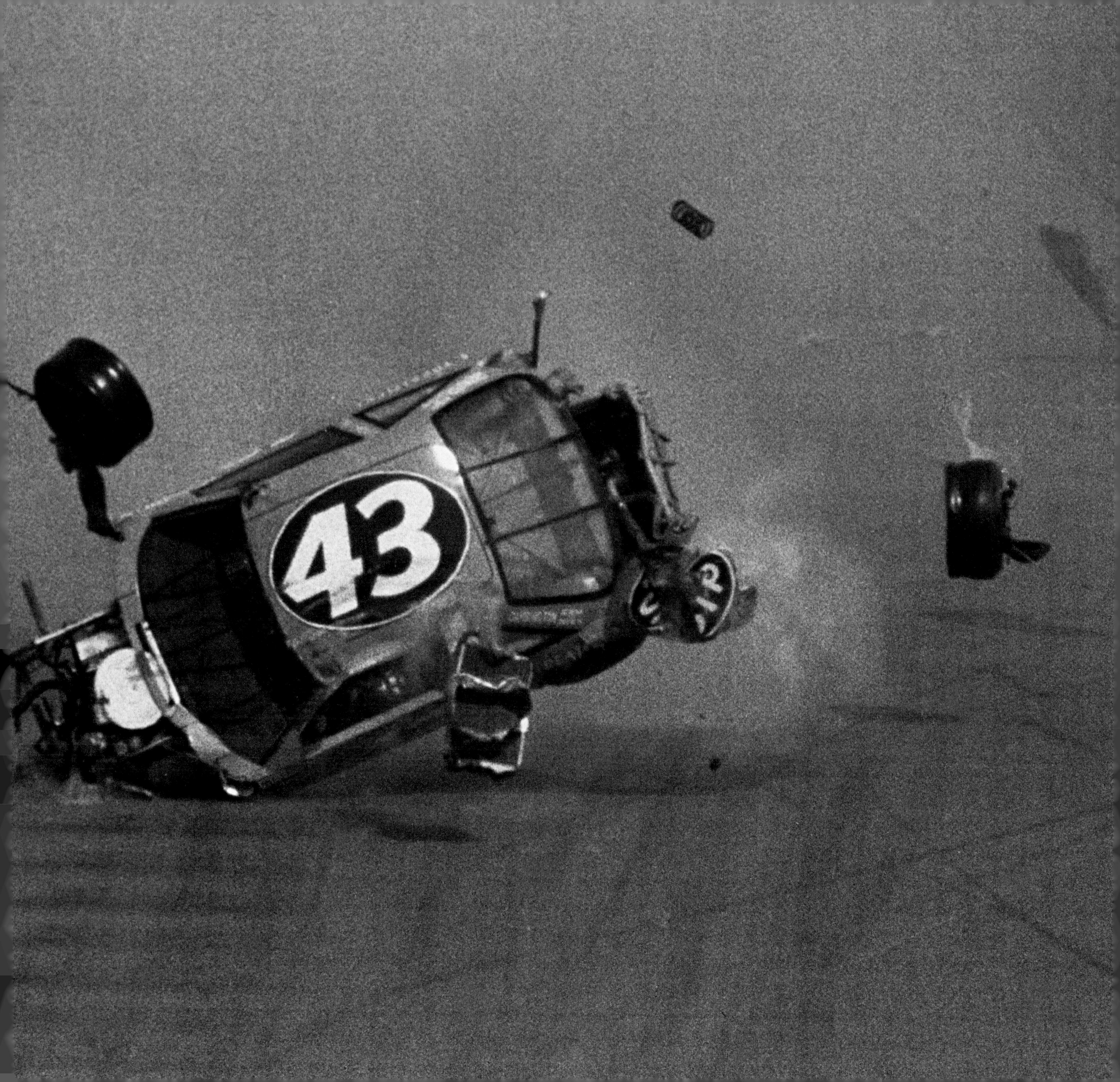
43

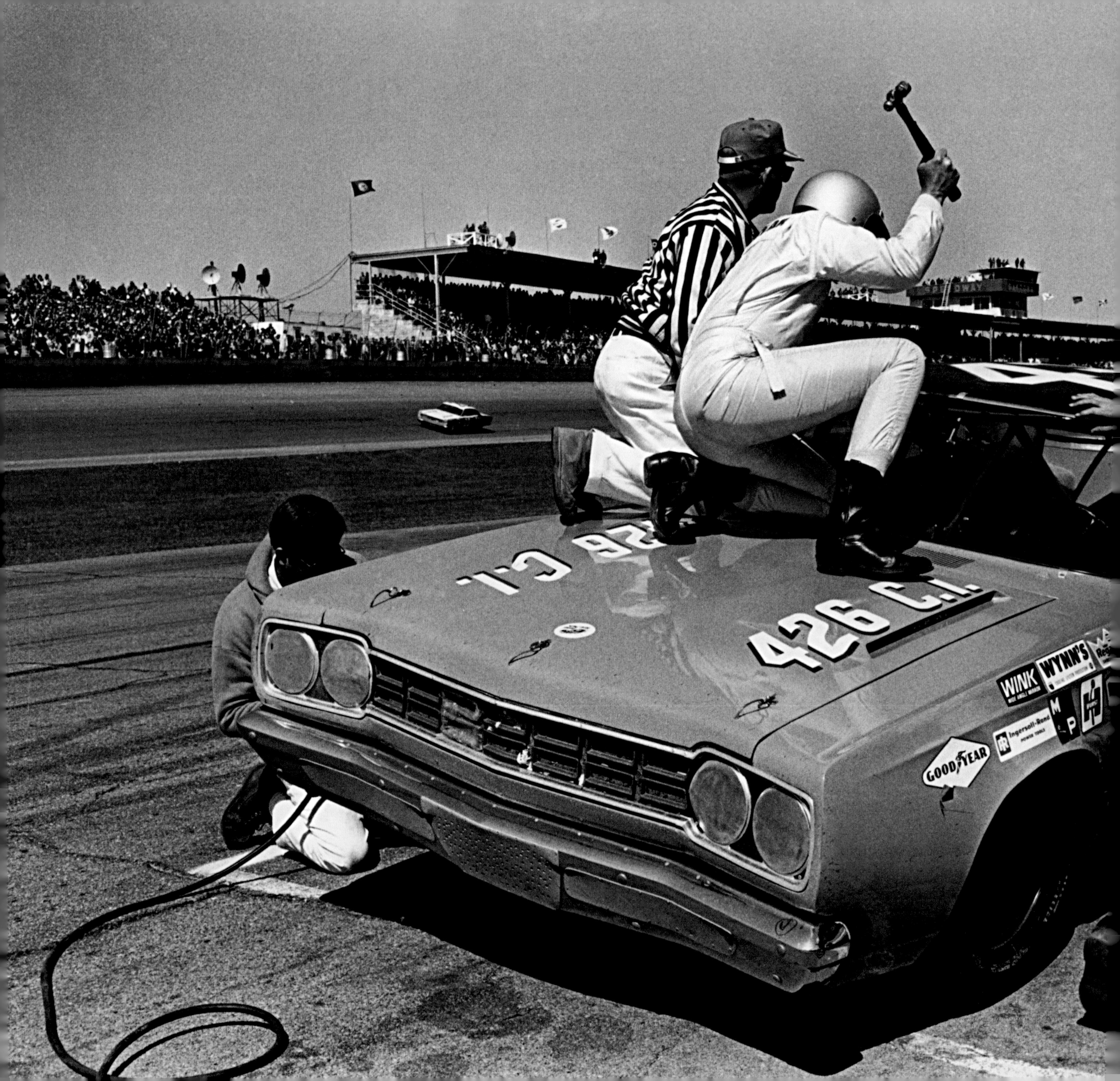
426 C.I.
WYNN'S
WINK
Ingersoll-Rand
GOODYEAR

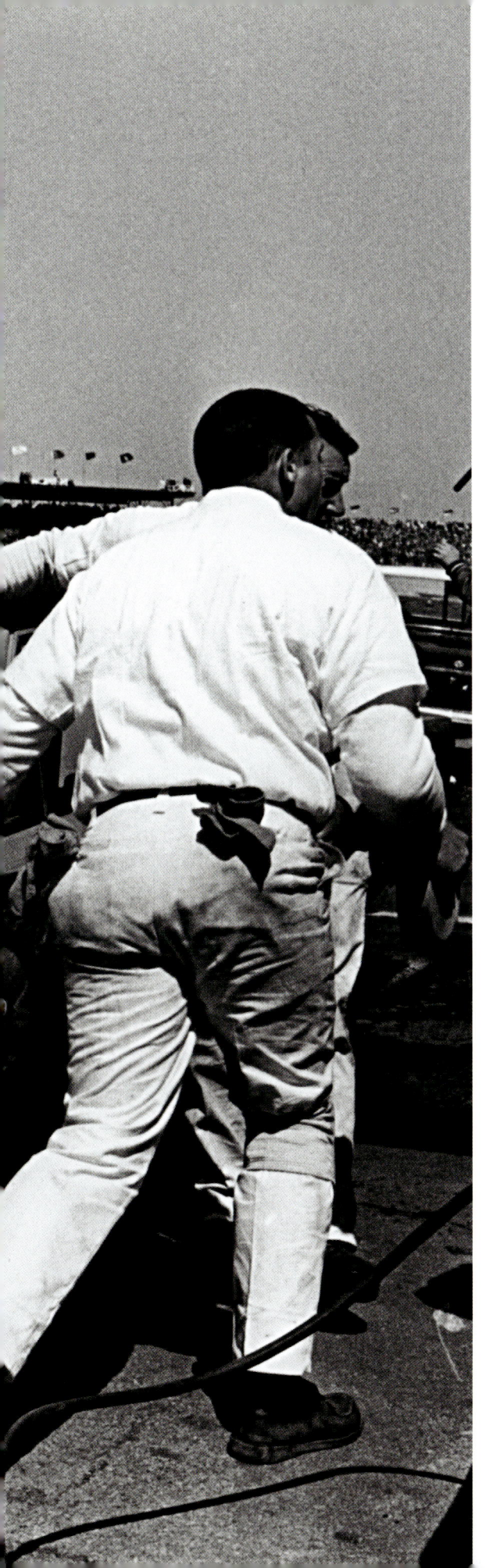

You don't see this often – the driver getting out of the car on a pit stop and beating the mercy out of it with a hammer. That would be Richard Petty, thumping on the vinyl roof covering, which was popping up and acting like a sail and slowing his car down.

people that helped me and stuff, it was a gradual deal. It wasn't a deal where you didn't do anything one year and you come out and win 10 or 12 races next year or a championship or something like that. It grew, and I grew up with NASCAR. It just kept adding on day after day after day and it just built into what it is now."

In the 1970s, Petty strengthened his marketing persona when he donned a pair of STP sunglasses and wore a Charlie 1 Horse cowboy hat. The glasses and hat became the symbols of NASCAR's king of all drivers, a trademark pushed not only by Petty, but by keen marketing people at STP and R.J. Reynolds Tobacco Company, whose Winston cigarette brand became Grand National's title sponsor in 1971. Petty said he was positioned in the right place at the right time when big-time stock-car racing started to spread its wings.

"Between RJR and STP, the first thing you knew, people in New Hampshire knew about us and people in Wisconsin and people in Texas or whatever," he said. "So we were thrown out there and the people just

Far left Richard Petty celebrates his most unexpected Daytona 500 victory in 1979 with his wife Lynda. Petty was nearly a half a lap behind race leaders Donnie Allison and Cale Yarborough. On the last lap of the 500, Allison and Yarborough crashed, opening the door to Petty's sixth victory in NASCAR's biggest race. While Petty celebrated in Victory Lane, Yarborough, Donnie Allison and his older brother Bobby Allison slugged it out near the crash site.

Left Petty scrambled out of his burning stock car after crashing in his final career start at Atlanta in 1992. Crew chief Robbie Loomis and his pit crew pieced it back together so Petty could ride under his last checkered flag.

Right Petty had an unusual habit of holding a wet rag in his mouth during races, which helped quench his thirst during a race. It would be impossible today, since drivers are required to wear full-face helmets by NASCAR.

had heard about it, and then it come along with a little TV and then come along out there with a big TV deal and put us out there in everybody's deal, and then they started building racetracks in other parts of the country – Chicago, Kansas City, Phoenix, all around. So first thing you know, we go all around the country but we are already pre-sold because a lot of our sponsors have been using us as a nationwide sponsorship, even though the majority of the races came in the South or Southeast.

"So all of those things together, just a little bit at a time, just like taking one step at a time, some of the steps are two or three, you skip a couple of steps and jump up big. There's not any one thing that made anything happen. It's just a bunch of people over a period of time and a lot of them working independently just to make their part of the series better. And as they join all together, NASCAR today is what you have."

To celebrate his last year as a NASCAR racer in 1992, Petty Enterprises Inc. and STP organized a season-long "Fan Appreciation Tour." It is estimated he signed at least one million autographs. Once, in Nashville, the man who has signed thousands upon thousands of hats and shirts and photos, signed a duck. A live, web-footed, quacking duck.

His last day in the cockpit was November 15, 1992, in the Hooters 500 at Atlanta Motor Speedway. Petty had not won a race in eight years and nobody expected a miracle finish on that cold afternoon in Hampton, Georgia. Petty knew his driving career should have ended in the 1980s, as he indicated in 1992. "The Good Lord gave me 25 good years of racing and I tried to stretch it out to 35," he said from behind the ever-present cowboy hat and sunglasses. In the '92 finale, Petty crashed the No. 43 Pontiac, which caught on fire. With the car towed behind the pit wall, his team worked frantically on the car as the race progressed and finally got it operational, which allowed "The King" to end his career taking one last checkered flag. He finished 35th, four positions behind a kid racer by the name of Jeff Gordon, making his first run in the Winston Cup Series. As one brilliant career ended, another was about to begin, one that would take NASCAR to new heights, and truly bring out the personalities in the sport. ■

Paying homage to "King Richard"   87

Where this madness started

When recalling the Daytona Beach & Road Course, William C. ("Bill Jr.") France would respond with a hearty chortle. "We would lease the land for the race and charge people to stand on property that didn't belong to us. My father was a genius."

NASCAR Modifieds thunder through the North Turn on the Daytona Beach & Road Course in this photo from the early 1950s.

Car owner John Holman (left), NASCAR founder and president William H.G. France (center), and his son William C. France discuss the driver revolt in the days leading up to the 1969 Talladega 500, the first race to be held at Alabama International Motor Speedway. Professional Drivers Association members boycotted the event, which had the sanctioning body in a scramble to assemble a field for the inaugural race.

France's dad was William H.G. France, the founder of NASCAR, the first lion of stock-car racing. "Big Bill" France used the beach and A1A as a temporary race course from 1938 to 1958, excluding the war years. The Daytona course – which actually moved south into neighboring Ponce Inlet over time because of development along the coast – was approximately four miles long and a favorite of racers. But the elder France knew in the early 1950s that beach racing would someday become extinct due to the houses and motels being built in the area. The beach was just becoming too clogged with construction. France reasoned that the only way to keep big-time stock-car racing in the community was to construct a stand-alone race course that would rival Indianapolis Motor Speedway in size and scope.

As early as 1953, France had his eyes on a piece of swampland adjacent to the airport in Daytona. Dan Warren, a young city commissioner then, said he went to the proposed site with France and city engineer Charlie Moneypenny, who had recommended the area and designed the course. Ideas were one thing. Building a super-sized racing facility in the middle of nowhere, on the outskirts of a town light in the wallet, was another. France tried to secure public money, but ran into a dead end. He pitched his speedway-in-the-swamp dream to moguls, tycoons and industrialists, who all turned him down. "Big Bill" just would not take no for the final answer. "He was the most unusual person I ever met in my life," Warren told the *Daytona Beach News-Journal*. "He was the extreme optimist. He used to say, 'Everything is gonna be all right.'"

Even a blind frog will catch a fly if it flicks its tongue often enough. In France's case, it was blind luck. By chance, France met businessman Clint Murchison – the man who started the NFL's Dallas Cowboys franchise – and gave the Texas oilman an airplane ride to Miami. France owned a small prop plane that he used for quick trips in the South and up the East Coast. Since there were no parachutes in the aircraft, Murchison had no escape as France delivered his entire superspeedway spiel. Murchison

Race fans love to brag about their favorite drivers and a flag is the perfect way to express love of a driver. This is a flag cluster from the 2005 Daytona 500.

"He was like a bulldog, as far as getting something done . . . If he hit one dead end, he'd go down another alley."

agreed to a $600,000 loan. Coupled with money from the sale of International Speedway Corporation shares and "Big Bill's" personal savings, the project was started in 1957. The estimated cost to build Daytona International Speedway varies from $1 million to $3 million, but everyone agrees France had just enough money to get the facility open for the 1959 Speedweeks program. "He was like a bulldog, as far as getting something done," Bill France Jr. told the *News-Journal*. "If he hit one dead end, he'd go down another alley." The younger France was part of the construction crew, working heavy equipment, like a motor grader used to shape the foundation before the asphalt was laid.

The new track had few amenities – limited women's restroom facilities, for instance – and the Speedway was not prepared for the stampede of passenger cars that flocked to the track on February 22 for the inaugural Daytona 500. Horrified, teenaged parking attendants, dressed in white jumpsuits, soon abandoned their positions as aggressive spectators claimed the first open patch of grass or gravel they could find behind the long, main grandstand. According to the official race report, 41,921 race fans crammed into the bleacher-type seats or were scattered in the vast Speedway infield. The first three rows of seating were the first that sold out; race fans figuring the closer, the better, like most sporting events. Lou Fuchs (pronounced "Fox"), who had a front row seat for the inaugural Daytona 500, said he was covered in dust and rubber fragments when the 200-lapper was finished. "I was wearing sunglasses," he said. "When I took them off, I looked like a raccoon because my face was covered with dirt and oil that blew off the cars and into the seats."

It was that excited throng, estimated to be twice as large as any race on the Beach &

90 Man-made Thunder

Daytona International Speedway added a lighting system in 1998 at the cost of $4 million, or about $1 million more than it cost to build the entire track in 1958. Daytona now runs about half its racing events at night because it adds to the drama of the event.

Road Course, which kept "Big Bill's" dream alive. France delivered the pre-race prayer via the track's crude public address system. He was hardly the religious type. After blessing the 59 drivers about to risk life and limb in a high-speed chase, he abandoned the normal "amen" to end his prayer. Instead, with head bowed, he concluded with: "Sincerely, Bill France." The next year he recruited a preacher, the Reverend Hal Marchman, to deliver the pre-race benediction. It was the good-natured Marchman who best described the annual Speedweeks ritual as "Redneck High Holy Days."

Now Daytona Beach's racing history can be clearly defined in three stages: From 1903–35, there were Land Speed Record runs on the beach; from 1936 to 1958, stock-car races were staged on the Beach & Road Course; and from 1959 until today, there has been that formidable speedway course that "Big Bill" built in a slough.

When stock-car drivers conquer Daytona, they not only add their names to the Speedway's relatively short list of winners, but extend the century-long tradition of automobiles going fast in the seaside town. It is that history which makes a Daytona trophy special. It's

> "If the [first] race had been rained out, we were bankrupt."

that mystique that helped bring Richard Petty, a seven-time Daytona 500 champion, into the national sports spotlight. "Richard Petty wouldn't be Richard Petty without all those Daytona wins," he said. In the first few years of its life, the Speedway lived a dicey existence. It could have been reclaimed by the Florida bog, if not for the intrigue it offered spectators who pushed through the turnstiles in droves. Fifty years after "Big Bill" opened the gates to this speed paradise, Warren recalled the earliest days and the frail financial ground upon which Daytona International Speedway sat. "Bill told me, 'If the [first] race had been rained out, we were bankrupt,'" Warren told the News-Journal, "That's how close it was." ∎

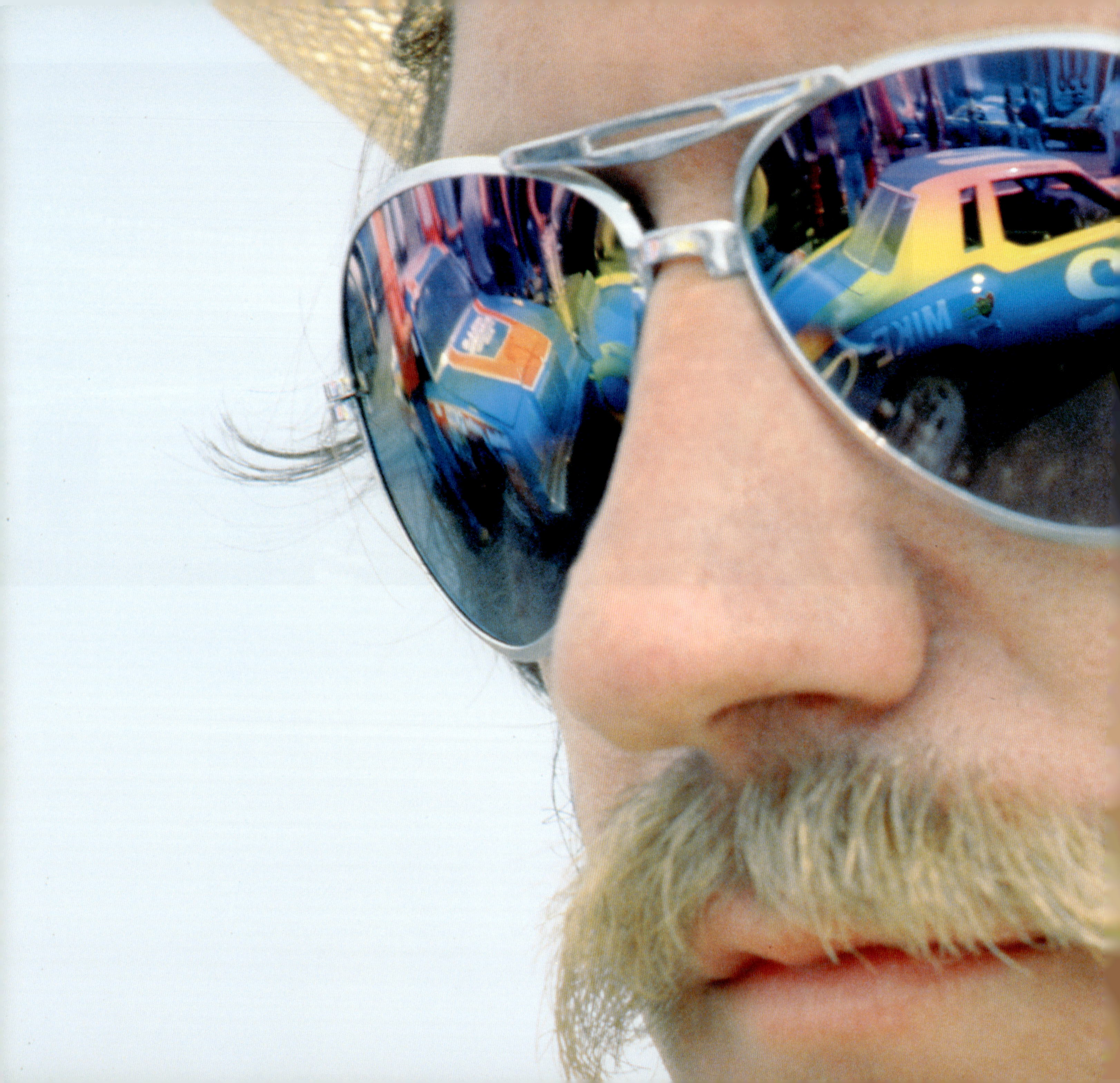

Man in black

4

Previous page Dale Earnhardt, a rookie in 1979, keeps an eye on his No. 2 Chevrolet owned by Rod Osterlund.

A T-shirt salute to Dale Earnhardt from the 1986 season. Earnhardt was building his NASCAR image as the "Intimidator." NASCAR fans like to show support for their favorite driver by wearing shirts and jackets emblazoned with their name or image.

Junior Johnson has an interesting yarn he likes to spin about Dale Earnhardt, the man who won seven NASCAR Winston Cup championships and, maybe just as importantly, took motorsports marketing to a new level. As Johnson tells it, he went to Anheuser-Busch's marketing department, hoping to sell them on the idea of letting him hire Earnhardt as a driver for the 1984 season. The folks at A-B brew America's favorite beer, Budweiser, and they have a gigantic sports marketing budget. At the time, they had agreed to fund Johnson's two-car Cup Series team.

"Well, when Budweiser was my sponsor there, they did not particularly like Dale's profile, you know," Johnson says in a slow, southern drawl. "He was an outspoken, you might say redneck, southerner, is what he was. And they, well, they kinda shied away from him. That's one reason I didn't ever have Earnhardt as a driver – because I was with Budweiser." And so, Earnhardt and his Wrangler sponsorship went to Richard Childress Racing, where the two men masterminded six championship runs and used Earnhardt's personality to their advantage. What the business folks

"That's one reason I didn't ever have Earnhardt as a driver – because I was with Budweiser."

at Budweiser didn't realize when they passed on Earnhardt was this: Under that gruff exterior, there was a Monet on the canvas. If Earnhardt was art, the A-B businessmen only saw the modern-day American classic *Dogs Playing Poker*. The decision makers at A-B thought Earnhardt was backward, too country, had no polish and would be a poor spokesman for their mass-produced hops-and-barley creation. At that time, they had no idea what they were letting slip through their hands.

It seems that the Budweiser trust missed the data showing that Earnhardt's redneck persona would play in Peoria. His was a snarling image that the driver would massage and develop into NASCAR's face of the working man. He would become nothing short of a stock-car icon.

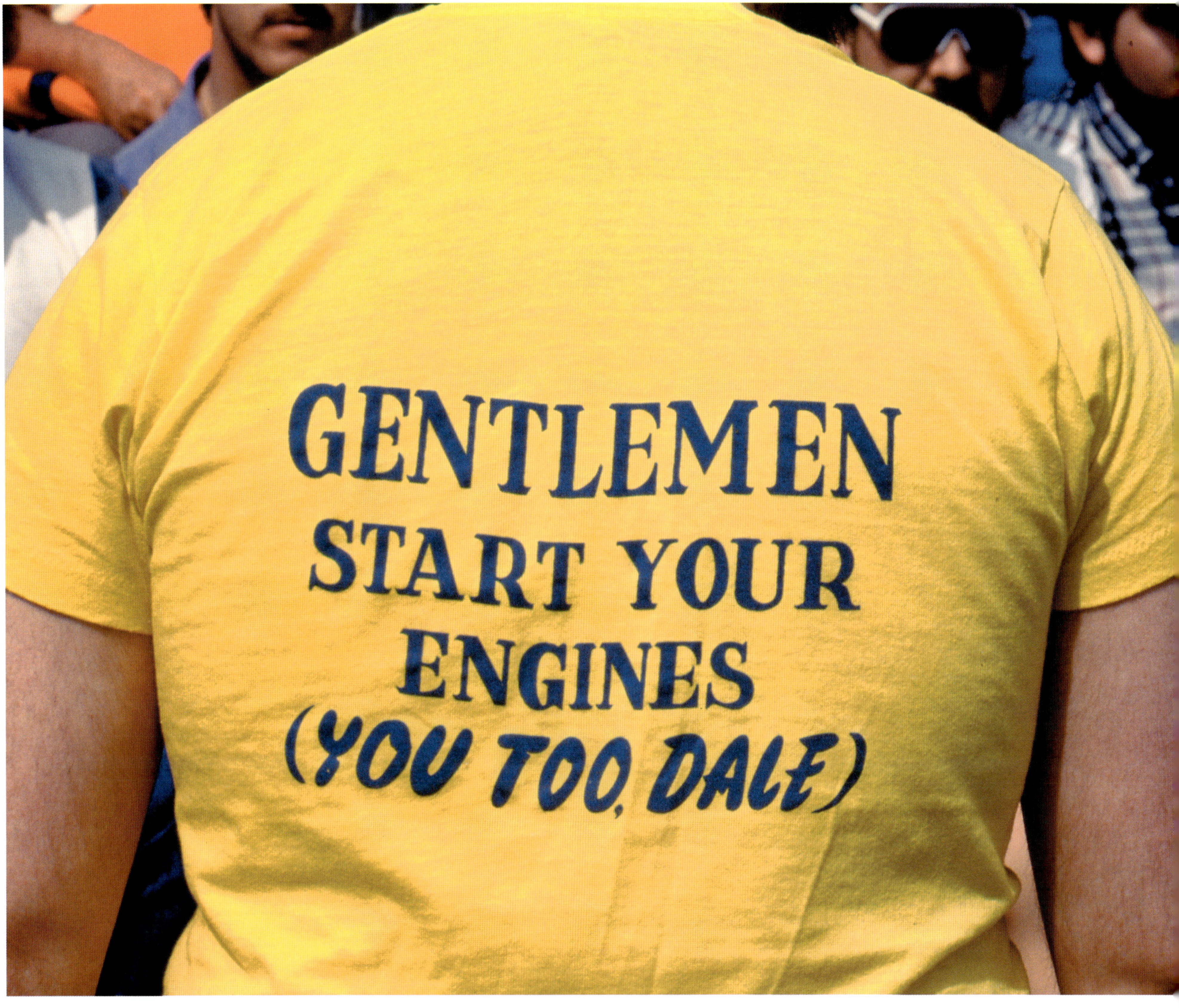
GENTLEMEN
START YOUR
ENGINES
(YOU TOO, DALE)

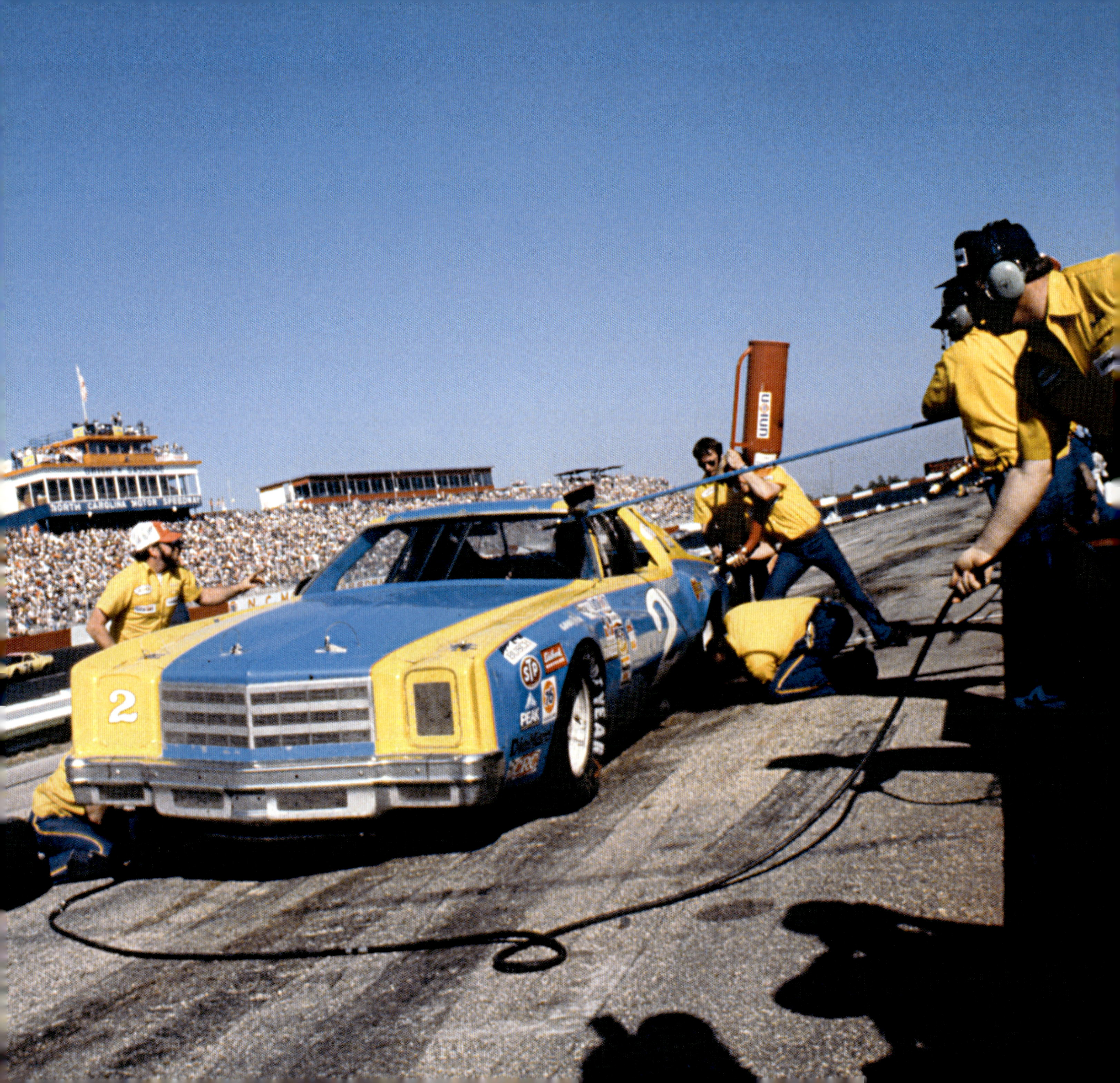
2
STP
PEAK

Left Dale Earnhardt brings his Wrangler-sponsored No. 2 Chevrolet to pit road for service. Rod Osterland was the car owner who plucked Earnhardt from the short-track circuit to run NASCAR's big-league tour.

Right Dale Earnhardt (right) and Doug Richert, his crew chief at the time, discuss stock-car setup at Charlotte Motor Speedway during the 1986 season.

They missed all of that in the St. Louis headquarters of Anheuser-Busch. Of course, back then, Earnhardt was rough around the edges, but learned men of racing, such as Johnson, knew he was something special. It took three years for the Earnhardt-Childress tandem to hit complete stride, but they made stock-car magic, as well as history. Earnhardt had captured his first NASCAR crown with car owner Rod Osterlund in 1980. Midway through the 1981 season, Osterlund sold his franchise to Jim Stacy, a deal unacceptable to Earnhardt. He bolted from the team to run 11 races with Childress, himself a former driver.

After the '81 tour was finished, Earnhardt wound up at Bud Moore Engineering, in the No. 15 Ford, but never got in the groove with Moore, a World War II hero-turned-racer whose shop was located in Spartanburg, South Carolina. After leaving Moore's team, Earnhardt found himself working with Childress again, because Johnson could not get Budweiser's approval to hire him. "I feel more comfortable in Chevrolets," was Earnhardt's explanation for leaving Moore. RCR's first championship came in 1986, and the team defended it in '87. The next year, Wrangler was out, and GM Goodwrench was in. The No. 3 went from blue and yellow to a menacing black with white and silver trim. With the money and success, Earnhardt, who turned 37 in 1988, had become more business savvy and aware that his name was becoming a powerful brand in NASCAR. With his third wife, Teresa, whispering in his ear, Earnhardt began gathering back all his name and image rights from various contracts he had made through the years. That list included Childress and the mothership, Chevrolet. He even started his own company (Sports Image Inc.) to handle sales of his souvenirs and clothes, and developed a new revenue stream like no other driver had enjoyed. Earnhardt's oldest daughter, Kelley, worked at Sports Image after her college years, and now manages the career of Dale Earnhardt Jr., NASCAR's most popular driver.

"In the Wrangler car, he was looked at like a bully," Kelley said of her father. "He wasn't as well-liked by the other competitors." The best example of that bullish mentality came at Charlotte Motor Speedway in

Man in black 97

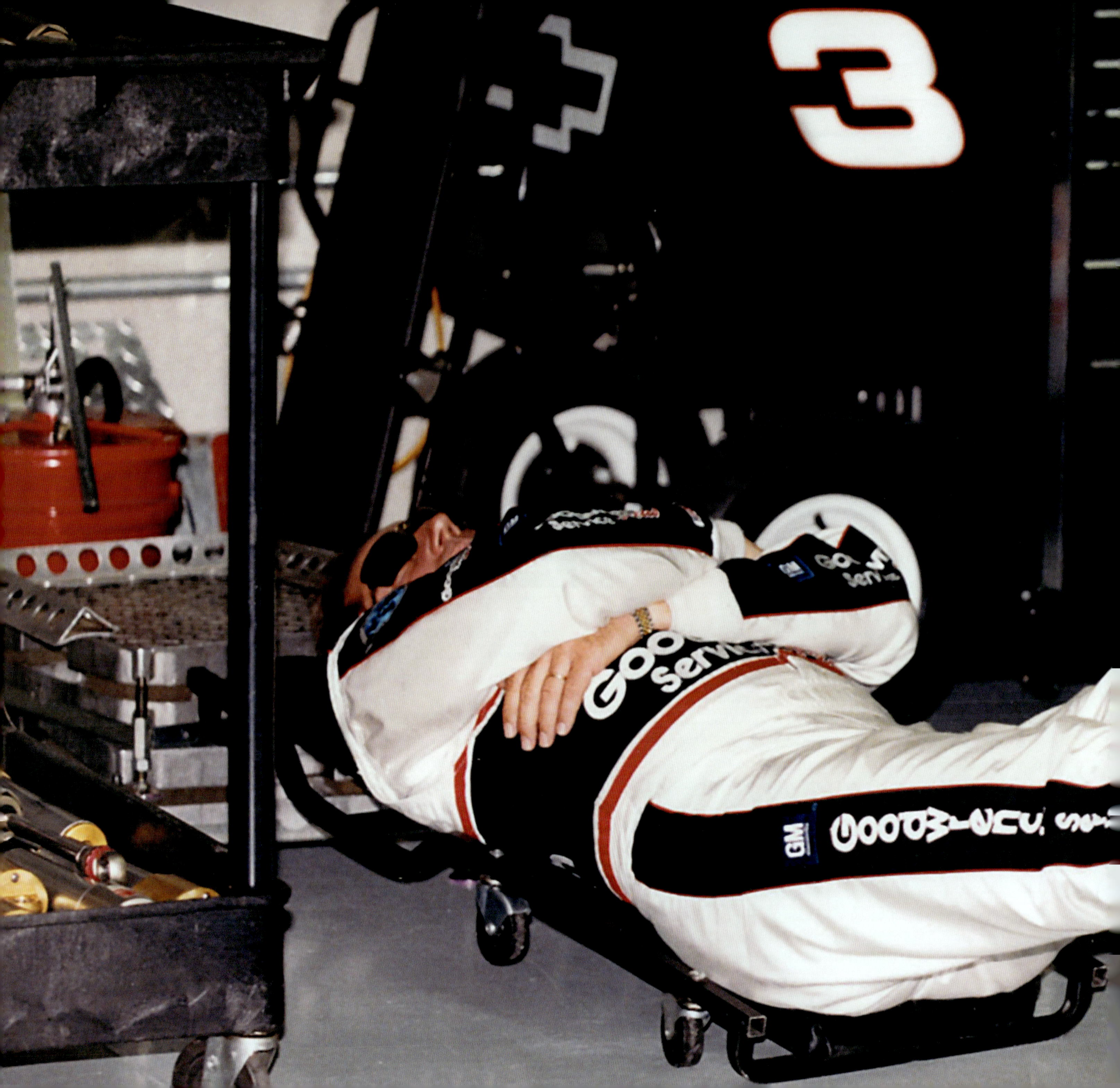
3
GM

Dale Earnhardt catches a nap in the "Gasoline Alley" garage stall at Indianapolis Motor Speedway in 1994. The NASCAR schedule is so hectic that drivers rest whenever they can. Driver Ken Schrader used to catnap in his car while waiting in line to qualify.

Man in black 99

Dale Earnhardt was a master wheel at Darlington Raceway. He scored nine career wins at the track competitors say is "too tough to tame." Darlington was built in 1950. The turns on either end of the track are banked at different levels and have a different turning radius, making the perfect stock-car setup nearly impossible. That is why Darlington is the ultimate "driver's track."

May, 1987, at the expense of veteran superstar Bill Elliott. The race was a high-profile annual exhibition, "The Winston," something of an all-star race featuring an abbreviated field. The cars of Earnhardt and Elliott touched at full speed, and Earnhardt's car was pushed off the asphalt and into the grass. But Earnhardt never cracked the throttle, never relinquished his lead. The incident became known as the "pass in the grass," though it technically wasn't a pass, but a holding of his lead. It made a point regardless, and it was that kind of hell-bent driving and attitude that made Earnhardt a favorite of the blue-collar working-man set that filled most grandstand seats.

"He was a dream for anybody that had him, you know, the outspoken roughness that he was," Johnson said. "He had to be the ideal person for the fans 'cause they wanted to see people fight, run over each other, and bang each other's car up. He made the races, really. He was the best guy at that particular time for the sport." The black car seemed to play a role in changing Earnhardt's stature. It was a symbol of strength. Now Earnhardt was cast in a different, somewhat intimidating light – not unlike the black-and-silver-clad Oakland Raiders of the NFL, a team whose best days were built on attitude as well as ability.

When Earnhardt went to the black color scheme on his car, the media dubbed him the "Man in Black." A few years earlier, in 1985, a vendor named Hank Jones had come up with a line of shirts that described Earnhardt as the "Intimidator" and reportedly made about $200,000 selling T-shirts to fans outside racetracks. Both those nicknames stuck to Earnhardt like peanut butter on a kitchen wall, especially the "Intimidator" moniker. The black car, the GM sponsorship, the nicknames – all helped form Earnhardt's racetrack personality and created a bigger-than-life image for the driver. "The GM Goodwrench/Earnhardt marketing campaign was one of the most brilliant in American marketing. Not sport marketing, just marketing," said H.A. "Humpy" Wheeler, the former president of Lowe's Motor Speedway, who helped reshape NASCAR's top series. "Earnhardt was the real thing and it just fit what they did perfect."

100   Man-made Thunder

Man in black

Before Daytona International Speedway installed a light system in 1998, the track staged its Pepsi 400 summer race in the blazing sun. Here, Dale Earnhardt gets a bit of shade thanks to his umbrella-toting wife Teresa before the start of the 1995 Pepsi 400.

102   Man-made Thunder

Right Winning never got old for Dale Earnhardt, here celebrating his record-tying seventh NASCAR Winston Cup Series championship with his third wife, Teresa, and car owner Richard Childress at North Carolina Motor Speedway in the fall of 1994.

Far right Homemade signs are common at the racetrack, and no driver in NASCAR history had more than Dale Earnhardt, who elicited the most passion – good and bad – from race fans across the country.

For a time there, Earnhardt was the driver people loved to hate. During driver introductions, he would be booed by spectators, and he in turn egged them on by waving his arms as if to say, "Bring it on!" While developing business acumen, he was also producing numbers at the track; back-to-back Winston Cup Series championships in 1986–87, 1990–91, and again in 1993–94. He was becoming a regular at the Presidential Suite – complete with a butler – inside the Waldorf-Astoria hotel in Manhattan, where NASCAR's annual awards banquet is held each December. Series sponsor R.J. Reynolds Tobacco Company, footed the bill for the champion's stay.

Even with the wealth and fame, there was a void in Earnhardt's spectacular career. Up to 1998, he had never won the Daytona 500. He'd lost NASCAR's biggest race at least six times in the closing laps of the event. He won a lot of races at Daytona International Speedway, an all-time high 34, when counting various events. The 500 was another story. The best example of his bad luck was in 1990, when he had led 155 laps and had his familiar black car out front on the last circuit, screaming toward the checkered flag. As he entered Turn 3 on the final lap, his car slowed and moved toward the top of the banking. He'd run over a piece of metal and punctured one of his rear tires. He limped home a disappointing fifth, the victory going to upstart Derrike Cope. Earnhardt said he thought he ran over something thrown from the "chicken-bone grandstands," or cheap bleacher-style seats, in Turn 3. The debris actually was a bell housing dropped from another car on the track. Childress had the shredded tire mounted at the race shop.

Every year, Earnhardt faced the same line of questions from the media in Daytona. When will you win this race? How are your chances this year? What happens if you never win? "The 500 is a unique race," Earnhardt told the media in the days leading up to the 1998 Daytona 500. "It's a race that has eluded me. You could write a big book on everything that has happened to me the last 19 years in the Daytona 500." Despite the aggravating line of questions, Earnhardt stayed stoic. "Every year when

Man in black 103

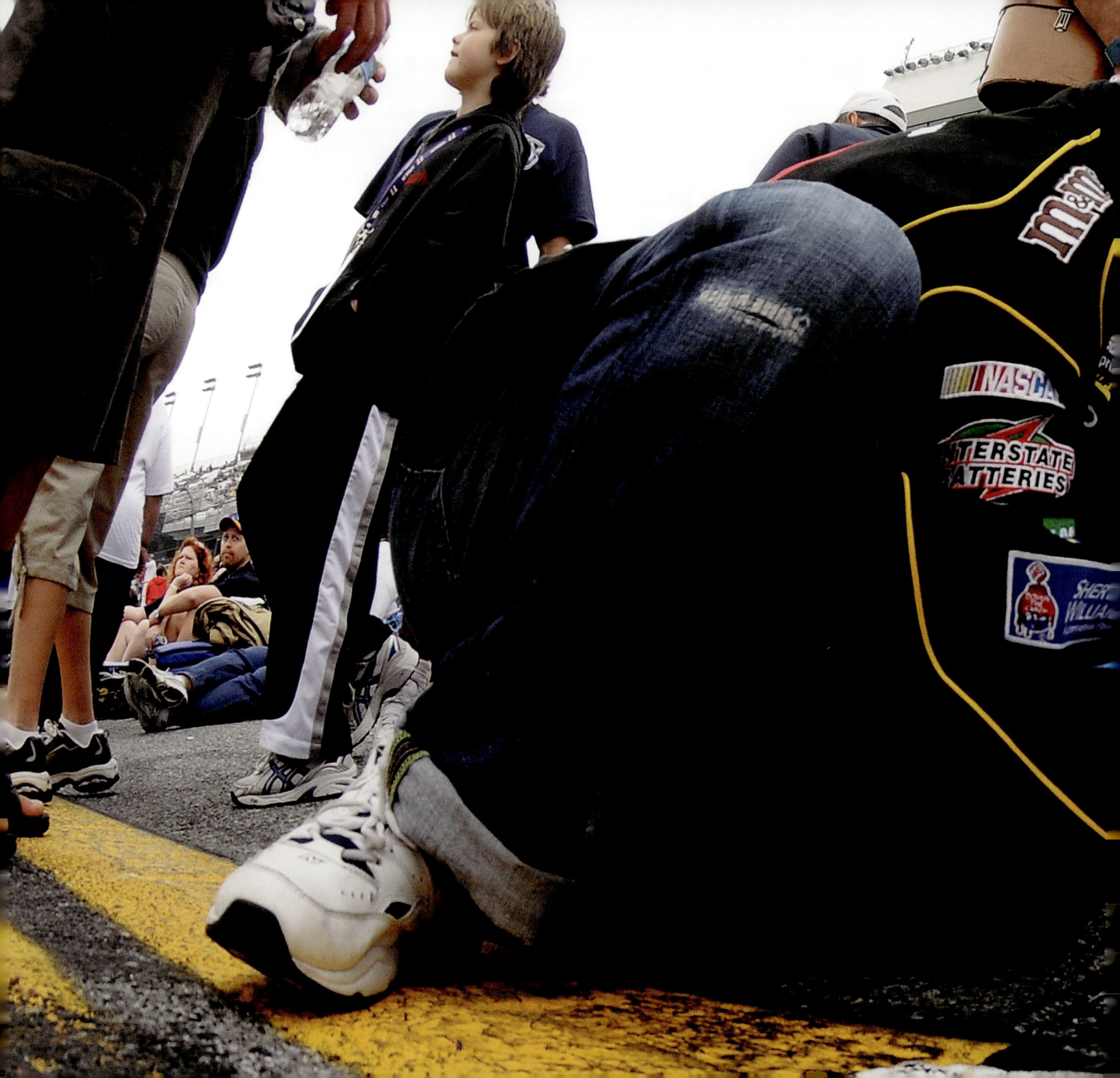
NASCA
NTERSTATE
ATTERIES

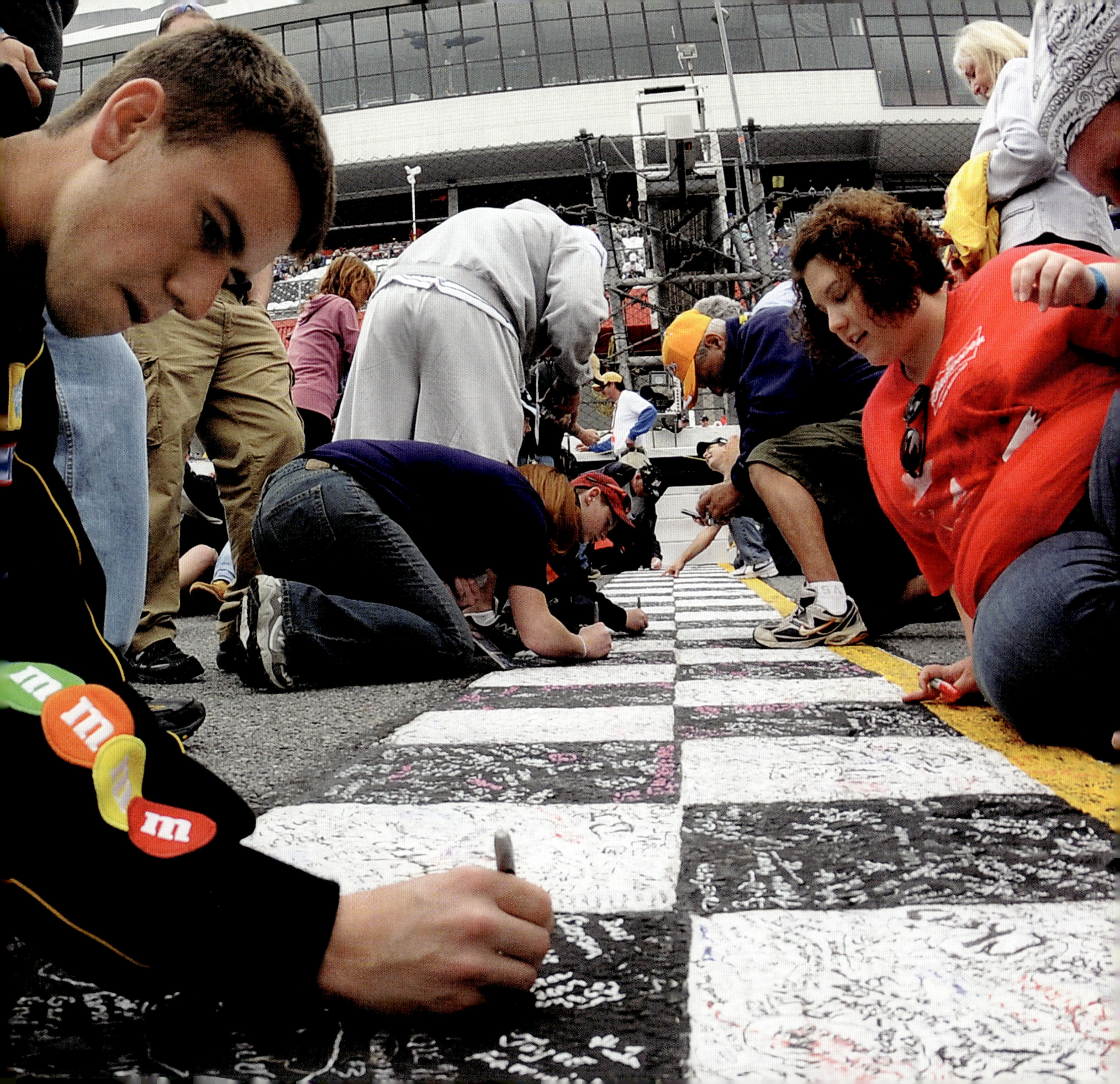

Previous page Race fans sign their names on the start-finish line at Daytona International Speedway before the start of the 2009 Daytona 500. Race fans have the advantage over their football and baseball counterparts because many tracks allow fan access on the "playing field" before an event.

On his 20th attempt, Dale Earnhardt celebrates his first Daytona 500 win with a fist pump out of the driver's side window. Soon after, Earnhardt was congratulated over his two-way radio by "Captain Jack," who was NASCAR president Bill France Jr.

How important was this victory? In Victory Lane he crooned, "It tops 'em all, buddy. It tops 'em all."

you come into the Daytona 500, you feel like you've got everything going for you," he said. "You feel like you've got the best team, the best car, the best engines, everything is working great for you. I feel like this is a great year for us. I'm very confident right now."

Earnhardt got the 500 monkey off his back in 1998, on his 20th Daytona 500 attempt. How important was this victory? In Victory Lane he crooned, "It tops 'em all, buddy. It tops 'em all. To come and get that checkered flag is a feeling you can't replace." The giant victory came after two disappointing years of racing, including a slump of 59 straight events without a victory. The Earnhardt brand received yet another boost and his expanding legion of fans reached a new state of euphoria. "I remember

106   Man-made Thunder

Man in black 107

108   Man-made Thunder

Left Dale Earnhardt, in the No. 2 Chevrolet, knocks Richard Petty, in the No. 43 Chevy, out of the way at Martinsville Speedway in 1980. Earnhardt was labeled a bully by fans for knocking heads with the veteran drivers of the day.

Right Tim Richmond, shown here in 1985, was one of Dale Earnhardt's greatest rivals, although their track battles didn't last very long. Richmond was very different from his NASCAR contemporaries. He came from the Indy-car ranks, had Hollywood looks and didn't have a southern accent. Car owner Rick Hendrick said, "He was about 20 years ahead of his time. He had a condo in New York; a girlfriend from California; lived on a boat in Fort Lauderdale. All the guys [back then] had on cowboy boots, big buckles and cowboy hats. He comes in with a New York hairdo and a silk suit and a cane and purse."

Right It's become a NASCAR tradition for the sport's bigger events – the military fly-over during the last stanza of the national anthem. Nothing pumps a race crowd up more than seeing air force fighter jets making a low pass over a speedway.

the last couple of laps of it like it was yesterday," Childress says today. "We'd been there before and lost it before." And that night after the victory, Childress says, "[Earnhardt] just kept saying, the one thing he kept saying, 'We done it, we done it.' "

Earnhardt is an important link in the NASCAR continuum, bridging the last glory years of Richard Petty to the future success of Jeff Gordon. Petty won the last of his seven NASCAR titles in 1979, the same year Earnhardt earned Rookie of the Year honors. Earnhardt's first championship came in 1980, a year after Petty's seventh and final crown. Petty's last race as a driver was in 1992, the same event where Gordon made his Winston Cup Series debut. Earnhardt snatched the baton from Petty and Gordon took it from Earnhardt. It's the way of stock-car racing.

Earnhardt loved Daytona, had a passion for the place, because of its history and speed, and because of his respect for William C. France, the son of NASCAR's founder. There is a tragic irony. Three years after his tops-'em-all victory, Earnhardt crashed in Turn 4 on the last lap of the

Earnhardt is an important link bridging the last glory years of Richard Petty to the future success of Jeff Gordon.

Daytona 500. He died instantly from a basilar skull fracture. Later that week, his image was on the cover of *Time* magazine, testament to the great loss suffered by the sports world, and to the national popularity stock-car racing was enjoying.

Before Earnhardt left, he had got the last laugh on Anheuser-Busch. In 1999, he negotiated a sponsorship deal for the Budweiser brand (probably five times greater than the money Junior Johnson would have been paid) to fund the No. 8 Dale Earnhardt Inc. Chevrolet, driven by his son, Dale Jr. That sponsorship deal lasted eight years, and cost tens of millions of dollars. "They [Bud] come back and eat him up at the end," Johnson said with a chuckle. ∎

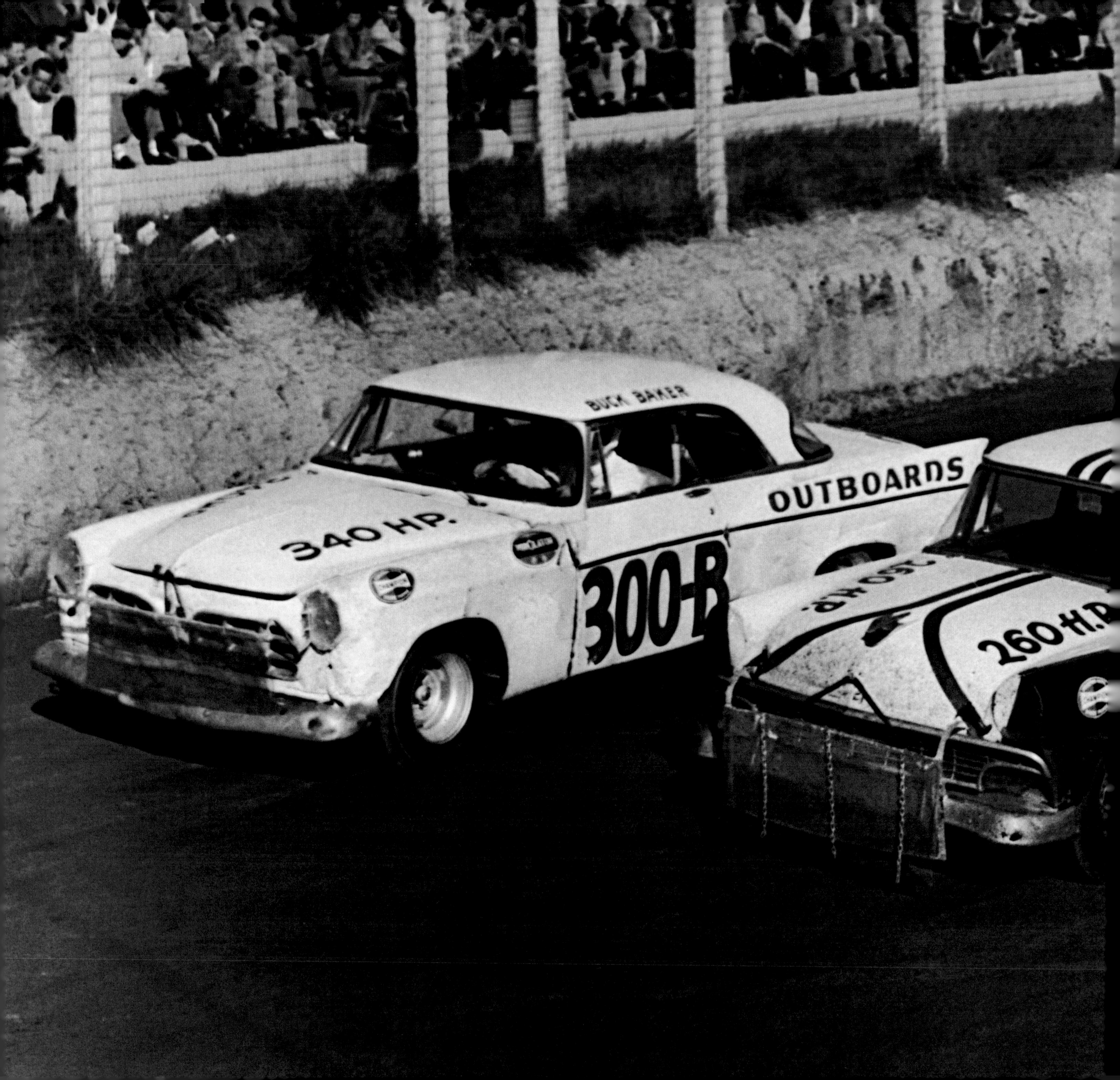
BUCK BAKER
340 HP.
OUTBOARDS
300-B

Ralph Earnhardt, in the No. 22 Ford, prepares for the green flag against Buck Baker, in the No. 300-B Chrysler owned by Carl Kiekhaefer, at Hickory Speedway in 1956. This was Earnhardt's first Grand National Series start. He scored his career best NASCAR Grand National Series finish in this race, finishing second to Speedy Thompson.

Mill town racer

Ralph Lee Earnhardt was the father of five. He worked 12-hour shifts in the textile factories in and around his hometown of Kannapolis, North Carolina.

Needless to say, it wasn't much of a life. "Mill town people had a work ethic," Marshall Brooks told *All Race* magazine. Brooks was owner of Marshall Motor Company in Concord, North Carolina. He was friends with the Earnhardt family. "When the mill worked six days a week and 12 hours a day, you worked." Ralph Earnhardt wanted a way out and found it by starting a stock-car racing career. Through the years, Earnhardt built a grassroots organization, working out of an expanded garage at his house. His forte was short-track dirt racing, and at the age of 28, he captured NASCAR's coveted national Sportsman Championship. "Racing was a hobby," Frank Dayvault told *All Race*. "It was cheap to race

Man in black 111

Richard Petty discusses his 1981 Daytona 500 win in Victory Lane with Ned Jarrett, a former NASCAR champion turned CBS television announcer. Between them, they had nine championships and 250 wins.

Ralph Earnhardt was considered the epitome of a true race car driver.

then. It wasn't a business. But Ralph was different; to Ralph it was a business. He was able to make a living at it when not many people could."

In Ralph Earnhardt's International Motorsports Hall of Fame biography it says he was known "as one of the hardest chargers of the old school racers and respected by the drivers and car owners alike. Ralph Earnhardt was considered the epitome of a true race car driver. Foregoing the travel demands of the NASCAR circuit, Ralph chose to race primarily on the North Carolina short tracks around his home – allowing him to focus his attention on his race cars and family – although not particularly in that order. He mastered these short tracks compiling hundreds of victories and countless state and track championships. . ."

Ralph, who had three sons and two daughters, passed the racing bug on to son Ralph Dale Earnhardt. Unfortunately, Ralph never got to see Dale reach the pinnacle of racing success. He died of a heart attack in 1973 while working on a race car at his house. Dale was a mere 22-year-old kid, who shared the same speed dream as his father, and continued the Earnhardt racing legacy. Father and son only raced each against each other one time. Dale Earnhardt told the National Press Club about his most memorable experience.

"The one time I did race with him, was at a dirt track, and I was racing the Six-Cylinder Division, and they were short in the Sportsman's race that night. So, the promoter at the track said, 'OK, the top five in the Six-Cylinder Division tonight can line up in the Sportsman tonight, and run the Sportsman race after the Six-Cylinder race.'

"So, we did. I lined up second – I ran second in my race, so I lined up second. And I was racing the same guy that I had raced, trying to win, all night long. And here comes my dad, leading the

112   Man-made Thunder

NASCAR's brightest and best that Ford had to offer in the 1965 season. From left to right: drivers Dick Hutcherson, A.J. Foyt, Fred Lorenzen, Cale Yarborough, Ned Jarrett, Curtis Turner and Junior Johnson, with car owners Ralph Moody and John Holman.

Ralph and Dale Earnhardt had another magical moment in 1998 when both were named to a list of 50 all-time best NASCAR drivers...

race, and he comes up behind us, and he just falls in racing with us, you know? And I was watching, trying to get out of his way, and he kept getting in behind me, and I couldn't figure out what he was doing. Finally, he started bumping me around, so finally I said I better hold this thing straight down the straightaway anyway.

"So I got it straight down the straightaway, and he pushed me by this guy. And I beat the guy, and then daddy drove on past me. The guy protested that the race was fixed, 'cause daddy helped me pass him. And I ran third in the Sportsman race that night, as a matter of fact, so he felt like it was rigged. So, I got one exciting time racing with my daddy, and it was pretty neat to do that. I would have liked to have done more of it."

Ralph Earnhardt had two trademarks. First, he built solid racing equipment at the short-track level, and second, he was a hard-scrabble, tough-nosed competitor who wouldn't give an inch on the racetrack. As two-time NASCAR champion Ned Jarrett once said, "Ralph Earnhardt was absolutely the toughest race driver I ever raced against. On the dirt and asphalt short tracks in Sportsman competition, when you went to the track you knew he was the man to beat."

Ralph and Dale Earnhardt had another magical moment in 1998 when both were named to a list of 50 all-time best NASCAR drivers, coinciding with the sanctioning body's 50th anniversary. Later that week, Dale Earnhardt captured his first and only Daytona 500. "I wish he could have been here to see all of this," Dale Earnhardt said. ■

Racing bloodlines

Why racing? The question was posed to Richard Petty, NASCAR's all-time leader in wins, co-leader in championships, and considered stock-car racing's top ambassador.

Left A case of brotherly love. Kyle Busch leads big brother Kurt Busch at Atlanta Motor Speedway in 2007. They are the only brothers who currently race on a regular basis in the Sprint Cup Series.

Right Kyle Petty, driving the No. 42 Pontiac, bounces off the wall in front of his father, Richard Petty, No. 43 Pontiac, during The Winston, an all-star race at Charlotte Motor Speedway. Kyle finished last. One of the dangers of racing families is rubbing sheet metal during an event.

"My daddy did it, and I just done what he done"

His answer is simple. "My daddy did it, and I just done what he done," he says. "It's just a family business. My daddy done it, I done it and my kids done it. It's been passed down the line. I guess if my daddy had been a farmer, I would be a farmer, too. That's all there is to it."

There is no other sport in the United States, other than thoroughbreds used in high-stakes horse racing, where bloodlines play such an important role in the history and future of the game. For instance, there's the Petty lineage – Lee Petty begat Richard Petty, who begat Kyle Petty. All three men were all-out racers who pushed aside their personal lives to advance the sport in their own way. The Pettys and NASCAR have been in lockstep since 1949, when the sanctioning body hosted the first "Strictly Stock" event (now Sprint Cup Series) on a dustbowl track in Charlotte, North Carolina. Lee, who lived about 90 minutes north of the race site, was intrigued by the prospect of racing his family sedan against other Detroit pedigrees. Lee crashed that day, but didn't give up. He won a race that first year and continued forward to win 54 events and three titles. He only retired because he got busted up so bad after crashing at Daytona. Richard got 200 wins and seven titles, giving the Petty clan 10 championships. There were no championships for Kyle, but he did win eight races and became one of the sport's most popular drivers.

There are several father-son combinations that have given different generations of race fans somebody to cheer for, but only one other father-son combination that produced two generations of championships. Ned Jarrett won a couple of titles before retiring at the ripe old age of 34. Ironically, Ned's youngest son, Dale, didn't win his first Winston Cup Series race until he was 34. Ned was a young whiz, while Dale was slow to bloom. Of Dale's 32 career victories, 24 came when he passed age 40. And unlike his father, who had no wins at Daytona International Speedway, Dale scored three Daytona 500

Man in black 115

Body building is not required to be a NASCAR driver, as evidenced by Donnie Allison, left. His brother, Bobby Allison, middle, would drive his passenger car around town with the heater on in the summer to build up his stamina to heat. Davey Allison, right, was Bobby's oldest son and won 19 races. Together, they formed part of the heralded "Alabama Gang."

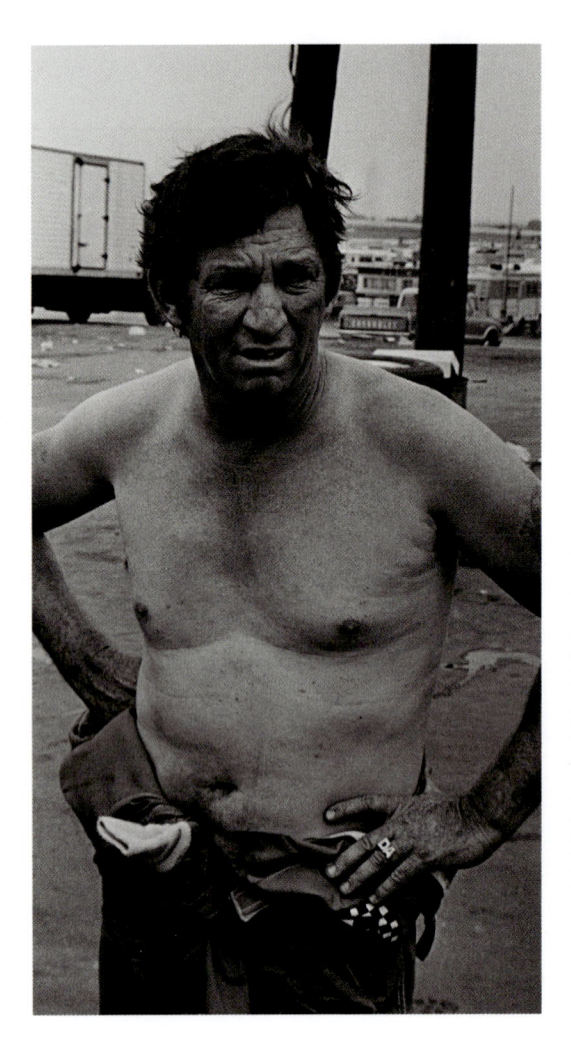

victories for two different car owners. His lone championship was enjoyed in 1999 at the age of 42. "I used to be introduced as 'Ned Jarrett, two-time NASCAR champion,'" says Ned. "Now I'm introduced as 'Dale Jarrett's father.'"

Buck Baker, who stood like a short pile of iron, won a couple of championships, while his son, Elzie Wylie (better known as "Buddy"), excelled in NASCAR's biggest races. To this day, 6-foot-5 Buddy Baker holds the record (177.602 mph) for the fastest average speed in a Daytona 500, set in 1980. Baker led 143 laps that day, and after he emerged from Harry Ranier's No. 28 "Grey Ghost," he slapped the roof of the Oldsmobile so hard, he put a dent in the car. To this day, he can't find the words that adequately describe that afternoon in Daytona. "I wish I could," he said. "I have tried every way in the world. I do a lot of after-dinner speaking and I have my own satellite [radio] show, and that question is impossible for a race-car driver to answer. It is exhilaration, it's, 'OK, you've won the biggest race that we have in NASCAR,' the years of frustration waiting to get into that spot and it finally happening – the emotion was to a point where you almost felt nauseous. It's hard to explain." It was a feeling Buck Baker never got to experience.

It should not come as a surprise that there are three father-son combos who have conquered Daytona. The first was the Pettys, who felt like Daytona was a second home. Then there was Bobby and Davey Allison. Bobby won three 500s. The last time he took the checkered flag, in 1988, Davey was on his rear bumper. Davey won NASCAR's biggest race in 1992. Then there was Dale Earnhardt and Dale Earnhardt Jr. Earnhardt won his in 1998, on his 20th attempt. Dale Jr. captured the flag in 2004, on his fifth try. "Glad that's outta the way," Junior said the night of his victory, relieved that he would not have to carry that burden like his father did for two decades.

And, oh brother! The NASCAR Cup Series has always featured sibling combinations. The list is endless. Some of the more notable include Donnie and Bobby Allison; Darrell and Michael Waltrip; Rusty, Mike and Kenny Wallace; Geoff,

116   Man-made Thunder

Lee Petty gives son Richard Petty some racing advice during the 1965 NASCAR Grand National Series season.

Below Dale Earnhardt raced both his sons only once, in the Pepsi 400 Presented by Meijer at Michigan International Speedway on August 20, 2000. The half-brothers both have the middle name Dale. Dale Earnhardt Jr.'s first name is Ralph. Kerry Dale Earnhardt is to the right of his father.

Brett and Todd Bodine; and all the Flocks – Tim, Bob and Fonty. The chain of brothers continues today with Kurt and Kyle Busch. NASCAR's all-time, overachieving stock-car wheeling siblings are Terry and Bobby Labonte. They are the only brother combination to each win a NASCAR Cup Series title. Terry had two (1984, '96) while Bobby got his in 2000, and they provided NASCAR with one of its biggest family moments on November 10, 1996. Bobby won the season finale at Atlanta as Terry clinched his second championship, then offered some insight into the life of racing families. "Bobby and I are a little different than other brothers in racing," he said that day in Atlanta. "We actually like each other." ∎

Man in black 117

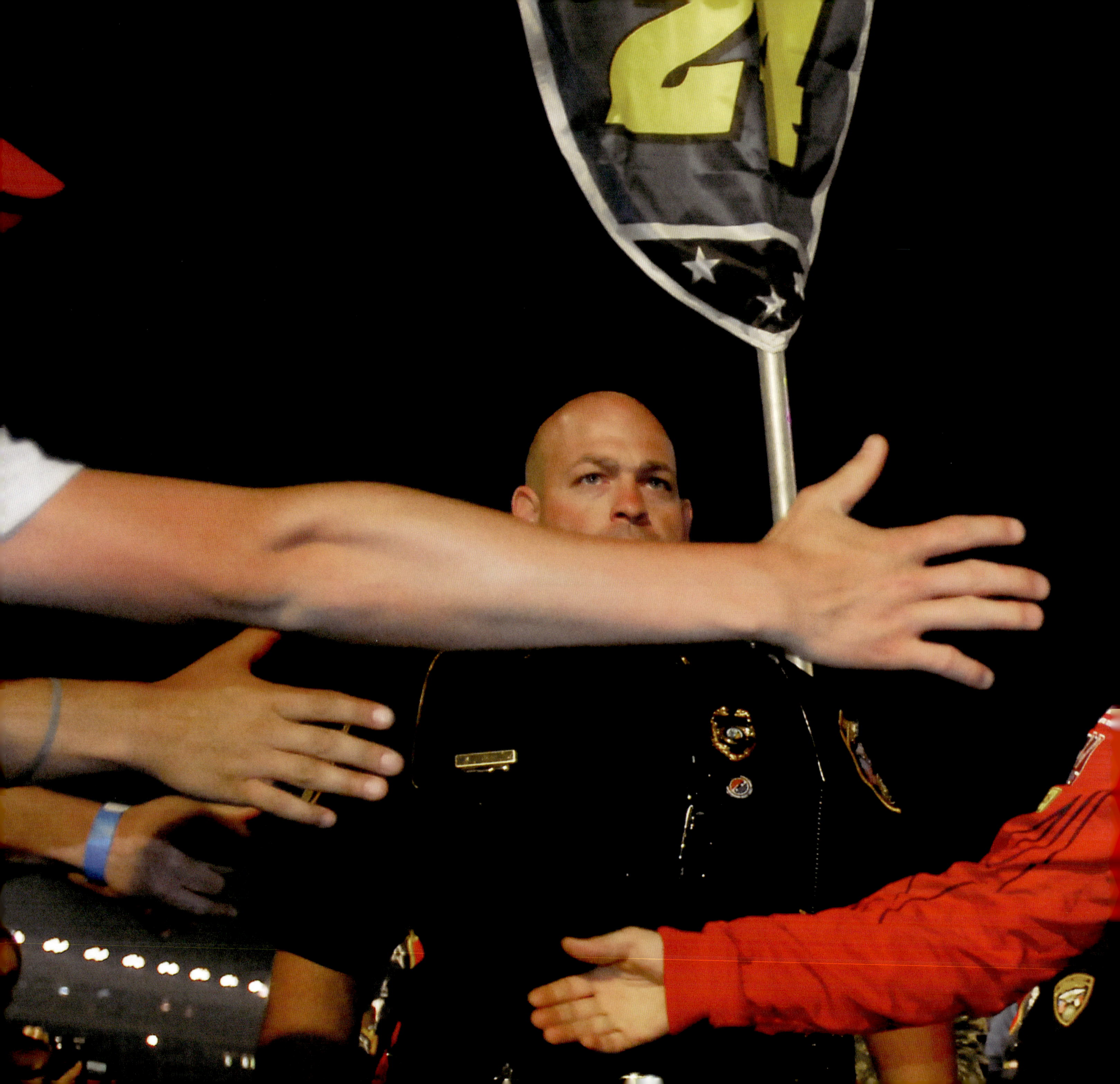
24

5

Modern-day prototype

Previous page After being introduced to the crowd at Lowe's Motor Speedway, Jeff Gordon takes a "celebrity walk" from the stage on pit road to his race car before the 2007 NASCAR Nextel All Star Challenge.

Right An 18-year-old Jeff Gordon, complete with a mullet haircut and poor excuse for a mustache. Not growing a thick mustache was Gordon's lone failure in racing.

Far right Jeff Gordon gets an early education in media training as a television crew shoves a camera into his face on pit road before a NASCAR Busch Series race in 1992. Gordon and other drivers must constantly deal with a demanding media.

From the start, Jeff Gordon's NASCAR career has been a streaming headline – or, in this new media age, a 24/7 blog detailing events and highlights that helped catapult today's Sprint Cup Series into a dizzying state of hyper-exposure. The epidemic began in 1992 when the stock-car racing trade papers, sort of a paparazzi in print in those days, screamed the news that Chevrolet had parachuted into the camp of its most-hated archrival, Ford, extracted the young Gordon and delivered him to the "Bow-tie Brigade" safety zone. Gordon, only 20, had shown the skill of a veteran down in NASCAR's Busch Series – NASCAR's top "minor league" circuit, known today as the Nationwide Series.

Over the course of the 1992 Busch Series season, Gordon, who was born in California and raced sprint cars as a teenager in his adopted Indiana, won three events, including the Atlanta 300 at Atlanta Motor Speedway. It was on that day, at that race, that mega-watt car owner Rick Hendrick was entertaining corporate clients in a speedway suite and instructed his guests to watch Gordon, predicting he would crash.

"He was racing with [Dale] Earnhardt and [Harry] Gant," Hendrick recalled. "I told the people that I was with, 'Watch that car. He's gonna bust his butt.'" But that didn't happen. Somehow, some way, Gordon kept that white No. 1 Ford, complete with the logo of its candy-bar sponsor Baby Ruth, off the concrete walls and took the checkered flag. He was greeted in Victory Lane by his Busch Series team owner, large and bespectacled Arkansas native Bill Davis – they hugged and laughed and posed for the customary photographs. Hendrick liked the driving style he saw that afternoon on the track, and wanted more information about this young sensation. By chance, Gordon's roommate was one of Hendrick's employees. "I said [to the employee], 'It's a shame that kid has a contract.' His roommate that worked for us said, no, he didn't have a contract," Hendrick said.

Hendrick pounced on the opportunity. Two days after the race, Hendrick invited Gordon over to the shop. They sat down at a table, had a few sodas, some light conversation, loosened their shirt collars, one

120 Man-made Thunder

Modern-day prototype 121

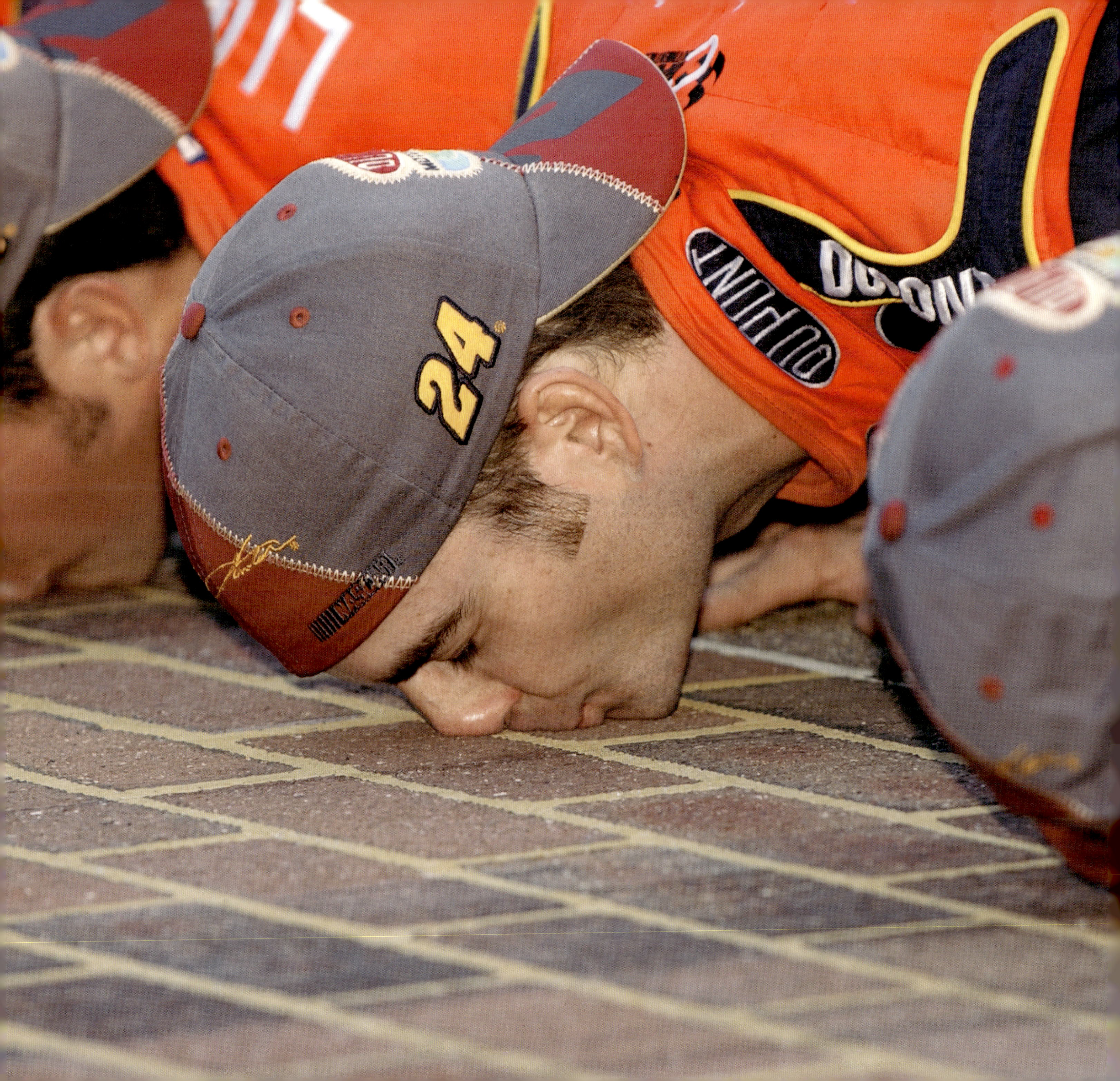
24

Jeff Gordon and his race team kiss the "yard of bricks" after winning the 2004 Brickyard 400 at Indianapolis Motor Speedway. Gordon has tasted brick and mortar four times at the famous racetrack.

It was juicy, hot, rippling gossip that ignited a classic Chevy-Ford feud in the media...

thing led to another, and VOILA! The young Busch Series sensation had a NASCAR Winston Cup Series contract with the sport's most progressive and dynamic car owner. In what many believe was the last major news-story scoop of the weekly racing trade industry, the *National Speed Sports News*, edited by the venerable and vivacious Chris Economaki, shocked the world with an account of how Chevrolet made Ford look like the last guy in the forest on a snipe hunt.

It was juicy, hot, rippling gossip that ignited a classic Chevy-Ford feud in the media, with verbal salvos fired for weeks between top racing officials. It pushed Gordon from the quiet and overlooked Busch Series results page to the front cover of many national sports dailies. This was a good storyline: Two Detroit industrial titans in a game of intrigue and ruthless pursuit of resources – a win-at-any-cost scenario, which grabbed the attention of sports editors from coast to coast. Gordon was just a pawn on the NASCAR chessboard. Back then, Gordon was a relatively little-known entity, with a lot of talent. He had the look of a pale and slight high school sophomore, which included an extremely thin, brushy mustache. No matter. Inside a race car, he resembled a hardened asphalt graybeard, and that's what intrigued the media and Hendrick, who created a third Cup Series car, the No. 24, for the rising star.

After his Winston Cup Series debut at Atlanta in 1992, which ended in a crash, Gordon got an avalanche of off-season, wintertime hype. When he showed up at Daytona International Speedway in February, 1993, his car was awash in a rainbow of colors, thanks to a new sponsorship with DuPont, the auto-paint industry giant. Because of his extreme youth, he became something of a teeny-bopper heartthrob, someone that would even get mom's attention. Because of his speed, he stayed on the

There is very little difference in stock-car bodies because the cars are built according to strict NASCAR specs. The manufacturers are allowed to add their own nose and opera window (side window on back of cars) design and build their own motors. Upper left, No. 82 Toyota Camry of Scott Speed; lower left, No. 44 Dodge Charger of AJ Allmendinger; upper right, No. 17 Ford Fusion that carried Matt Kenseth to victory in the 2009 Daytona 500; lower right, No. 42 Chevrolet Impala SS of Juan Pablo Montoya.

124   Man-made Thunder

NASCAR Sprint Cup Series drivers are identified by the color schemes on their stock cars. The No. 82 Toyota is owned and sponsored by Red Bull, so Scott Speed's car resembles a can of the high-energy drink. AJ Allmendinger's No. 44 Dodge is splashed with the famous "Petty Blue" for the 2009 Daytona 500. DeWalt's company colors are yellow with black trim, as sported by Matt Kenseth's No. 17 Ford. Target's corporate colors are bright red and white and that translates to Juan Pablo Montoya's No. 42 Chevrolet.

Modern-day prototype 125

In a bygone era of racing, NASCAR drivers were more involved with the setup of their stock cars. Here Richard Petty makes notes about a race engine at Petty Enterprises Inc. Today's cars are designed by computer and constantly massaged by teams of engineers. The driver offers input, but rarely is seen with a wrench in hand.

Every stock-car generation has that innovative nuts-and-bolts guy who does things a little differently and shakes up the sport.

media's radar. The Earth, moon and stars continued to align in Jeffrey Michael Gordon's favor at that Speedweeks when he captured a 125-mile qualifying race and, after one last left turn that took him through a gate into Victory Lane, met his future ex-wife, who was smiling and waving in her role as model for series sponsor Winston. Four days later in NASCAR's showcase event, the Daytona 500, Gordon started third, led two laps, and finished fifth.

The guy pulling the levers and turning the knobs behind the scenes for Gordon was crew chief Ray Evernham, then in his late 30s. The rail-thin Evernham was a short-track racer turned mechanic, who challenged every NASCAR measurement. Yes, an evil genius, always looking for the mechanical advantage. Evernham built a race car one time that carried Gordon to a dominating victory. Afterwards, NASCAR officials told Evernham never to bring that particular car back to the track. It was legal – "too legal," if there was such a thing. Every stock-car generation has that innovative nuts-and-bolts guy who does things a little differently and shakes up the sport. In the late 1950s and early '60s, it was the highly esteemed Smokey Yunick; in the 1970s, the nod went to Junior Johnson and his boys in Ingle Hollow, North Carolina; in the 1980s, California-bred Gary Nelson; in the 1990s, Evernham; today's crown is worn by Chad Knaus, who engineered three consecutive Sprint Cup championship runs with driver Jimmie Johnson. Knaus was twice suspended by NASCAR during that string of titles.

In 1993, Gordon was gold, but more like plain ingot; there was rare talent but no refined skill. That first year in The Cup Series saw moments of brilliance and several wadded race cars. On the performance see-saw, Gordon posted seven top-five finishes but suffered 11 DNFs (as in "did not

Modern-day prototype 127

Left NASCAR boasts it is the top, fan-friendly sport in the country. Here, four-time Sprint Cup Series champion Jeff Gordon signs autographs for a group of fence-hugging fans before qualifying for the 2006 Pennsylvania 500 at Pocono Raceway.

Right A.J. Foyt is the model of old-time, tough-guy driver, unlike the dashing Jeff Gordon. Here the scruffy, old-school driver participates in the one media opportunity that he actually enjoyed – the winner's interview from Victory Lane.

128   Man-made Thunder

> **... NASCAR fans found out just how different Gordon was from the usual, leather-necked, steely-eyed, good-ol'-boy race driver.**

finish"). It was Evernham who patiently worked and shaped and molded the boyish stock-car jockey into a champion, an assignment that required nearly 18 months of effort but was worth every ounce of sweat. The two men averaged 8.4 wins and enjoyed three titles between 1994 and 1998. Evernham left before the end of the 1999 season to become point man for Dodge's return to big-league racing. From 2000 to 2008, without Evernham, Gordon averaged 3.6 wins and had one crown (2001). In 2008, for the first time since his rookie year, Gordon had no wins. Yes, the man with the wrench in his hand does make a tremendous difference.

Gordon had his breakthrough victory on May 29, 1994, in the Coca-Cola 600 at Charlotte Motor Speedway, thanks to some fancy, late-race pit strategy by Evernham. That's when NASCAR fans found out just how different Gordon was from the usual, leather-necked, steely-eyed, good-ol'-boy race driver. When Gordon got to Victory Lane, he broke down and cried. It happened again that year on August 6, when Gordon nabbed the inaugural Brickyard 400 at prestigious Indianapolis Motor Speedway, previously off limits to stock-car types and their cars. Gordon had lived in the Indianapolis area in his early teens and skipped high school several times to watch Indianapolis 500 qualifying. He had dreams of some day competing in the Indy 500, and now found himself in the Winner's Circle at the famed Brickyard. Trying to avoid another public display of emotion, Gordon said he took an extra spin around the 2.5-mile course to cry in the cockpit. "I took an extra lap so I could wipe away the tears," he confessed soon after the race. "I don't want to be a crybaby or anything, but I just get emotional. At Charlotte, I about hyperventilated and almost needed oxygen and I didn't want to do that again." The win had a real fairytale spin to it, so much so, that Disney signed Gordon to one of those famous "I'm

Unlike Formula One, where cars launch from a sitting position, NASCAR races begin with a controlled, rolling start behind a pace car. There are a number of reasons why this technique is employed. First, it allows the drivers a chance to warm-up their racing tires to provide maximum grip to the track surface, and if there's any sort of fluid leak in the car, NASCAR officials have the chance to detect it and order the car to pit road for inspection. The speed of pace laps varies from track to track, from 60 mph at Daytona, to 30 mph at short tracks.

The tears and money flowed and a new breed of stock-car star was created.

going to Disney World" television commercials. The tears and money flowed and a new breed of stock-car star was created.

Gordon, 23 when he conquered Indianapolis, quickly matured and realized the marketing bonanza before him. The mustache was now gone. His hair was neatly cropped. He dressed better. Gordon started to look more like a rising Hollywood star rather than a stock-car journeyman. His success, charm and good looks, coupled with a new nationwide interest in the NASCAR brand, attracted new spectators – fans well beyond NASCAR's base of the Deep South. "I think the sport was on a steep incline at that time anyway, but he just brought a different audience," Evernham says today. "You know, people say he was different and Jeff didn't want to be like this guy and he didn't want to be like that guy . . . he certainly knew how to drive a race car and had unbelievable talent, but he also just had a little bit more . . . probably . . . knowledge of the sport and of sponsorship and of marketing, maybe [more] than some of the guys who were more connected down here."

Gordon was comfortable in front of a camera, and humble around race fans, and became quite rich and famous in short order. The Winston Cup Series entered into a new phase of enlightenment in 2001, when NASCAR's $2.4 billion, six-year television contract was activated. With the majority of Cup races now on network TV, The Series was picking up race fans like a subway snatching passengers along a Manhattan route. With that new-found attention, and drivers reaching new heights of fame, the gossipy tabloids took notice. When Gordon's first wife, Brooke, filed suit for divorce in March, 2002, the racing trades weren't the only media outlets reporting the story. The national tabloids – those magazines in the checkout line at the grocery store – were all over it like hungry hounds

Modern-day prototype 131

132 Man-made Thunder

Left Janet Guthrie was well ahead of her time in the world of professional motorsports. To this day, she's the only female driver to compete in both the Daytona 500 and Indianapolis 500. The aerospace engineer turned race driver made 33 NASCAR Winston Cup Series starts from 1976 to 1980. She also made three appearances in the Indy 500, her history-making first in the 1977 event. In the 1960s and early 1970s, women were not allowed in the pits (the infamous "no t*ts in the pits" rule) during a race because females were deemed a distraction by NASCAR.

Right Women have a variety of jobs in NASCAR, including wives, who take an active role in the career of their husbands. Here Jeff Gordon gets a big hug from his second wife, Ingrid, after winning the 2007 Aaron's 499 at Talladega Superspeedway. Since many married drivers have private jets and motor homes, the family tags along to most Sprint Cup Series events.

> **When the National Enquirer or one of its counterparts starts sifting through your curbside garbage, you know you have reached true celebrity status.**

fighting for a pork chop. In her paperwork, the former trophy queen stated that the marriage was "irretrievably broken as a result of the husband's marital misconduct." In some eyes, he was the "boy next door" no more.

The legal proceedings dragged on for more than a year, with all sorts of unseemly details bubbling to the surface along the way. Brooke caused a real hullabaloo during Speedweeks '03 when her team of lawyers attempted to issue subpoenas at Daytona International Speedway to several high-profile personalities, including Evernham.

Speedway security held the legal team at the gate. It was done to embarrass Gordon (mission accomplished), who had guest-hosted *Saturday Night Live* about five weeks earlier. "It's out of my hands," he told the media. "It seems kind of ridiculous to me and uncalled for." He described the subpoena attempts as "disgusting." In June, 2003, the divorce was settled, after 12 hours of private mediation. Brooke reportedly got a $15 million settlement from Gordon's $48 million fortune.

There was a silver lining. Like his defection from Ford to Chevy, his early successes, the four championships and all those race victories in between, the belly-up marriage marked another milestone event that the media covered from the top button of Gordon's shirt to the tacks in the soles of his shoes. When the *National Enquirer* or one of its counterparts starts sifting through your curbside garbage, you know you have reached true celebrity status. NASCAR and the Sprint Cup Series, and of course Gordon, had reached yet another level of recognition. ∎

Tug-of-war

There has always been this natural cycle in NASCAR's marquee division. A driver or team has a string of success, then gradually melts back into the pack.

Jeff Gordon celebrates his record fourth Brickyard 400 victory at Indianapolis Motor Speedway in 2004. Gordon captured this checkered flag on the 10th anniversary of winning the inaugural Brickyard 400 in 1994, a triumph that catapulted the young driver into instant stardom.

When Ray Evernham was given the reins of the No. 24 Chevrolet team by car owner Rick Hendrick, he had this checklist poster made and hung in the team's race shop. After winning the 1995 NASCAR Winston Cup Series championship, Evernham, who has vast motivation skills, applied the check mark to the box where it reads "From Winner To Champion" to the delight of his team, celebrating the title in Victory Lane at Atlanta Motor Speedway. Gordon's crew was nicknamed the "Rainbow Warriors." Evernham, a self-confessed micro-manager, called himself the "Rainbow Worrier."

There was the exchange of power between Dale Earnhardt and Jeff Gordon in the 1995 Winston Cup Series season, but for Earnhardt it was more like an unwanted tooth extraction without Novocain. Earnhardt, who turned 44 that year, went into the season tied with Richard Petty as a seven-time NASCAR champion. He had won two consecutive crowns. He was motivated and primed to win a third straight title with Richard Childress Racing and become NASCAR's all-time champion. Dale Earnhardt was lord and master of the stock-car ring, defeating a string of opponents as he climbed to the pinnacle of the sport. In 1995, he must have been looking too closely at the big prize on the horizon and not at the pint-sized challenger

He never saw this knockout punch coming; it caught him right between the eyes...

before him. He never saw this knockout punch coming; it caught him right between the eyes, followed by a 10-count in the middle of the ring. When he lifted his head off the canvass, there was a 5-foot-8 figure above him that looked like a Macy's-window display mannequin, not a hair out of place, thanking all with a mild, nasally voice and tears in his eyes.

Jeff Gordon's rapid rise in Winston Cup Series racing was a shock even to those in his camp at Hendrick Motorsports. His crew chief at the time, Ray Evernham, says, "Our team wasn't prepared to win a championship." But Gordon's progression was obvious – success in the Busch Series in 1992, Cup Rookie of the Year in '93, two high-profile Cup wins in '94. Now this. It seems surreal to this day; NASCAR's wide-shouldered, menacing and mustachioed "Intimidator" chopped down by a well-dressed, 24-year-old who looked more like a Tommy Hilfiger television model. "We had to beat Dale Earnhardt for the championship that year, and it came down close," Evernham says. "He was the guy that we were racing. That's also the year we switched to the 1995 Monte Carlo from the '94 Lumina and certainly our team – I wasn't and probably Jeff wasn't – wasn't ready to win a championship, but Hendrick Motorsports was. I think the resources that Rick Hendrick gave us to develop that '95 Monte Carlo faster than some of the other guys are what got us the advantage. And so, largely the technology that Rick Hendrick had in place was probably more of the reason for us winning the first championship, because we didn't know how to race for a championship. We just wanted to go and win races. And that was the year when we weren't supposed to beat Dale Earnhardt and we beat him." Beat him by a scant 34 championship points.

Earnhardt's car owner, Richard Childress, said his veteran driver took the title loss in his stride, and accepted young Gordon as viable

What the sport needed was an honest rivalry, and NASCAR found it with this Earnhardt-Gordon tug-of-war.

competition, even though they were on opposite ends of the spectrum on just about every imaginable level – age, background, hobbies, body size. "Yeah, Dale had a lot of respect for him, and that's just competition," Childress says today. "He came in and won the races and won the championship, but I still think for the sport that's what it needed at that time." What the sport needed was an honest rivalry, and

NASCAR found it with this Earnhardt-Gordon tug-of-war. Earnhardt may have groused about Gordon, and taunted him by calling him "The Kid," but in '95, Gordon and the No. 24 team drew a line in the sand. Said Childress: "He was just another team you had to beat. We never focused in on any one person. We raced everybody, and we raced 'em all hard. He just happened to have the talent, the money behind him, the team."

From 1995 through '98, Gordon supplanted Earnhardt as the driver to beat in Winston Cup racing. He scored 40 victories and three crowns, finishing second in points to teammate Terry Labonte in 1996. Earnhardt had eight wins and three top-five points finishes, including that

136 Man-made Thunder

Jeff Gordon and Dale Earnhardt may have had a rivalry on the track, but they also had a curious case of mutual respect. Gordon, who was in his 20s, became NASCAR's top driver in 1995, after Earnhardt, who was in his 40s, had won back-to-back championships in 1993–94.

When Dale Earnhardt looked like this, it was best to keep your distance. Earnhardt appears not to be happy with his No. 3 Chevrolet after the final practice for a 1995 Winston Cup Series race at Michigan International Speedway. When Earnhardt was NASCAR's most dominant driver, and his car was fast, he would run a few laps of practice, go the garage, cover the car and leave. He was a master of the mind game.

runner-up showing to Gordon in '95, in the same four-year stretch. When the '95 championship race was settled, Earnhardt wondered aloud if Gordon was old enough to drink champagne and participate in the Winston Cup awards banquet festivities in New York City. During his championship remarks, Gordon stopped to toast Earnhardt, who was sitting at his team table looking up at the stage in the Grand Ballroom at the Waldorf-Astoria. Gordon pulled a tall glass of milk from under the podium and raised it in Earnhardt's honor.

They were never classified as friends, but Earnhardt and Gordon had a mutual respect, and they played off each other very well, building a rivalry that captured the attention of race fans in America, and beyond. Earnhardt had a native intelligence and understood money. He had a seat on the New York Stock Exchange. Earnhardt realized Gordon was good for the bottom line. "Jeff has his own personality," Childress said. "He's done one hell of a job doing what he's done. He's helped the sport. He brought in different fans and newer fans. When Jeff Gordon came along, he had the Hollywood look, the smile. He was so much different than what Earnhardt was: The blue-collar guy, the working man's person. Jeff came in with more of a different, polished look and attitude and everything. He brought a lot to our sport. He did a lot for our sport and he'll go down in history as one of the greatest drivers yet." ∎

Modern-day prototype 137

Multiheaded mania

The old prevailing logic in NASCAR racing, in terms of team structure, was this: One car owner, one crew chief, one team, one driver.

Left Rick Hendrick has a strong driver lineup for the 2009 NASCAR Sprint Cup Series. From left to right, Dale Earnhardt Jr., Jimmie Johnson, Jeff Gordon and Mark Martin, here holding die cast collectible cars, or toy-like replicas of their race cars, near the start-finish line at Daytona International Speedway. Selling collectibles is a big money-making venture for NASCAR's top drivers.

Right Master engine builder Waddell Wilson builds a motor at the Holman Moody racing complex in the early 1960s. Holman Moody was a Ford factory team in the 1960s. The team had so much cash, they built their own office areas at bigger racetracks, such as Daytona. When Ford pulled its funding out of NASCAR in 1970, Holman Moody had to release hundreds of mechanics and eventually ceased operations in 1973.

Far right Carl Kiekhaefer's entries for a Grand National Series event at Asheville-Weaverville Speedway in 1956. Kiekhaefer was the first car owner to employ the shotgun approach, by entering several stock cars in a single race, thus insuring greater success. In '56 Kiekhaefer won 30 races over the 56-race schedule. Buck Baker led the charge by winning 14 races and the championship that season. Kiekhaefer got out of the sport after only two years, but his cars won 52 races and two championships over the 1955–56 seasons.

There were variations along the way, such as Carl Kiekhaefer's mad rush into – and subsequently away from – the NASCAR Grand National Series over the 1955–56 seasons, when he used 11 drivers in a fleet of Chryslers and sent Tim Flock and Buck Baker to the championship on a wave of greenbacks. Kiekhaefer was independently wealthy as owner of Mercury Outboards, which manufactured boat motors. In the 1960s, it was Holman Moody which used the multi-driver concept. But, like Kiekhaefer before them, Holman Moody was more like a clearing house of cars and drivers. The team won two championships in 1968–69 with David Pearson. Four years later, when Ford pulled its funding,

Hendrick Motorsports started NASCAR life as a one-team/ one-driver operation...

the team disappeared from sight. There are other examples of multi-car teams, but none had the staying power of Rick Hendrick.

Hendrick Motorsports started NASCAR life as a one-team/one-driver (Geoff Bodine) operation, but two years later turned into a two-headed beast when Hendrick added Tim Richmond to his lineup. The new guy on the team won seven races and finished third in points, while Bodine won twice, finished eighth in the standings, and was not happy at all. It

got even more crowded the following year when three-time NASCAR champion Darrell Waltrip joined the Hendrick roster. Waltrip left after the 1990 season and Hendrick spent the next two seasons as a two-car operation. In '93, it was a trio again with the addition of Jeff Gordon, who joined Ricky Rudd and Ken Schrader on the driver roster. In 2002, Hendrick went to a four-car operation. The point is obvious: Hendrick, through thick and thin, mostly thick, has stayed the course with a multi-car operation, while others have come and gone. Hendrick's rationale for the multi-car team format was easy: More resources to win more races and improve the odds of contending for a championship.

Left Car owner Carl Kiekhaefer's No. 500 Chrysler 300 leads the pack at Charlotte Speedway during a Grand National Series race in 1955. Charlotte was a three-quarter-mile dirt oval where the inaugural NASCAR Sprint Cup Series (then "Strictly Stock") race was held in 1949. Drivers say Charlotte had a rough, unforgiving surface. Five years later, Charlotte Motor Speedway, a 1.5-mile paved oval, about 30 minutes from the city, was opened.

Right After an eight-year run with Dale Earnhardt Inc., Dale Earnhardt Jr. went to drive for car owner Rick Hendrick. Here the driver and team owner share a moment on pit road prior to the 2008 Aaron's 499 at Talladega Superspeedway.

It can be prickly and tricky at times. Gordon wasn't real happy about Terry Labonte winning the championship in 1996. Hendrick talked him through it, explaining Labonte was at the end of his career, and Gordon was just beginning. As the two battled for the championship in the closing races, Hendrick said he ate enough aspirin to "kill a man." Late in 2006, lame-duck Hendrick driver Brian Vickers, on his way to his first career victory, crashed teammate Jimmie Johnson out of the UAW-Ford 500 at Talladega Superspeedway. It was the last lap and Johnson was running for the championship as well as the race win. He dropped to eighth in the standings. After that fracas, Hendrick offered no input to the

Hendrick and other multi-car teams quickly adopted the unified team concept.

media. Said Johnson, later that week: "I think it's tough for him. He's happy. He's bummed. It's the same way I am."

Hendrick may be the father of the modern-day multi-car team concept, but give credit to Joe Gibbs Racing for putting their successful spin on the idea. When Gibbs paired drivers Bobby Labonte with Tony Stewart in 1999, all the JGR stock cars were prepared in the same shop, under the same roof, by the same mechanics. Both cars worked as a true team. Gibbs Racing, owned by former NFL head coach Joe Gibbs, won three Cup Series championships between 2000 and 2005. Hendrick and other multi-car teams quickly adopted the unified team concept. Single-car teams are near extinction in NASCAR's top tour. The last single-car driver to win the title was Dale Earnhardt in 1994, driving for Richard Childress Racing. RCR went to a four-car team format in 2009. ∎

Man-made Thunder

Modern-day prototype 141

Ray Evernham
First person

Ray Evernham, Jeff Gordon's Winston Cup Series crew chief from 1993 to 1999, on the relationship between Dale Earnhardt and Gordon.

Left Ray Evernham was a car owner when this photo was taken in 2003. Here he's watching drivers Bill Elliott and Jeremy Mayfield make laps at Michigan International Speedway.

Right Kasey Kahne, who replaced Bill Elliott in the No. 9 Evernham Motorsports Dodge in 2004, here at speed during a race at Las Vegas Motor Speedway in 2006. Race team owners are very proud of their equipment. If you look closely at the headlight on the right, you see Evernham's name, almost like a signature. These are not real headlights. They are just decals that look like headlights to give stock cars more of a street-legal look.

" Not that I want to hurt the legacy of that rivalry, but I think that some of that rivalry was staged for the fans as much as it was for anything else. Dale Earnhardt and Jeff Gordon had a tremendous amount of respect for one another, I think, on and off the racetrack. I think that competition-wise, they wanted to certainly beat each other. I know that Jeff knew that Earnhardt was 'the man.' So when he beat Earnhardt, he beat the best. And I think Earnhardt, in some ways, really looked at Jeff almost like another Tim Richmond. I think Earnhardt really enjoyed racing Tim Richmond because Tim was extremely talented and I think Earnhardt felt the same way about Jeff. I know that Earnhardt really introduced Jeff to a lot of business things outside of the racing so that Jeff could continue to be part of things. In many ways, Earnhardt was a rival to Jeff, but also a pretty good mentor.

"And I can remember when we won the Indy in '94 and then Earnhardt won in '95. He said something like, 'I'm the first MAN to win this race,' implying that Jeff was a boy when he won. That was just fun, you know what I mean? That was Earnhardt's way of having fun. If Earnhardt didn't do those things to you, that meant he didn't respect you. If he kidded you, he respected you. There's probably certain people that he didn't say anything about. These are probably the people he didn't respect. I know . . . from being inside of that, there was a ton of respect that flowed both ways. And you know, there were a lot of people that were jealous of Jeff Gordon when he first came on. A lot of good drivers that were jealous of Jeff because he was good-looking, had a lot of talent. You know, he got the trophy queen. He was getting money, getting attention. Earnhardt was plenty confident that he was Dale Earnhardt and he didn't look at Jeff with jealousy. I think Earnhardt, again, from what I can see from the outside, Earnhardt appreciated people with talent, and racers, and he could pretty much pick out somebody that was real and someone that wasn't. "

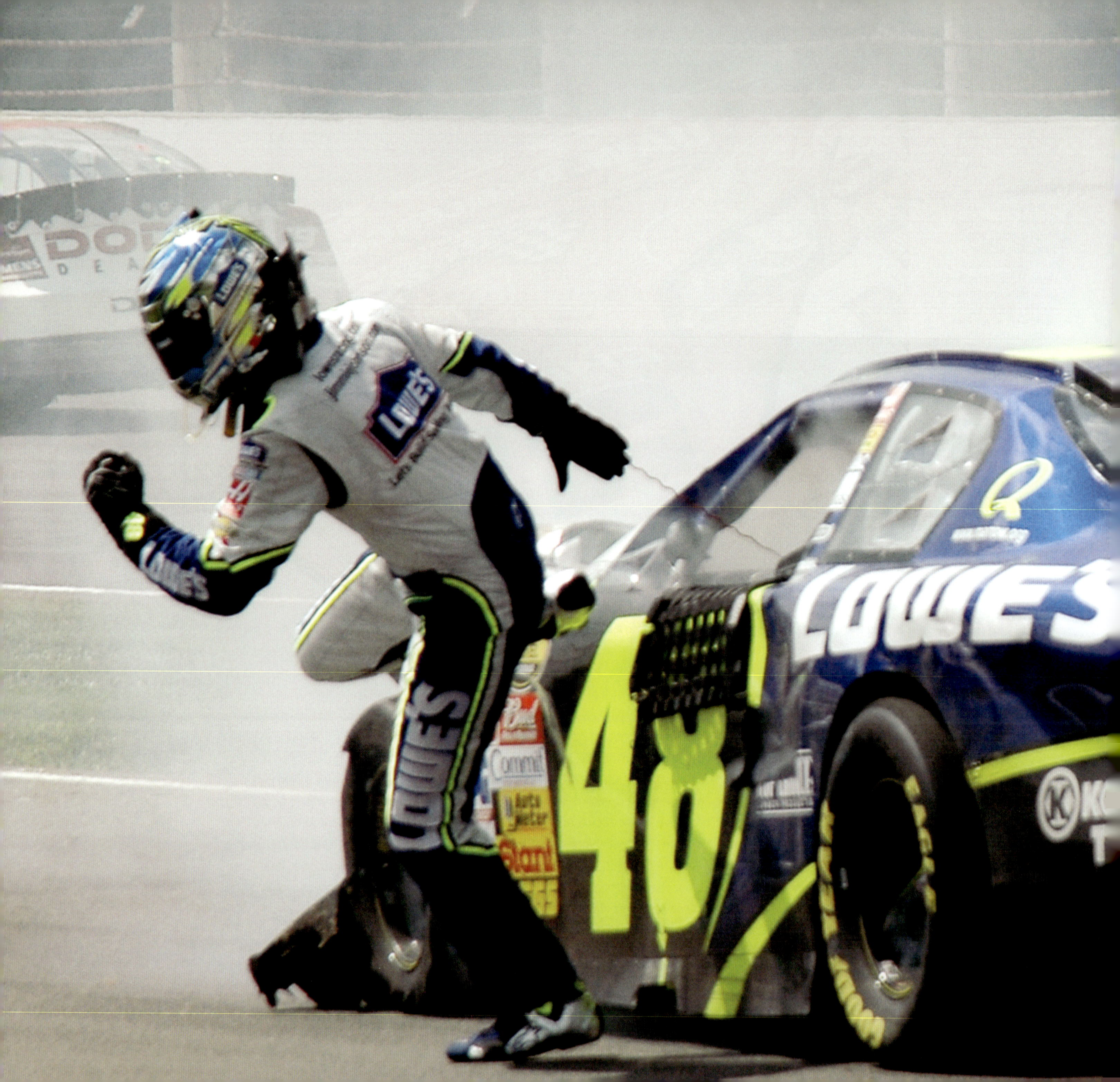
LOWE'S
48
Lowe's
Commit
Stant

A caged personality

6

Previous page Jimmie Johnson does a quick exit from his burning car during the 2007 Allstate 400 at the Brickyard. The three-time Sprint Cup Series champion was not injured in the blaze.

What you are about to read and digest, a few pages from now, is akin to Mary Poppins flashing Constable Jones and Uncle Albert as she floats out of sight, umbrella in hand, over the London skyline. "Goodbye children!" This has to do with Jimmie Johnson and the public perception of the mild-mannered driver, who races away not only from controversy, but from the fear of failure. If you win, you can't fail, so you keep winning, and keep failure in your rear-view mirror. Johnson is pretty good at winning and avoiding disappointment. In 2008, he did the unthinkable, claiming a third consecutive Sprint Cup Series championship, putting him in the elite company of Cale Yarborough, the cockpit bulldog from Timmonsville, South Carolina.

Up until '08, Yarborough had a page to himself in the NASCAR record book as the only man in stock-car history to earn a title trifecta. He collected his three crowns over the 1976 – 78 Winston Grand National Series seasons, driving the No. 11, Junior Johnson–enhanced entry. Nobody in the short line of stock-car greats could catch him. Not Dale Earnhardt (the "Intimidator"). Not Jeff Gordon (Wonder Boy). Or Richard Petty (The King). Or Darrell Waltrip (Jaws). All won back-to-back championships, but stumbled and fell on their third attempt.

That made Yarborough unique among NASCAR's conquerors, made him special, gave him braggin' rights. Other drivers may have seen more wins, or had more championships, or made more money, or run around with more women, but only Yarborough was able to string together three straight title runs, like popcorn on a Christmas tree. "It's an awful difficult thing to do," the Hall of Famer said in '08. "I think it may have been harder to win 'em back then than it is today because you had to compete against everybody back then." The fighting spirit, the competitive nature, the very soul in Yarborough at first didn't take kindly to the fact that he would have a roommate in the Chronicles of NASCAR. He enjoyed the elbow room in the category of "the only driver ever to . . ."

Johnson tried to reach out to Yarborough, but they never connected before the NASCAR clan gathered in New York to honor its 2008 champion.

146 Man-made Thunder

NASCAR racing is not a sport for claustrophobics because there is not a lot of wiggle room inside a NASCAR Sprint Cup Series car. Here we see Jimmie Johnson tucked inside his No. 48 Chevrolet. Not only is Johnson covered from head-to-toe in fire-resistant wear, but he's cinched tight into his seat and up close to his steering wheel. The steering wheel is close to the driver so his arms only have to hang down to avoid fatigue. During some summer races, the temperature inside the cockpit climbs well over 100 degrees.

A caged personality 147

Pit road fills up at Atlanta Motor Speedway during the 2007 Kobalt Tools 500. This was shot during a caution period when all the lead-lap stock cars pit at the same time. Mass stops like this produce controlled chaos on pit road, since the average four-tire stop takes under 15 seconds. Drivers appreciate a fast pit crew because a fast stop can improve their position on the track. Pit road rules changed dramatically after the death of Mike Rich during the 1990 Atlanta Constitution 500 at Atlanta. He was pinned between two cars while working on Bill Elliott's Ford that day. The speed of stocks entering and exiting pit road is now tightly regulated.

Teammates, but friendly foes. That's how Jimmie Johnson, right, describes his relationship with Jeff Gordon, who is actually listed as Johnson's car owner. Both race for Hendrick Motorsports and have seven NASCAR Sprint Cup Series championships between them. Gordon has four. Johnson nabbed three straight (2006 – 08). Here they share a moment on pit road at Martinsville Speedway in 2007.

The southern gentleman locked inside Yarborough's stout frame would eventually win the mental war inside his head. When it came time to present the 2008 championship ring at the NASCAR Awards Banquet, it was William Caleb Yarborough who walked on stage and hand-delivered the jewelry box to his modern-day equal. "As far as it lasting 30 years, I just wonder how come it took so long for somebody to win three in a row," Yarborough said. "That was a long streak. Thirty years is a long time, but I was happy to hold it." And now, happy to share it, with a man who is his polar opposite, in physical stature, speech, roots, dress, approach to racing and just about everything else.

Yarborough was pure Carolina country, while Johnson grew up in Southern California. Yarborough tolerated the media, much like a horse deals with flies – he didn't run, but wasn't afraid to swat 'em away. Johnson is completely TV-refined; he could retire as a driver and become a network news anchor. If Yarborough was a cracklin' AM radio, then Johnson is a high-def, plasma screen. Yarborough was tough. Johnson is patient. Yarborough went over the fence at Darlington Raceway once, and came up the hill, red-faced and cussing. Johnson went violently and headlong into a wall at Watkins Glen International and emerged from the car with a spontaneous celebration of life, joyously waving his arms over his head like a triumphant Olympian.

"When I was climbing out of the car, the fans were going nuts," Johnson says of that Busch Series wreck in 2000. "And what I experienced internally, I thought I was dead. When I was airborne, going into that wall, I thought it was concrete. I didn't know it was Styrofoam. And the speed I was going, this was gonna be ugly. I hit and it's soft. I get out and the fans are going nuts, and I'm overwhelmed with the feeling. 'Hell, yeah! I'm alive!'"

Johnson did not have a stellar Busch Series career. There is no highlight reel. He says race fans actually remember the crash at The Glen more than his lone career victory the following season at Chicagoland Speedway. In his first year of full-time Busch Series competition, he led two laps of competition, failed to qualify for one race and had no top-five finishes. In his

A caged personality 149

This has been a common sight in the 2000s – the No. 48 Chevrolet of Jimmie Johnson racing side-by-side with the No. 24 of Jeff Gordon. Rick Hendrick has never issued "team orders", which are common in Formula One, where one team driver has preference over another to win a race. Hendrick's standing order? "Just don't wreck each other," he says.

Everybody was beating the motorsports bushes for the next-big-thing driver, the next Jeff Gordon…

second at-bat in 2001, Johnson had that one victory and eight other top-10 finishes. Still, those are not the kind of stats that attract much attention among elite car owners with the fat checkbooks over in the Sprint Cup Series garage; yet when Rick Hendrick decided to expand to a four-car team, and created the No. 48 entry, he picked the 25-year-old driver from El Cajon, California. Well, actually, it was the co-owner of the No. 48, Jeff Gordon, who selected Johnson to fill that seat.

The irony here is rich, because at the dawn of this new century, car owners were scouring the land for young, dashing, well-spoken asphalt jockeys who could create the same winning momentum that Gordon brought to Hendrick Motorsports in the mid-1990s. Everybody was beating the motorsports bushes for the next-big-thing driver, the next Jeff Gordon, if you will, and many of them were scouring the same shrubbery from which Gordon had sprouted – the open-wheel, short-track leagues of America's Midwest. Hendrick was now looking elsewhere.

When Hendrick got his hooks in Jimmie Johnson, he couldn't have been sure what he was bringing ashore, and Johnson couldn't have been sure where or even why he was the one going – but go he did, willingly. To everyone's surprise, Johnson won three races in 2002; and 29 races into that defining, 36-race season, led the Winston Cup Series points standings as a rookie driver – a previously unimagined possibility. He has never lifted off the accelerator. In seven seasons of competition, he has 40 wins, those three championships, and has never finished lower than fifth in the points standings. That makes Jeff Gordon, the car owner, happy. It makes Jeff Gordon, Johnson's teammate, second fiddle at Hendrick Motorsports. Their cars are prepared under the same roof at the Hendrick racing campus. They share the same engineers, get the

A caged personality 151

NASCAR NEXTEL CUP SERIES
LOWE'S
KOBALT
TOP CHOICE
GOODYEAR
DELPHI
Hendrick MOTORSPORTS
LOWE'S
Let's Build Something Together
Johnson
LOWE'S
DELPHI
GOODYEAR
BOSCH Spark Plugs
LOWE'S
LOWE'S
LOWE'S
HAAS
BOSCH Spark Plugs

Jimmie Johnson stands alongside the most important person in his life – crew chief Chad Knaus, who is known for stretching the NASCAR rule book like a rubber band. During Johnson's three-straight championship run, Knaus was suspended twice for making unapproved modifications to Johnson's No. 48 Chevrolet. In the old days, the crew chief was the chief mechanic on the race car. These days, crew chiefs are managers who direct team operations. Johnson and Knaus were paired by team owner Rick Hendrick in 2002 and have enjoyed unbelievable success in the Sprint Cup Series.

same motors, and their crew chiefs compare notes going into every race. There are no secrets. Johnson has thrived in this environment, which is both head-to-head and hand-in-hand.

The 2007 and '08 seasons were particularly brutal for Gordon. In '07, he had just won at Talladega Superspeedway and was leading the points race in the Chase for the Nextel Cup. There were just six races left to contest. Johnson won four consecutive races to leapfrog Gordon and win the championship. In '08, Gordon failed to win a race, which had not happened since his rookie season. Meanwhile, Johnson won seven times and captured his third straight crown. Yes, Gordon and Johnson are personal friends, and yes, such things can grate on a relationship.

"There certainly are complications that come through," Johnson said. "There's been a handful of times that he's called me mad as hell, shot me the bird at the racetrack. There's times I've called him and said, 'What the hell were you thinking?' I've shot him the bird on the track. Even though you're teammates and we all are going in the same direction, we're all still

Johnson won four consecutive races to leapfrog Gordon and win the championship.

competitors and we do have respect for one another. In any competitive sport, you're gonna have conflict among teammates; coach to player; driver to crew chief; driver to driver; player to player; there's so many relative situations there."

But it goes back to 2001, when Gordon and Hendrick started putting the pieces of the No. 48 together. It was Gordon who pressed for Johnson's services in that car; he created this oval beast. "I was so shocked when he picked me to drive for him, and very insecure about my own talent and what I could do in a race car," Johnson said. "I've been beaten down by crew members and things over the years about just not having 'it.' That stuff, after a few years, sinks in. Then I got my chance with the right

S. ARMED FORCES
RECRUITING STATION
ONE WAY
GRAY LINE
POLICE
LOWE'S
48
IMPALA SS

The "Victory Lap," featuring the top 10 drivers in season-ending NASCAR points, was a special event during NASCAR's Champions' Weekend in New York City. The stock cars would wind their way through midtown Manhattan for several blocks as a publicity stunt. The parade lap was discontinued in 2008. In order to give stock-car racing greater visibility, NASCAR began holding its annual award banquet at the Waldorf-Astoria hotel in 1981. The celebration has been staged there every year since.

A caged personality 155

> Jimmie Johnson waves the checkered flag just earned at Martinsville Speedway in October, 2007. Martinsville is a bittersweet track for Hendrick Motorsports. While Johnson has enjoyed many wins at the half-mile oval, car owner Rick Hendrick suffered a devastating loss near there in 2004. A Hendrick plane crashed en route to a race at Martinsville killing 10 people, including John Hendrick, Rick's younger brother, Ricky Hendrick, Rick's son, and John's two daughters.

company, the right cars, the right people, and, BOOM!, off it went. [But] when Jeff picked me there were many nights I went home and thought, 'What the hell is he doing putting me in this car? I hope I get the job done.'"

Gordon won his fourth championship in 2001, and most of those race cars were passed down to Johnson for the '02 season. Hendrick selected Chad Knaus – bright and ambitious – as the crew chief. Throw in the millions of dollars invested by the team sponsor, Lowe's Home Improvement, and Johnson was feeling more than a pinch of anxiety. It was more like a giant crocodile taking a chomp inside his belly. Johnson had seen several young drivers thrown into a Cup car, get sucked into the talent grinder, come out chewed up, then shoved out the back door of The Series, left on the curb with other debris. Why? Their performance numbers were flat. Once-rejected drivers are lucky to find a job in NASCAR's lower divisions. Johnson calls it "a short window."

"When you go to one of the big teams, you might get a year. Show some hope, you'll get a shot at a second year. If you don't produce, you're almost tainted at that point. You don't miss one rung after you leave a big-time team. There may not be a bottom; you may keep falling."

So Johnson went into the 2002 Winston Cup season with that mental monster riding shotgun. Basically: You don't win, you don't stay. He figured this was his one and only shot, and he made the most of the opportunity, not only by leading laps and winning, but by presenting himself in a professional manner. Johnson isn't flashy. He doesn't swear or talk trash. He avoids conflict like the pox. He is very mindful of his image. He says he sends every thought and emotion through a mind-sift before he utters one word in the garage area, or along pit road, or in the team hauler, or when he receives visitors at the race shop. Johnson takes his at-the-office appearance quite seriously, giving the perception that he is duller than Richard Nixon's joke writer. In public, he hides behind an invisible cloak, his actions so self-restricted that those filters act more like a bank vault – absolutely nothing gets out.

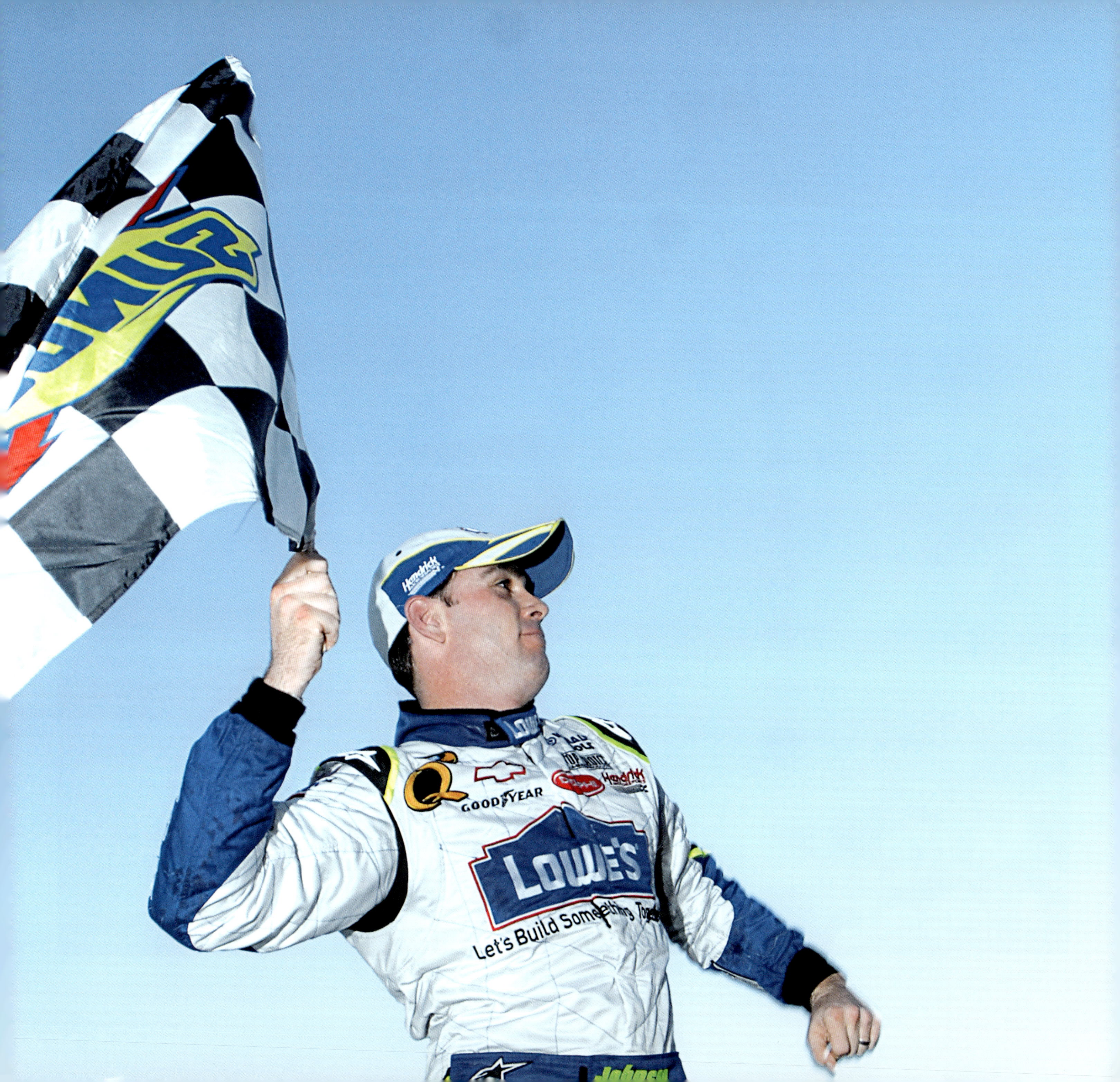
GOODYEAR
LOWE'S

158 Man-made Thunder

Burnouts are the celebration of choice for many younger NASCAR Sprint Cup Series drivers. Here Jimmie Johnson burns rubber after a win at Martinsville Speedway in 2007.

"He loses it, gets into me. I almost lose it and almost wipe out our second car, and we're racing for the championship. So I go looking for him."

"It's just the way I'm wired," he explains. "I certainly melt down and cuss like a sailor and throw fits and do all the things that take place. But for whatever reason, before it comes out, it runs through a filter. There's some filter that's kept me out of trouble . . . Over a long period of time, I'm happy I had a filter, because I've seen some of the issues that [Tony] Stewart's been through with Kurt and Kyle [Busch]. I wouldn't want to listen to that crap."

Move Johnson one space over from his normal public routine, jostle that perfectly combed hair a bit, and he will shock you with true confessions of his private life. On this day, Jimmie Johnson was at the track, but playing with a sportscar, not his No. 48 sponsored-to-the-gills Chevrolet. He had been shaking down the No. 99 GAINSCO/Bob Stallings Racing Pontiac Riley over the 3.56-mile road at Daytona International Speedway, not the 2.5-mile tri-oval in the corporate-heavy stock car. This Jimmie Johnson had three days' growth of beard and was wearing old jeans. There were no restrictions, no restraints. He let his "real" personality out of the cage and let it run around the garage area for a few refreshing moments.

Johnson talked about one fit of rage he experienced with the on-course actions of another driver in 2007, at a road course, during a practice session. "I went after Michael Waltrip [who stands 6-foot-5]," Johnson said with a hearty laugh. "This was in the garage area after practice. I get stuck running in practice, side-by-side, for like three laps, and I'm overtaking him and he's just being a d*** about it. He loses it, gets into me. I almost lose it and almost wipe out our second car, and we're racing for the championship. So I go looking for him. Well, I just got out of the car and left, and my guys could tell I'm pretty mad. Now I'm in his [Waltrip's]

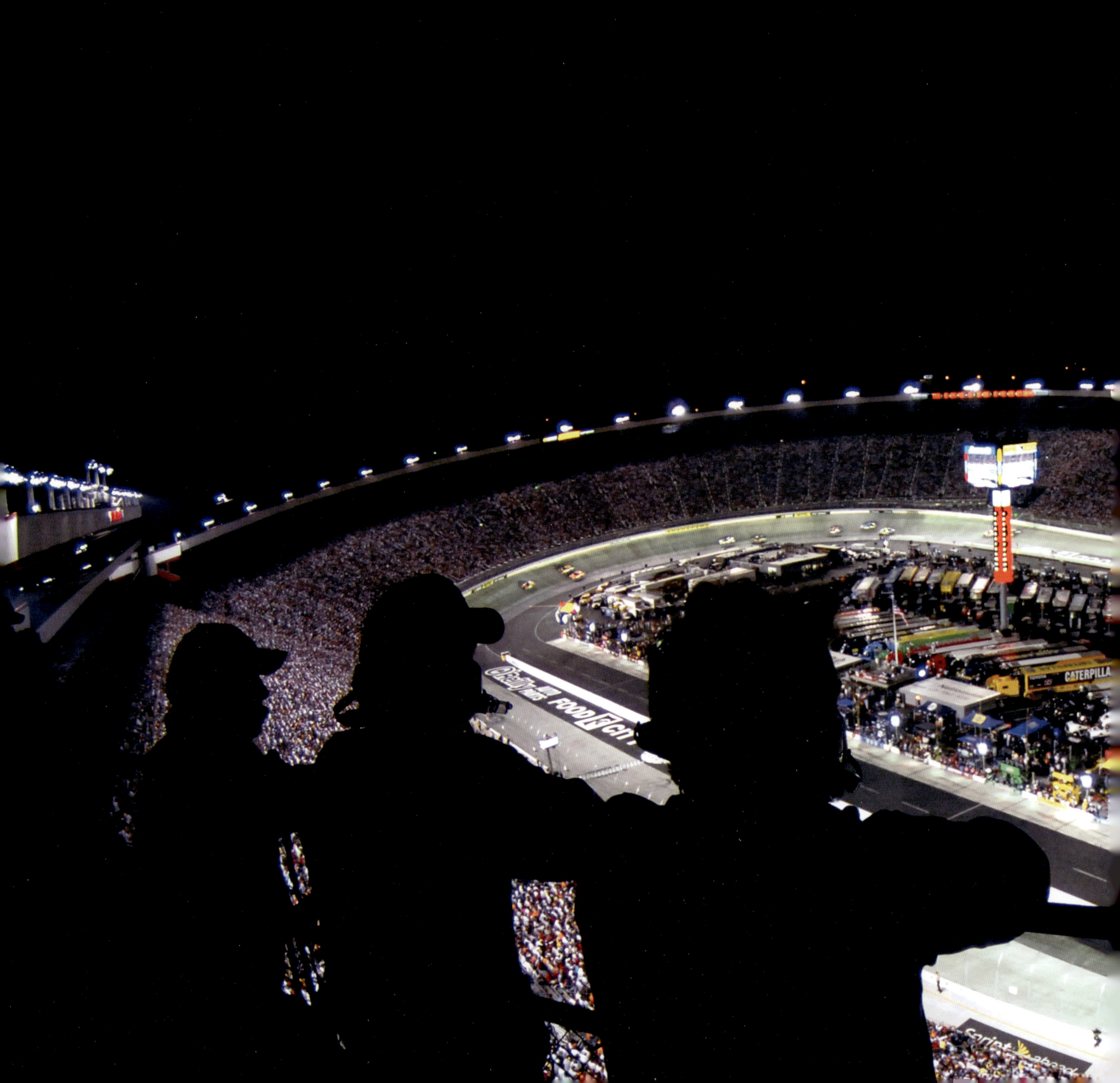

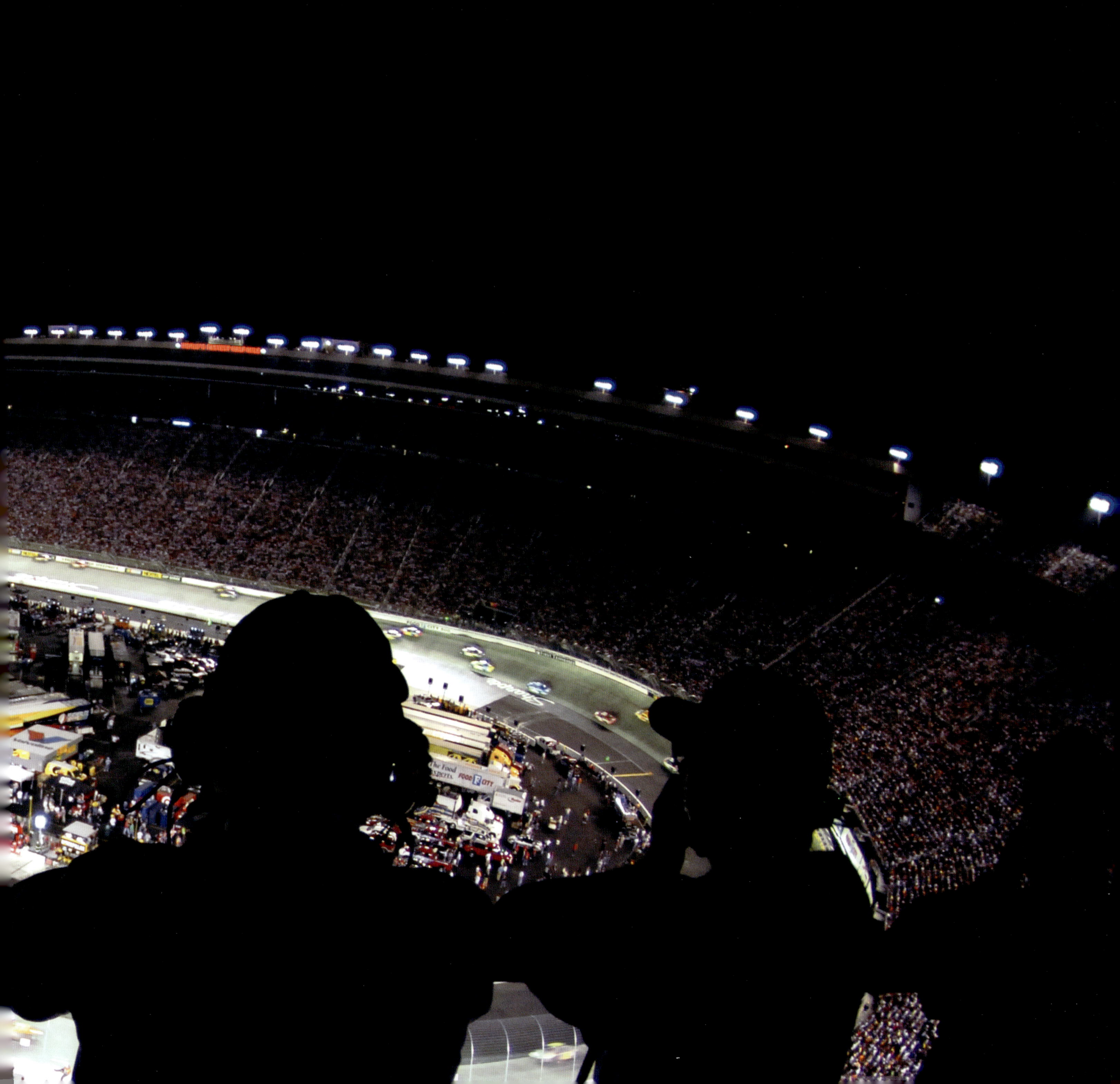
The Food Experts.
FOOD CITY

Previous page Sprint Cup Series spotters get a bird's-eye view of Bristol Motor Speedway during a race in 2007. Spotters are now mandatory, for safety reasons, anytime the stock cars hit the track for practice or race laps. Armed with a two-way radio, they communicate directly with their drivers. Their job is to help drivers navigate through traffic because there are so many blind spots in a Sprint Cup stock car. They can also warn their drivers of accidents up ahead.

It takes about six weeks to build a Sprint Cup Series stock car, but only seconds to destroy one. Jimmie Johnson's mangled machine is carried off the track after crashing at Daytona International Speedway.

garage stall with all of his guys. Michael is trying to get out of the car to yell at me; we're gonna get ready to start screaming and pushing and shoving. That big son-of-a-b**** gets out of his car and I'm like, 'Oh God. This is a bad decision.' I look around and I'm seeing all his guys there, and I'm like, 'You're here. Say what you're gonna say.' That stuff happens. People don't expect it from me so the cameras don't follow it, and I don't go on the [two-way team] radio and raise hell about what went on. I just get out and go deal with it."

And this other Jimmie Johnson likes to have his fun. We all got a glimpse of that via a news report dispatched from Florida in December, 2006, when Johnson fractured his wrist after falling from a golf cart. Actually, he didn't fall out of the cart, he fell off the roof of the cart while horsing around with friends during a golf outing. "I want to do the right thing," he said. "It doesn't mean I don't think any different. It doesn't mean that when I'm away from workspace that I don't let loose just as much as anyone else. One thing that people don't understand, it's fun when you get away from the track and get to have some fun. I personally think you should take a couple shots of tequila each night you go out. It just floors people. I get out there, have some fun, get crazy, have some shots of tequila, let 'er rip. And people are like, 'Really?' Hell, yeah."

He stops talking a moment, rubs the thickening whiskers on his face, and considers how his attention to public image probably wouldn't allow such growth on a normal race weekend. "It's just, again, that good-student thing pops up and I'm like, 'Ah, I probably should shave. I probably shouldn't say that I got s***-faced with my buddies over the off-season.' Those things don't come to mind in my workspace. Even talking to you, I get nervous to say stuff. I don't know why. I've just always had this thing about being a good student. Over the years, I guess I'll get out of it."

And when that Liberation Day comes, the racing community will see the whole of the man, and not just his cardboard-cutout image. Someday, but probably not tomorrow. ■

162 Man-made Thunder

A caged personality 163

The original three-peat

Hard as a South Carolina pine tree, but only tall as a stump, Cale Yarborough has always been bigger than life in the minds of history-minded NASCAR Sprint Cup Series fans.

Left Cale Yarborough gets a Victory Lane kiss from a Union 76 trophy girl. Union 76 supplied NASCAR teams with free gas for 50 years before yielding the duty to Sunoco in 2004. Yarborough, who won 83 races during his career, was constantly wiping lipstick off his cheeks.

Right From 1949 through 1970, dirt tracks were part of the NASCAR Grand National Series schedule, and those dirt-racing stock cars needed extra modifications, such as the plastic piece bolted to the nose of the car to keep the grill clean. If the grill was clogged with dirt, it would choke the air flow to the radiator and cause the engine to overheat. Here a crew cleans the mud off the grill and windshield. To the left in the black shirt is car owner Junior Johnson doing his part to help the clean-up efforts.

Up until 2008, Yarborough was the only man in the stock-car timeline able to win three consecutive NASCAR championships. In the first 59 years of racing, since the Cup Series debuted in 1949, there have been 13 times drivers have won, then defended, a title. The list reads like a Hall of Fame roster and includes Buck Baker, Lee Petty, Joe Weatherly, David Pearson, Richard Petty, Jeff Gordon, Darrell Waltrip and Dale Earnhardt. Richard Petty won back-to-back crowns twice, while Earnhardt did it three times. Only twice, in 1978 by Yarborough, and again in 2008 by Jimmie Johnson, has there been a three-peat winner.

After 31 years, Johnson was able to match Yarborough's once unthinkable record.

Yarborough was so tough, he could have chopped wood with his fists.

"Thinking back with Petty and Earnhardt, Gordon, you would think that some of those guys would have put three together within those 30 years," Yarborough said. "But thank goodness they didn't." There aren't many similarities between Yarborough and Johnson, as far as their backgrounds. Yarborough was born and raised in rural South Carolina and was always on the athletic side, playing football in high school. Johnson was born and raised in urban Southern California and claims to have had "nerd" tendencies as a teen. He said he got into two fights in high school and both times broke a hand after making contact with his school-yard opponent. Yarborough was so tough, he could have chopped wood with his fists. Even though he was undersized, Yarborough was a fire-plug of muscle and got a football scholarship offer from Clemson University, a big-time program in the South. He never played a down for coaching legend Frank Howard because of a disagreement over, you guessed it, racing.

"I was just about to win the track championship," Yarborough says. "I went to Coach Howard and told him I needed

A caged personality 165

Right Drivers have always had to pay their dues in NASCAR's lower divisions before working their way up to a full-time, big-league ride. Here Nelson Stacy (No. 29), Cale Yarborough (No. 50) and Norman Edwards (No. 7A) battle on the high banks of Daytona International Speedway during the 1962 Modified-Sportsman race. Yarborough made it. He won 83 Cup Series races and three titles. Stacy had four Grand National Series wins. Edwards never made it to the elite stock-car division.

Far right Wood Brothers Racing pushes the No. 21 Ford back to the garage area after Cale Yarborough won the 1967 Atlanta 500 at Atlanta International Raceway (now Atlanta Motor Speedway). The Wood Brothers team was quite familiar with Victory Lane procedures. The team has won 97 NASCAR Cup Series races since the 1960s.

to go home to race one more race that I'd be through with it. He said, 'If you go back, pack your clothes, don't come back. You either go and race or play football.' So I packed my clothes and left. He says, 'Son, you'll starve to death [as a race driver].'" As Yarborough advanced in racing, he became friends with Howard, who joined him once in Victory Lane at Talladega Superspeedway following a checkered flag. "He walked up to me and put his hands on my shoulder, and he always called me 'boy,'" Yarborough recalled. "He said, 'Boy, I ain't never been wrong many times in my life, but I want you to know I was wrong this time.'"

The common ground between Johnson and Yarborough is probably the quality of their race teams and each driver's brand of tenacity in a race car. Yarborough drove for Junior Johnson, who had special skills deciphering the NASCAR rule book, and prepping superior cars. Between 1976 and 1985, Johnson's entries won six championships and 80 races. Rick Hendrick, who redefined the car owner job description, has eight titles with three drivers since the 1995 season. Yarborough was go-hard-every-lap, while Johnson has become NASCAR's top money-lap driver. Johnson showed his real grit at Texas Motor Speedway in 2007. Instead of settling for second-place championship points, he pushed past Matt Kenseth, after a stirring side-by-side battle, to win the Dickies 500. It was his third-straight victory during a four-race winning streak that launched him to the '07 crown.

"We're all dedicated drivers," said Yarborough, who had 83 wins in his career. "Jimmie is a dedicated driver and has a lot of dedicated competition he's running against. That's what it takes to run races and win championships, to have that dedication and determination to get it done." It is a shame Yarborough and Johnson raced in different generations. It would have been an intriguing matchup. "The only thing I can say is Jimmie better be glad I'm not racing with him today," Yarborough said with a laugh. ∎

Right Cale Yarborough had a considerable fan base as he piled up victories and NASCAR Cup Series championships. Before race teams got involved with collectibles, race fans showed their pride with homemade signs and posters cheering on their favorite drivers.

166 Man-made Thunder

A caged personality

One season of glory

It only takes a single championship to make an entire career glimmer.

Bobby Allison is all smiles in Victory Lane after winning a NASCAR race in the mid-1970s. Allison's 1983 NASCAR Winston Cup Series championship is one of the most revered in stock-car history because it came late in his career, at the age of 45. Allison was born in Hialeah, Florida, but moved to Hueytown, Alabama as a young man to pursue a stock-car racing calling. Allison, his younger brother Donnie, Red Farmer and Neil Bonnett were the original members of the notorious "Alabama Gang," Alabama-based drivers who had many stock-car successes from the 1970s through the mid-1980s.

Bobby Labonte prepares for battle in the No. 43 Petty Enterprises Inc. Dodge moments before a 2007 race at Dover International Speedway. Labonte won the 2000 NASCAR Winston Cup Series championship driving for Joe Gibbs Racing. Bobby and Terry Labonte are the only brother combination to win the Cup Series championship. Terry Labonte won his titles in 1984 and 1996, then cheered his younger brother to the crown in 2000.

NASCAR's list of Cup Series champions provides an odd phenomenon in the ranks of American pro sports. That roster is relatively short because the majority of names on the roll call won more than one title. Since 1949, there have been only 13 one-time champions, compared to 15 drivers with at least two NASCAR crowns.

This pattern was established in the first 20 years of racing, when The Series produced only three one-time winners and eight multiple titlists. It only took five years for NASCAR to produce its first two-time champion. Herb Thomas and Smokey Yunick teamed to win titles in 1951 and '53. Buck Baker was the first driver to win back-to-back championships in

Since 1949, there have been only 13 one-time champions, compared to 15 drivers with at least two NASCAR crowns.

1956 – 57. The Petty family boasts 10 NASCAR titles. Richard Petty won seven while his father, Lee, nabbed three over the first 10 years of the Cup Series.

Dale Earnhardt and Richard Petty are tied for most titles with seven, then comes Jeff Gordon with four, followed by a five-driver logjam with three championships – Lee Petty, David Pearson, Darrell Waltrip, Cale Yarborough and Jimmie Johnson. With so many drivers with multiple championships, the single-season winners tend to get overlooked. Red Byron took home the "Strictly Stock" trophy in 1949, which only had eight races. Bill Rexford won the following year. Rex White earned his one and only championship in 1960, the lone single-season champion in that entire decade. The 1970s had two drivers win the title one time, Bobby Isaac in 1970 and the beloved underdog, Benny Parsons, in 1973.

Since 1999, there has been a flurry of one-time champions, a list that includes Dale Jarrett ('99), Bobby Labonte (2000), Matt Kenseth ('03) and Kurt Busch ('04). In another 10-year span, 1983 through '92, there were four other one-timers, including Bobby Allison

('83), Bill Elliott ('88), Rusty Wallace ('89) and Alan Kulwicki ('92). Each of those drivers has a unique spin to their championship seasons; for instance, Jarrett turned 43 the year he won his title. Kenseth was the last driver to win the Cup Series title based on a season-long accumulation of points. Busch, Kenseth's teammate at the time, was the first driver to win in the Chase playoff format.

Allison's climb to the top was one of the more popular in NASCAR history, since he was 45 and had spent 20 years banging fenders in The Series. Elliott was overtaken late in the 1985 season for the championship by Waltrip, then rebounded in '88. Elliott won 11 superspeedway races in '85 and became a huge favorite of

> **Waltrip was furious and told Wallace what he could do with the prize money. "I hope he chokes on that $200,000"**

NASCAR fans. Wallace's championship season was highlighted by spinning Waltrip out of The Winston All Star race at Charlotte. Waltrip was furious and told Wallace what he could do with the prize money. "I hope he chokes on that $200,000," Waltrip fumed. Kulwicki was the ultimate underdog, a single-car team with limited funding. Kulwicki owned the car he drove, and nicknamed his Ford the "Underbird."

He went into the '92 season finale second in points and emerged as the champion, beating the heavily favored Davey Allison and Elliott. Sadly, Kulwicki was killed in a private airplane crash the following season. After his first Cup win in 1988, Kulwicki made a statement that could easily be applied to his championship. "It's been a long road and it's taken a lot of hard work to get here, but this has made it all worthwhile. When you work for something so hard for so long, you wonder if it's going to be worth all of the anticipation. Believe me, it certainly was." ∎

Left Kurt Busch tightens a shoelace before getting behind the wheel of the No. 2 Penske Racing Dodge. Busch has the distinction of winning the first NASCAR championship using the Chase playoff format. His championship run was dramatic, since he had to rally back from a lap down in the season finale to finish fifth and win the crown by a scant eight points over Jimmie Johnson.

Right Junior Johnson, left, never won a NASCAR Grand National Series championship and is considered by many as the top driver in stock-car history not to wear a crown. He exacted his revenge as a car owner, winning six championships, including three with driver Darrell Waltrip. Here, Johnson and Waltrip were putting the clock on opponents at North Carolina Motor Speedway in 1981.

Jimmie Johnson
First person

Jimmie Johnson on dealing with jealousy from his contemporaries.

Left Jimmie Johnson showed up for Daytona Speedweeks '09 sporting a new look – a light beard – which prompted several stories by the media. NASCAR's stars are now accustomed to dealing with tabloid-like issues.

Right Let's get this party started! Jimmie Johnson, standing on the driver's side window of his No. 48 Chevrolet, celebrates in Victory Lane after winning the 2006 Daytona 500. Numerology is big in NASCAR. In this case, it was the 48th Daytona 500 – the same number as Johnson's car. Darrell Waltrip won the 1989 Daytona 500 driving the No. 17 Chevrolet on his 17th Daytona 500 attempt and his youngest daughter was 17 months old. Matt Kenseth's 2009 500 win was his 17th career victory – in the No. 17 Ford.

"There's a handful of situations with guys that I started off racing in the Busch Series with, and even before that, that kicked my ass [at the racetrack] on a regular basis. And I was there for them. I was happy for them for their first wins. I went to their parties. I mean, truly, genuinely happy for their first wins, championships, and all that. I wasn't competitive with them, so everything worked. And then when the situation changed and it was my turn to have the spotlight, relationships fell apart. I didn't confront; I didn't raise hell about it. It certainly bothered me, but I let it be and kept to myself.

"At times I thought, 'Just go over there and raise hell with whoever that is. Go over and speak your mind, tell them what you think. But thankfully I haven't because every one of those situations have come back the other way and guys I see now, they recognize that they get those feelings, too, and they come and say, 'I'm happy for you. It was tough for a while. I probably haven't been the friend I should've been, but now I can be. I'm happy for you.' I've heard that from four guys in the last six months and it's like we're all back to normal now."

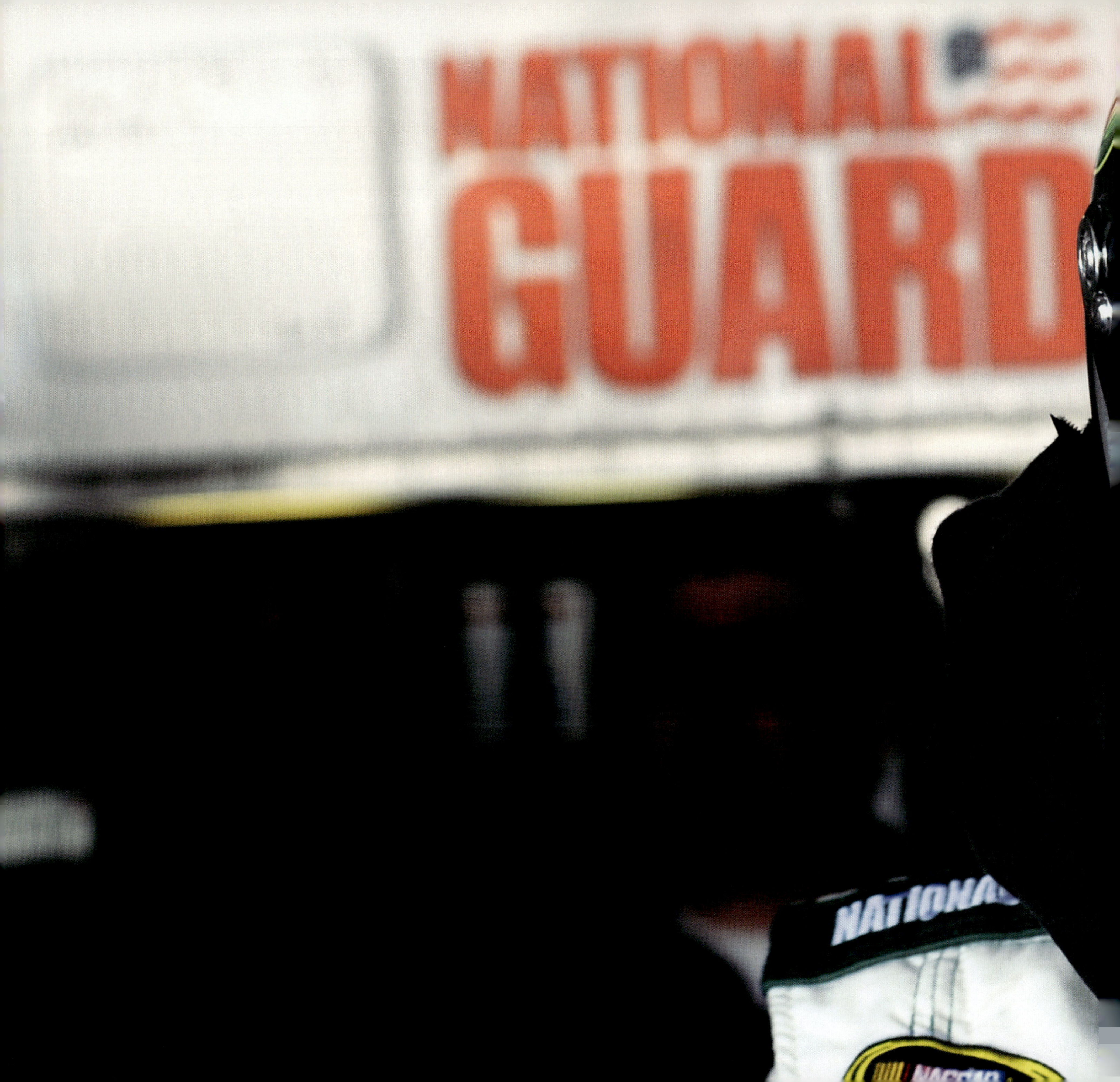
NATIONAL
GUARD

The driver you don't know

7

Previous page Dale Earnhardt Jr. – The man, the myth, the mystery, the son of a racing legend. Who is the real person behind this protective helmet?

The ride that Dale Earnhardt Jr. made famous – the No. 8 Dale Earnhardt Inc. Chevrolet. Here, it's being rolled out to the starting grid for the 2007 NASCAR Nextel All Star Challenge at Lowe's Motor Speedway.

You may be the most loyal fan of Dale Earnhardt Jr., but you probably don't know much about this man who is, without question, the largest name, the hottest star and the main attraction on the NASCAR marquee. He didn't ask for this distinction, and there are some who don't think he deserves the attention, but there's no denying that Earnhardt is the ringmaster at the stock-car personality circus. As crazy and loud events unfold around him at a rapid pace, Earnhardt remains the constant, never sweating under the intense white light that follows his every move; his hand never trembles, his voice never wavers.

The second son of everyman's champion, Dale Earnhardt, he burst onto the NASCAR Winston Cup Series scene in 2000, driving a blood-red car that sported the competition number (8) used by his late grandfather, sponsored by a beer (Budweiser) that defined a generation, and prepared at a race shop (Dale Earnhardt Inc.) owned by his famous father. Young Earnhardt (known simply as "Junior" to most, as "June Bug" to a few oldtimers) arrived on the big stage with two Busch Series championships, creating an enormous swell of anticipation from the sport's Southern hub, which was rapidly losing its NASCAR identity because of scheduling realignment.

Realignment is a benign-sounding word that NASCAR uses to describe the act of extracting Sprint Cup race dates from the South and moving them to places such as Loudon, New Hampshire, and Fontana, California. "Realignment" muffles the screams during the removal process. It was done for the betterment of the sport, to grow stock-car racing, but this withdrawal cut the grassroots NASCAR fan base to the bone. In 1990, 20 Cup stops in the 29-race schedule, or 68 percent, were held below the Mason-Dixon Line, and eight of those in the Carolinas. North Carolina native Dale Earnhardt won the title. Fast forward to 2008 where only 16 of the 36 races (44 percent) were held in the South, a scant three in the Carolinas, and the championship was earned by California's Jimmie Johnson. The Southern accent has gone almost extinct among drivers in the garage area, save Ralph Dale Earnhardt Jr., a.k.a. "Junior," "Dale

LOWE'S
Fresh Express
Budweiser
DaleEarnhardtInc.com
MENARDS
Miller Welders
FREIGHTLINER
EAGLE
GOODYEAR
JESEL
3M
Mobil 1

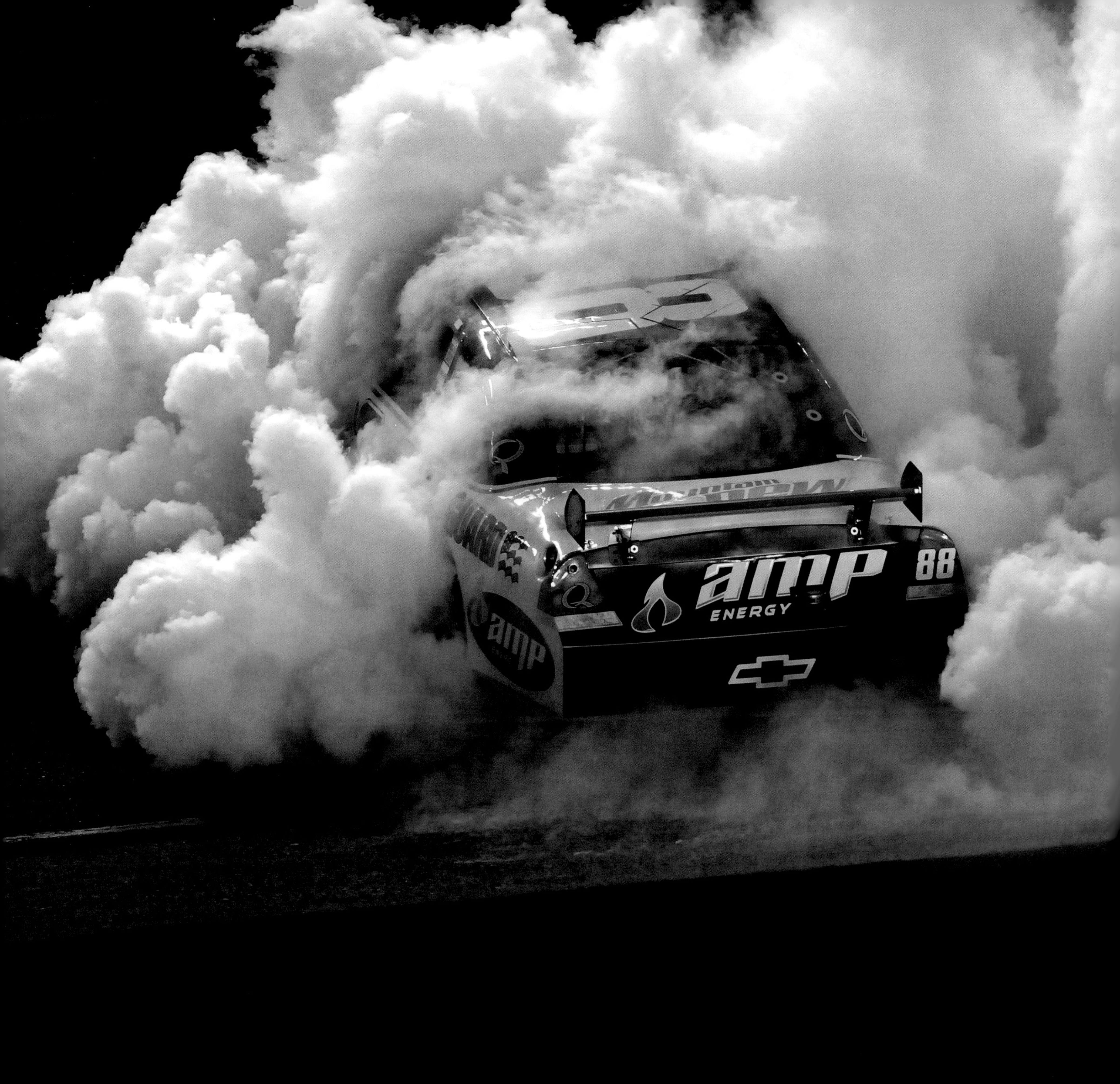
88
amp
ENERGY

Left Dale Earnhardt Jr. opened the 2008 NASCAR Sprint Cup Series in dramatic fashion by winning the Budweiser Shootout at Daytona International Speedway. It was his first race in the No. 88 Hendrick Motorsports Chevrolet. Earnhardt celebrated the victory with a burnout, his stock car halfway disappearing in the tire smoke. Car owners don't particularly like the burnouts because they can damage a perfectly good engine.

Right Dale Earnhardt Jr.'s No. 8 Chevrolet is pushed out of "Gasoline Alley" at Indianapolis Motor Speedway to compete in the 2006 Allstate 400 at the Brickyard. Earnhardt finished sixth that day.

Jr.," "JR," and "Little E." He is one of the few stock-car jockeys who can still whoop the "rebel yell;" who has permission to use "ain't" and "y'all" in his vocabulary; who can pitch blue jeans on television; who can sport facial hair; who can drive a roaring, gas-guzzling 1973 Chevrolet Camaro; and who can say things like, "I don't feel like I have had to reserve myself too much" and folks, plain folks, understand what he means.

Every weekend, Earnhardt enters the NASCAR battles while carrying the South on his shoulders with a unique combination of grit, charm, grace and determination. He's fighting every lap, not only for the same people that were drawn into the sport by his namesake, but for millions of fans that he has created throughout the Great Republic, thanks in part, to realignment. Ironic, isn't it. NASCAR abandons the Southern tier of states to settle in the nation's largest urban areas, and its superhero hails from the cratered race-date-mining zone.

Richard Childress, Dale Earnhardt's car owner from 1984 through that fateful February day in 2001, said Dale Jr. inherited the Earnhardt Nation after his father died. "When we lost Dale, he captured probably 80 or 90 percent of 'em," Childress said. "Some of 'em stayed with Childress Racing and Kevin Harvick, but he captured a tremendous amount of them." Even though father and son had completely different personalities, temperaments and marketing images, the Earnhardt base gravitated to their prince. So it should come as no surprise that Dale Jr. has captured the Most Popular Driver Award (as voted by the fans) every year since 2003. Yes, stock-car racing is a popularity contest.

Earnhardt has grown from a man-child, whose career start was carefully orchestrated by his father, into a full-blown adult driver. With the best possible equipment available on the market, and a skilled team of mechanics directed by Tony Eury (his uncle), "Little E" quickly blossomed into a driving sensation, winning 13 Busch Series races and a pair of titles in 1998-99. He got so good, so fast, that his father rushed to sign him to a written contract in '98, for fear of losing the boy to an enemy camp. The added bonus of this success was a late-in-life, father-son bonding. After years of Dale Sr. largely being an absentee father, the two finally shared common ground, as race drivers. In a piece he wrote for nascar.com in October, 2000, Earnhardt Jr. says of his father, "His friendship is the greatest gift you could ever obtain." That last handful of years with his father were some of the grandest of young Earnhardt's life. Says Kelley Earnhardt, Dale Jr.'s sister: "As he was doing well in racing, he and my dad started having a lot closer relationship, and so I think he felt kind of safe and tucked into that."

Kelley is Dale Jr.'s best friend, business partner, firewall and confidant. His slightly older sister is grounded and sensible and a good sounding board. She has been witness to his suffering, his joy and his heartbreaks. They grieved together when they lost their father, then six months later formed a partnership, well beyond their personal relationship. Over the last decade, she has watched him mature into this position as NASCAR's front man. There is nobody on this planet who knows Dale Earnhardt Jr. better than his protective sister. Nobody. Junior has said time and again that his sister is priceless and irreplaceable, the very foundation of his expanding empire, and the obvious cornerstone of his emotional well being.

"[I] don't have any worry whatsoever of my sister being able to get the job done or not being able to get the job done," he told the media in the spring of 2007. "I feel total confidence in her. We both learned a lot over the last several years and learned it together. But I wouldn't have her in that position if I didn't trust her, and she wouldn't want to be in it if she didn't feel confident. She wouldn't want to put herself or me in that position if she didn't feel like she could get it done." And it is here, with Kelley, and others within the glow of the inner circle, that we get the real snapshot of Dale Earnhardt Jr., who on one hand is as complicated as a probabilistic algorithm, and on the other, as simple as a chilled glass of sweet tea.

Any human being is a multifaceted mass. At the very base, we are made of carbon and water. At the first sublevel, we all walk upright, eat, drink, manufacture thoughts and spout visceral emotions. Most of us have

180   Man-made Thunder

Left It was a real family affair after Dale Earnhardt won a race at Darlington Raceway in 1989. Earnhardt is joined in Victory Lane by his third wife, Teresa, and three of his four children – 15-year-old son Dale Jr., and daughters Kelley, 17, holding her half sister, Taylor. The woman with the glasses next to Teresa is Earnhardt's mother, Martha.

Right After exiting his No. 88 Hendrick Motorsports Chevrolet during a rain delay in the 2009 Daytona 500, one of Dale Earnhardt Jr.'s assistants keeps him dry as he looks for cover along pit road.

Bud
DRAKKAR NOIR
CHAMPION
sparco
NEXTEL CUP SERIES
Budweiser

Left After winning the 2004 Daytona 500, Dale Earnhardt Jr. said he wanted to get an arm around the neck of his crew chief and cousin Tony Eury Jr. Earnhardt parked his No. 8 Chevy at the finish line and his team held an impromptu celebration before heading to Victory Lane. Earnhardt said he was relieved to win the Daytona 500, so he did not have to go through the frustrations of his father, who won his only 500 on his 20th attempt.

Right The 2004 Daytona 500 was a two-driver duel from the start. Tony Stewart, in the No. 20 Chevrolet, led 97 laps, while Earnhardt, in the red and white No. 8 Chevrolet, led the final 59, including the final 20. Stewart was happy for Earnhardt. Said Stewart: "Considering what this kid went through, losing his father here at the Daytona 500, and knowing how good he's been here, it's nice to see him get his victory here, too . . . there was no holding that kid back today."

hair and dislike dentist appointments. Then, on the human scale, come the diverse dividing lines. Social. Race. Economic. Talent. Not everyone can score 30 points in an NBA game. Not everyone earns a Nobel Prize. Not everyone can eat 59 hot dogs in 10 minutes. Not everyone can win the Daytona 500, like Dale Earnhardt Jr. did in 2004, like his seven-time NASCAR champion father before him in 1998. And that puts this particular race driver in a special category, gives him a unique sheen in this sport that revels in family bloodlines. From Day 1, Dale Earnhardt Jr. has been placed on a slide and probed under an electron microscope by the press, peers and other interested parties. They are always looking, always wondering. What they haven't figured out is this: Dale Earnhardt Jr. is both opaque and transparent. He casts an unseen shadow. There is actually more substance than image, but the projection of the man is vast; it swallows up reality, like a black hole gobbling up a galaxy.

The reality is that from 2005 to 2008 Earnhardt won three races and his last victory (Michigan, June 15, 2008) was a hold-your-breath-and-save -your-gas drama, his in-car camera showing the anxious driver turning his engine off and coasting behind the pace car several times to save precious fuel. On race chat sites across the land, the verdict that day for Earnhardt faithful was a resigned "win is a win," because it put an end to a disheartening 76-race losing streak. He was even defensive about it in his post-victory comments. "I know exactly what they are going to say Monday. But, to hell with it. I mean, there's going to be so many different [opinions]; my fans are happy and I'm happy for them. The other half are going to tear this apart on how we won this race . . ."

Winning does matter to Earnhardt, but it doesn't diminish his standing, because NASCAR is driven by personality, not performance, and he is the prime example of this phenomenon, which some will argue, was set in motion by his father, the dominant personality of his era. H.A. "Humpy" Wheeler helped raise the sport to new heights by turning his visions into reality. He's been active in the sport since the 1960s, most recently in a 30-plus-year run as president of Lowe's Motor Speedway. His opinion

Talladega Superspeedway, located in the heart of Alabama, measures 2.66 miles in length, but with more than 80 network cameras around the facility, every pass, crash and spin is recorded on video. These types of camera platforms are scattered all over the facility. It takes about 20 miles of wires and cable to televise a NASCAR race.

carries weight and he's watched Dale Jr. grow into the sport. "What's his popularity based on?" Wheeler asks. "He has been magnificently branded."

"What is the definition for Dale to be? " Kelley Earnhardt asks. "Some people say he is just an average driver with obviously a great name in the sport. Some say he is a really good driver. What's the definition of that? I think the definition for Dale is that he has so much greater expectation than a Matt Kenseth or Ryan Newman, somebody he's done more than. Some of them guys can be considered better than him by some people. It's just – I haven't figured it out yet. If he wins 17 championships, if he wins one championship, if he wins 50 races, or 17 races; what really defines what he is?"

Dale Earnhardt Jr. defies conventional definition. He's just Junior, a driver that transcends the everyday goings-on of a sport that delivers auto racing as an amusement value. Today's leading track promoter, International Speedway Corporation, which owns a dozen big-league racetracks and hosts 19 Sprint Cup Series events, bills itself as a "motorsports entertainment company." That tells the whole story of where the industry is at this very moment. Earnhardt is the star of the show, no matter how many times he makes it – or doesn't make it – to Victory Lane.

To Earnhardt's credit, he doesn't flaunt the title, because he's a common man trapped inside the framework of a superstar. He doesn't feed on attention; he deals with it. And yes, he has his fun along the way, which explains why he's a confirmed bachelor. He is one of the few students of NASCAR history; he can tell you a story about Junior Johnson, or Ned Jarrett, or Speedy Thompson, maybe even Possum Jones. But he's also in tune with the modern world: he enjoys video games and computer interaction; he's a fully integrated child of the data and Internet age. Most surprising, this man of the people, the leader of the vast Earnhardt Nation, is somewhat of an introvert.

"He's pretty quiet and to himself," Kelley said. "We don't do a whole lot of things as a family. I mean, when he is home he likes to be by himself

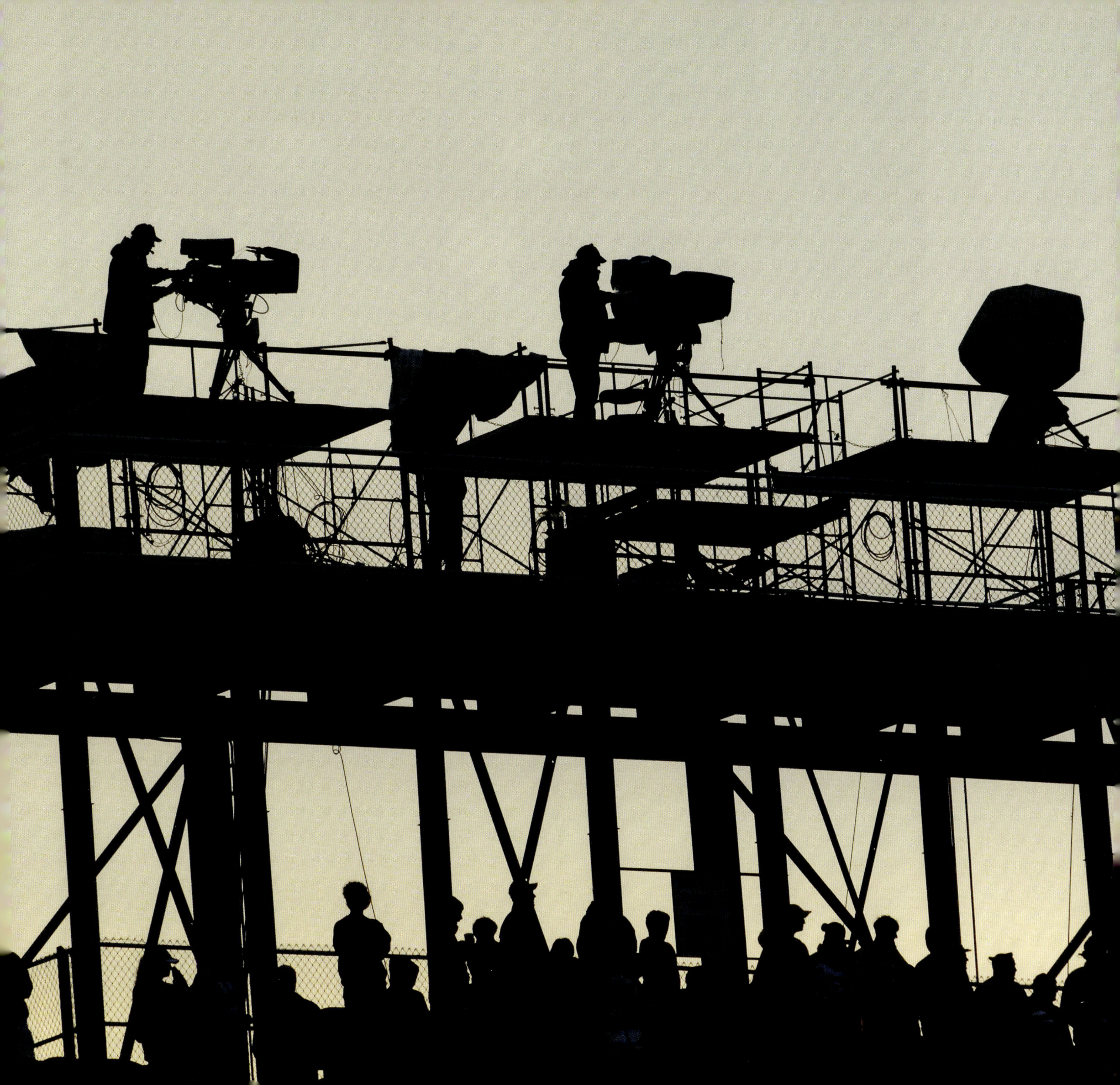

Dale Earnhardt Jr. comes into focus from behind the scoring tower at Bristol Motor Speedway during the 2007 Sharpie 500. His No. 8 was easy to find on the scoreboard after the race. He finished fifth that night.

186   Man-made Thunder

It's not uncommon for the same stock car to have different paint schemes over the course of a season. Either the primary sponsor is running a promotion or a secondary sponsor takes the hood for one or two races. This camouflage design Dale Earnhardt Jr. used at Lowe's Motor Speedway in 2007 drew the ire of then track president H.A. "Humpy" Wheeler. He talked to a race fan, who drove to Charlotte from Canada, and the fan complained he could not spot Earnhardt's car on the track because of the design. Said Wheeler: "He's a fan and he gets down here and he's trying to find Earnhardt and Earnhardt is in an 8, but it's camouflaged. I got so ticked off about that. I called Budweiser. I called Fox. I called [NASCAR chairman] Brian France. I was just beside myself. I was so p***ed off about that."

most of the time, playing on his computer, because he just doesn't get that very often. It's hard to balance his time across people, because he has so little of it. And whether he spends it with a friend or with the girlfriend or whether he spends it with a family member – sometimes I think he just chooses not to spend it with anybody because it's hard to manage it. He is a loner guy. He is a quiet guy."

Earnhardt has more money than he can count and owns a private jet that on a whim could whisk him anywhere in the country. Anywhere, anytime. And yet, he prefers the cocoon of home, which is outfitted with Mason jars for glasses, and paper products for plates, and all the latest digital gadgets you could imagine. Meanwhile, the plane sits at the ready in the hangar at the airport. "This past year was the first year he's even looked at it from the standpoint of, 'You know, I have this plane. I could take it on a personal trip.' He just doesn't. He's not frivolous. He's not fussy, fancy like that," Kelley says. "He doesn't have houses anywhere else. When he does choose to vacation, he goes and stays in a hotel. He doesn't have a mountain house. He doesn't have a beach house or a house in the Caribbean. He is just real simple."

And, there are two more personality traits that appeal to those in the garage area and the masses. When he speaks his mind, he tells the truth, and he packages it all with a keen sense of humor. You may not like what you hear, but you'll probably be laughing about it before he's done talking. It's endearing and charismatic. "The thing I admire about him, he's so totally honest and truthful," said Rick Hendrick, Earnhardt's car owner. "You ask him anything, he's gonna tell you what he thinks. It might not be what you wanna hear, but he's gonna tell you what he thinks.

"He's just a real guy. And he's funny. He's very, very funny. And the more you're around him, the more hilarious some of the things he comes up with are. He is just a good guy. And he's Junior, too. He doesn't want to try to be his daddy. He's like, 'I am what I am and I'm not Dale Sr., I'm not Jeff Gordon and I'm not anybody but me. And I'm comfortable being me.' I admire that about him." ∎

The driver you don't know 187

February 18, 2001

It was NASCAR's darkest hour, a grim day filled with grief and tears and questions.

Left Dale Earnhardt, moments before the start of the 2001 Daytona 500, on pit road, in his No. 3 Richard Childress Racing Chevrolet.

Right Dale Earnhardt racing side-by-side with Jeff Gordon (No. 24) and Sterling Marlin (No. 40) during the 2001 Daytona 500. Notice the air foil across the roof and how tall the rear spoiler is standing on all three cars. This was a new aerodynamic package mandated by NASCAR for this race. Earnhardt complained to his team via two-way radio that he didn't like the feel of his stock car that day.

It has become known simply as "Black Sunday." It was a day that started with a long kiss on pit road and ended with numbing reality at a hospital less than two miles east of Daytona International Speedway.

Dale Earnhardt was making his 676th start in the Winston Cup Series and 23rd in the Daytona 500, a race he had finally conquered three years earlier on a day awash in emotion and achievement. At the start of the 2001 Daytona 500, Earnhardt was lined up seventh in the 43-car field, and had allies all around. His teammate, Mike Skinner, was fourth on the grid, and the three Dale Earnhardt Inc. entries – carrying Steve Park, Michael Waltrip and Dale Earnhardt Jr. – were scattered between sixth and 25th at launch.

A day that started with a long kiss on pit road and ended with numbing reality at a hospital.

Before NASCAR's pit marshals ordered everybody off pit road, Earnhardt gave his third wife, Teresa, a long, passionate kiss before buckling into his mighty stock car for the 200-lap extravaganza over Daytona's white-knuckle, 2.5-mile tri-oval layout. Races at Daytona and its sister track, Talladega Superspeedway, fray a driver's nerves because the cars run in a large pack, often just inches from each other at speeds in excess of 190 mph. The cars are so close and running so fast that one hiccup or bobble can create an accident that swallows upwards of 10, 15 even 20 cars.

The "big one," as such large-scale wrecks are called, happened that day on Lap 174, and according to the official race report it involved a whopping 19 cars, including Tony Stewart's, whose No. 20 Pontiac went airborne and landed on the roof of the No. 18 Pontiac driven by his teammate, Bobby Labonte, the defending NASCAR champion. No one was hurt but the toll on equipment was staggering, an estimated $4 million in damages.

The elder Earnhardt led 17 laps, but during the course of the race he was occasionally coarse with his team, grousing via two-way radio communication, that he didn't like the

The driver you don't know 189

The crash that changed NASCAR. On the last lap of the 2001 Daytona 500, Dale Earnhardt's No. 3 Chevrolet hit the wall in Turn 4. Just before Earnhardt's car hit the wall, Ken Schrader's No. 36 Pontiac hit its passenger side. The crash killed Earnhardt instantly. He died of a basilar skull fracture and the nation went into mourning. To this day, Earnhardt has been the only driver fatally injured in NASCAR's premier race at Daytona International Speedway.

feel of his black No. 3 Richard Childress Racing Chevrolet. NASCAR had a new setup for these stock cars in 2001 that included an air foil on the roof toward the front of the car, and it made the cars jump around at speed.

After the cleanup was complete following the "big one," the race was flagged green on Lap 180. Earnhardt Jr. led a couple of laps and gave way to Sterling Marlin, who was passed by Earnhardt Sr. Then Waltrip, who had not won a race in more than 400 starts, driving the No. 15 Chevy owned by Earnhardt, forged to the front of the lead pack on Lap 184. On Lap 198 it was Waltrip, Dale Jr. and the elder Earnhardt at the front of the line. As the cars flashed past the start-finish line

He turned and frantically waved to the approaching Speedway safety team then walked away.

to begin Lap 200, Waltrip and Earnhardt Jr. separated from the others, with Earnhardt Sr. acting as a wing man, gumming up the traffic flow.

As the cars rumbled into Turn 3, the No. 3 was in the middle of the track with cars all around. Earnhardt Sr. dipped low, probably to block the charging Marlin and keep him a safe distance from the two front-running Earnhardt Inc. cars. Earnhardt's rear bumper touched Marlin's front bumper, and the No. 3 shot up the 31-degree banking in the Turn 4 area. Just before the No. 3 made contact with the concrete wall, it was hammered by the No. 36 Pontiac driven by Ken Schrader. Both the No. 3 and the No. 36 coasted off the banking and came to rest side-by-side in a grassy area inside Turn 4.

Schrader emerged from his car and checked on Earnhardt Sr. He turned and frantically waved to the approaching Speedway safety team then walked away. Meanwhile, the DEI cars of Waltrip and Earnhardt Jr. finished one-two at the checkered flag. Darrell Waltrip, who was announcing the race for FOX Sports, sensed

190 Man-made Thunder

The driver you don't know 191

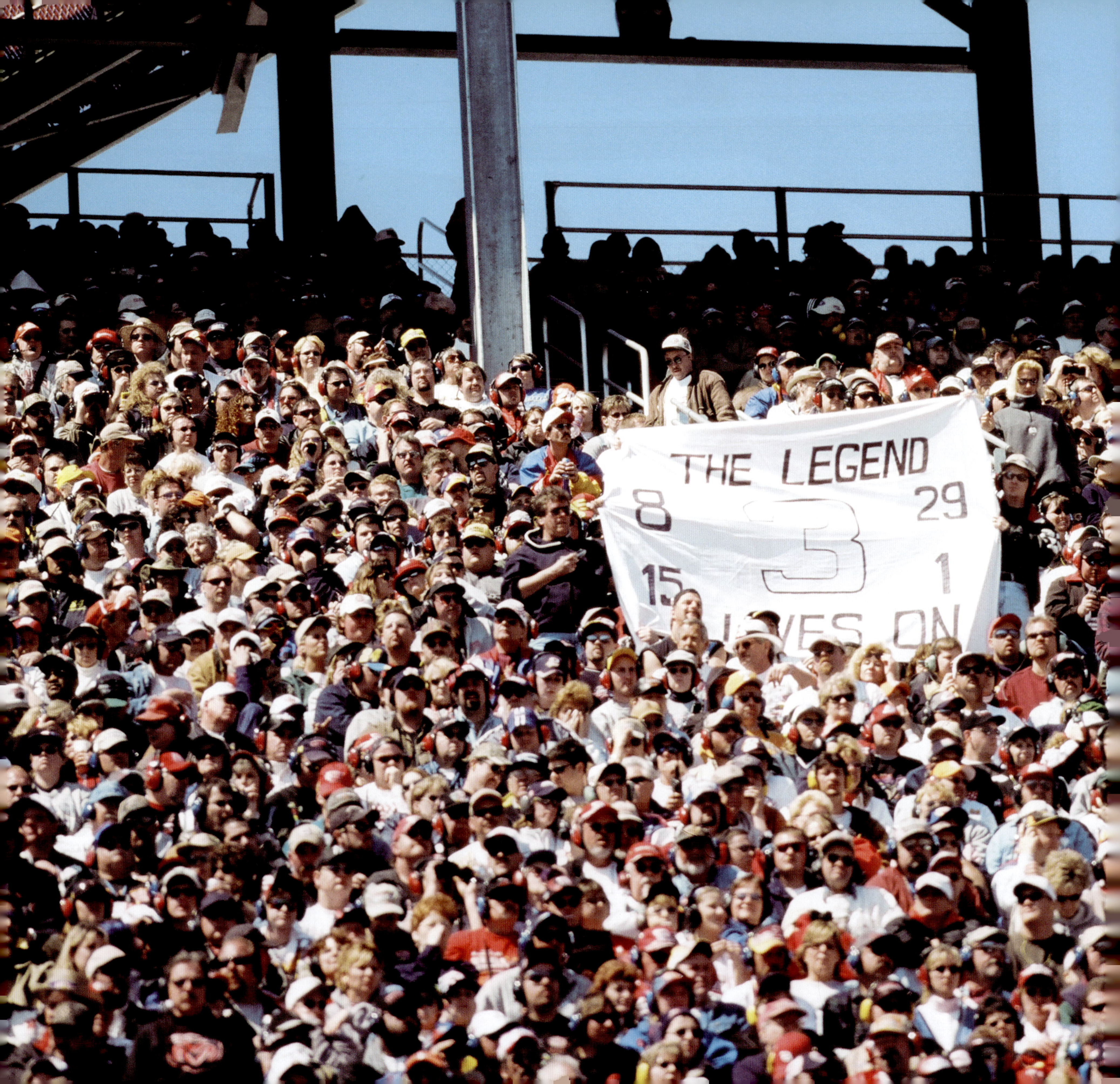
THE LEGEND
8
29
3
15
1

Left For months after Dale Earnhardt's death, race fans memorialized the racing giant. In the early stages of every race, those in the grandstand would rise and raise three fingers on the third lap as a tribute to the fallen, seven-time NASCAR champion.

Right In the days after Dale Earnhardt succumbed to a racing injury at Daytona, race fans from around the country journeyed to Dale Earnhardt Inc. in Mooresville, North Carolina, to place flowers, driver collectibles, candles and handmade notes in front of the race shop that bears his name.

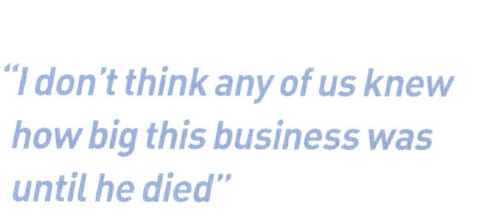

"I don't think any of us knew how big this business was until he died"

something was horribly wrong. His younger brother had just won the Daytona 500, but his face was ashen in the broadcast booth. "I hope Dale's OK," he said.

Hours later, NASCAR president Mike Helton, with tears in his eyes, made the horrific announcement that Earnhardt was dead. The seven-time NASCAR champion had suffered a basilar skull fracture and died instantly upon impact. The national media swarmed on the story. Later that week, Dale Earnhardt's photo appeared on the cover of national news magazines. It was that big. The day after NASCAR's biggest loss, H.A. "Humpy" Wheeler, then president of Lowe's Motor Speedway, went to pay his respects to the Earnhardt family at the DEI shop and watched dozens of weeping race fans leave flowers, candles, balloons, souvenirs and other memorabilia at the fence in honor of the "Intimidator."

"I don't think any of us knew how big this business was until he died," Wheeler says today. "I never thought I would ever see a race driver on the cover of *Time*. I don't care what he did, I never thought I'd see that." ∎

The driver you don't know 193

NASCAR's rush to improve safety

Dale Earnhardt won 76 races, seven championships and the hearts of race fans across the world, but his greatest legacy to stock-car racing was the ramp-up in safety research after his death at Daytona.

Left Before the 2001 NASCAR Winston Cup season had run its course, the sanctioning body had mandated that every driver be fitted with a head-and-neck device, designed to prevent the injury that killed Dale Earnhardt Sr. at Daytona. Here, Dale Earnhardt Jr. puts his helmet and HANS device on before the start of a Cup Series race at Michigan International Speedway in 2004.

Right Clint Bowyer's No. 07 Chevrolet is ablaze on the final lap of the 2007 Daytona 500. It got worse for Bowyer. The car flipped over and came to rest on its roof in the tri-oval. The good news? Bowyer squirmed out of the cockpit with no injuries. And since his car slid on its roof past the finish line, Bowyer was credited with a "running" 18th-place finish.

When the 49-year-old driver was killed on the last lap of the 2001 Daytona 500, the tragedy set in motion a new NASCAR approach to safety.

For the first time in its history, NASCAR sought help from outside experts to put a stop to a string of damning deaths over the 2000 – 01 racing seasons. NASCAR lost three drivers (Adam Petty, Kenny Irwin Jr. and Tony Roper) in its top three touring series in 2000. The final blow was Earnhardt, NASCAR's biggest star.

"It's a reality check," driver Tony Stewart said in 2006. "We lost Superman that day. Nobody is invincible." Mike Skinner, who was Earnhardt's teammate in 2001, agreed. "When the star of your series gets killed, everybody

"When the star of your series gets killed, everybody wants to know why"

wants to know why," Skinner said. "Everybody starts opening their eyes."

After Earnhardt's death, NASCAR went outside its inner circle of experts and hired independent engineers, scientists and doctors in the fields of crash reconstruction, biomechanical engineering and human kinetics to piece together a comprehensive report of the accident. The study was led by Dr. Dean Sicking of the University of Nebraska and Dr. James

Raddin from Biodynamic Research Corp. in San Antonio, Texas. Just how "independent" was this examination meant to be? "I'm not a racing fan," Sicking said in 2001.

The safety team studied Earnhardt's crash then made several recommendations to NASCAR so it could dramatically improve its standards. Before 2001 had run its course, drivers found themselves in a much safer race-car cockpit environment, including more padding, better restraints, netting, full-face helmets and head-and-neck safety devices. The HANS device, or similar gear, was made mandatory equipment by October 2001.

All NASCAR member tracks had so-called "soft wall" technology in place by the 2004

Soon after Dale Earnhardt's deadly crash, NASCAR engineers started on a project they called the "Car of Tomorrow." The next-generation stock car, built with a variety of safety features, debuted in 2007 on a limited schedule, then was raced exclusively in 2008. A group of the new cars are seen here crashing in the second Gatorade Duel qualifying race at Daytona in 2008. Similar design projects are in the works for NASCAR's Nationwide and Camping World series.

season. The walls are not soft at all. The Steel and Foam Energy Reduction (SAFER) system is actually a series of metal plates with foam backing placed in front of concrete walls. The SAFER barrier flexes and absorbs shock when a stock car impacts the structure.

The latest piece of the safety puzzle was introduced by NASCAR in 2007 with the "Car of Tomorrow." The COT, or next-generation stock car, was developed at NASCAR's Research and Development Center in Concord, North Carolina. It is built from the bottom up with safety improvements throughout. It was used in 16 events during the 2007 Nextel Cup Series, then became mandatory for all races in 2008.

Would Dale Earnhardt have died if some of these new safety features had been in place on the day of his accident?

Dr. John Melvin is a biomechanical engineer and a professor at Wayne State University and did consulting work with General Motors for 40 years. He lobbied NASCAR on safety issues. His pleas fell on deaf ears before Earnhardt's death. Now he is paid by NASCAR as an independent safety consultant. In 2008 he was asked a hypothetical question: Would Dale Earnhardt have died if some of these new safety features had been in place on the day of his accident?

"No," he said. "We know the severity of that crash was not all that great compared to some of the other crashes since. We'll never know for sure. We didn't have a crash recorder in that car. With the crash recordings we've had since then, we've seen much more severe crashes with good outcomes."

NASCAR may have been slow to implement new safety standards, but Melvin says, in all fairness, much of this research wasn't started until 1999. Earnhardt's death dramatically hastened the process. "A lot of the things we implemented wouldn't have been around much earlier than that," Melvin said. "We hoped to

196   Man-made Thunder

50
27
27
26
26
DODGE .COM
Crown Royal
CASK No16
JAMIE McMURRAY
IRWIN
BE A CHAMPION. DRINK RESPONSIBLY.
CASK No 16
IRWIN

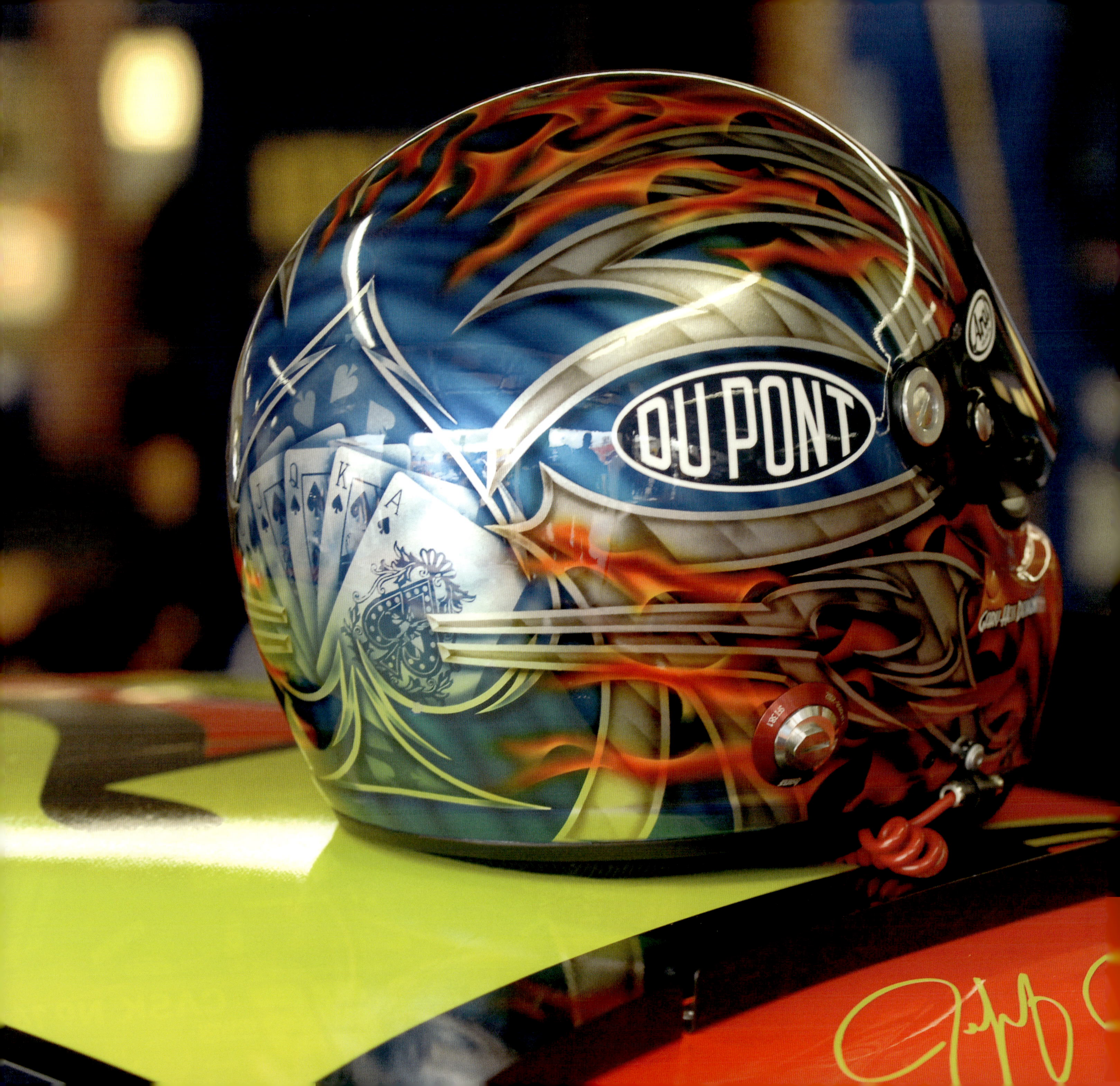
DUPONT

Jeff Gordon may have been one of the first Sprint Cup Series drivers to use a unique design on his racing helmet. This was a helmet he wore in the 2005 NASCAR Nextel All Star Challenge at Lowe's Motor Speedway. Gordon's royal flush, painted on his helmet, failed to produce a win in that race. He finished fourth, but his helmet was best in show.

implement these things by example and it would catch on, but Mr. Earnhardt's death accelerated that process way beyond any dreams that we had of getting that done. It just changed the sport."

Melvin said there have been many accidents over the last several years that could have produced catastrophic results for the drivers. In almost every one of those wrecks, the driver had minor injuries or was not hurt at all. Since Earnhardt's death in 2001, no driver has been killed in NASCAR competition. "That is very gratifying to me," Melvin said.

On the fifth anniversary of Earnhardt's death, NASCAR president Mike Helton was asked about the vast gains in safety, and he attributed the latest research-and-development gains to

Since Earnhardt's death ... no driver has been killed in NASCAR competition.

the loss of the sport's greatest competitor. "The safety effort was already there, and in our entire history safety has always been first and foremost," he said. "But there were two things that made this different. First, that bigness of Dale Earnhardt, and the icon that he represented – having lost that brought international attention to a lot of different areas. And in doing so, it brought a collaborative effort of everybody possible to make this sport safer." ■

Dale Earnhardt Jr.
First person

Dale Earnhardt Jr. in 2003, after being asked about the responsibility of being a fan favorite and being comfortable with that responsibility.

Left Dale Earnhardt Jr. employs the walk-and-sign strategy made famous by his father. If a driver with name recognition stops walking, he'll be mobbed by race fans. Earnhardt was walking to his race hauler after a practice session for the 2009 Daytona 500.

Right Dale Earnhardt Jr. is the No. 1 driver in NASCAR – based on fan popularity. Earnhardt won the Sprint Cup Series Most Popular Driver Award from 2003 to 2008. Since NASCAR and its teams are privately owned, there are no hard balance sheets available, but apparently Earnhardt makes millions of dollars each year just in the sale of collectibles, such as shirts, caps, jackets and die-cast cars.

"Well, there is some responsibility, but they are not very heavy, you know, to carry. When we're down there getting introduced to the crowd, it feels really, really good to get such a loud applause, and [there's] so much excitement for people to be excited for you to be here. It really, really feels good. And you really try not to compare it to other drivers or compare your popularity to other people. You try not to do that. You keep in the back of your mind the fact that it's not always going to be that way.

"One thing you always do is really be careful about what you do or what you say – try not to put yourself in a position, because you can lose it. It takes years to gain such respect or such

> "One thing that I have always done was just try to be honest, just try to be somebody that is easy to relate to, I guess"

admiration and it takes one second to lose it, which is amazing. One thing that I have always done was just try to be honest, just try to be somebody that is easy to relate to, I guess. And I think that's what's really the most profitable for me when it comes to creating my fan base – no matter who you are, there's something that you can relate to. That makes it easier for me. When I'm around the crowd of race fans, I don't feel uneasy or out of place. I feel like I'm standing in the same crowd that I stood with when I was in the infield at the speedway watching daddy run the track. I feel comfortable around the people.

"They might be excited or shaking or something – it's funny because I don't feel like there is a big difference between me or them. But they see something else. I have a lot of fun with the fans. I think even at this age I have an idea or a good appreciation for what they mean to me as a driver and the sport as well."

The driver you don't know 201

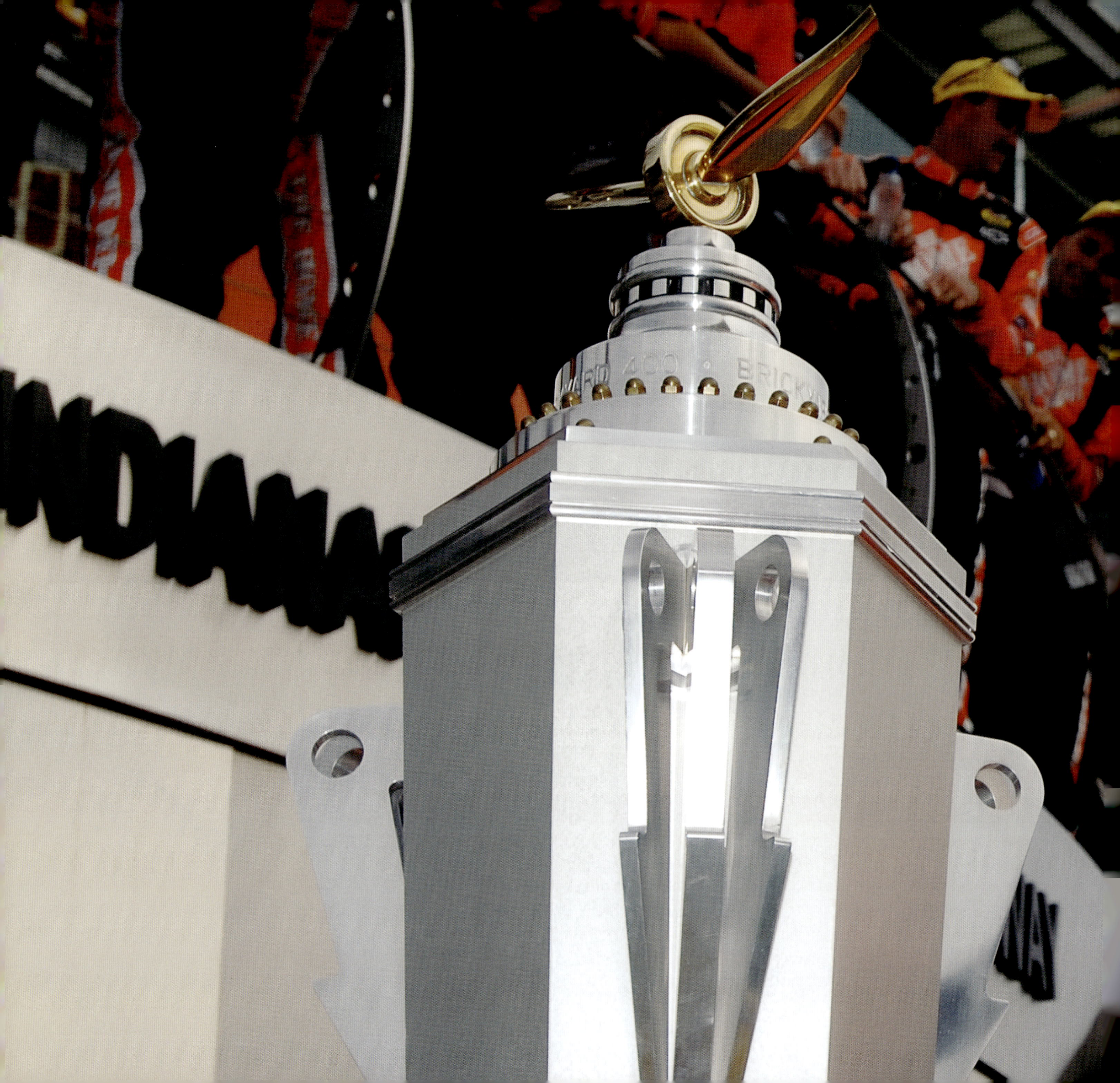

Smoke and fire

8

Previous page Tony Stewart, who dreamed of someday winning the Indianapolis 500, got to Indianapolis Motor Speedway's Victory Lane, but it was for his triumph in the Allstate 400 at the Brickyard.

Left This is the hauler that carried Tony Stewart's No. 20 Home Depot stock car around the country for 10 years. Race teams generally dedicate one of these 18-wheel transports for each car, each season. Between the schedule and testing, these haulers can easily log 70,000 miles a year on the highway. The sponsor gets their money's worth, because these haulers are like roving billboards. Race teams carry so much equipment, some bring an auxiliary truck to the racetrack to handle the overflow.

Tony Smoke Stewart arrived for 2008 Speedweeks at Daytona International Speedway packing extra pounds, sporting unruly hair and three days' worth of beard growth. He looked more like a Bruce Springsteen roadie than one of NASCAR's premier drivers. On the first day of business, group practice for the Budweiser Shootout, he wrecked with Kurt Busch, and the altercation continued as both cars limped onto pit road. Soon thereafter, both drivers were called to NASCAR's garage-area mobile office for a discussion of the incident. During the debriefing, in the presence of three NASCAR officials, Stewart smacked Busch in the head. Both drivers were put on probation for six races. It was a vintage Stewart episode.

Stewart's fans love the guy because they get him, understand what he's about – a throwback to a bygone era of race driver, cut from the same fabric as legend A.J. Foyt, who, not so surprisingly, is Stewart's racing hero. Stewart races hard, and he's not afraid to mix it up with other drivers on or off the racetrack. Stewart speaks his mind, usually in harsh

Stewart smacked Busch in the head. Both drivers were put on probation for six races. It was a vintage Stewart episode.

terms, and wears his emotions on his sleeve. He seems to have little use for the national racing media, and was once fined $10,000 by NASCAR for missing a mandatory press appearance following a race. Twice during his career, he's had physical contact with those in the Fourth Estate, shoving a photographer at Indianapolis, and knocking a tape recorder from the hand of a journalist at Daytona.

In 2003, Stewart felt persecuted by the media, and said: "What scares me is you guys. It always has. And it's not all of you. There are some people out there to me that hold grudges. Some of them that have chips on their shoulders; some of them that have something to prove when they write their articles. I met a lot of reporters. One thing I always said, I will

204 Man-made Thunder

Left Tony Stewart shows the gentle side of a gruff racer as he plays with a baby on pit road during the 2001 season. Stewart is a confirmed bachelor. Never been married, never had children.

Right Tony Stewart hoists the 2002 NASCAR Winston Cup Series championship trophy over his head in Victory Lane at Homestead-Miami Speedway. Three years later, he won the Nextel Cup Series championship for Joe Gibbs Racing.

Smoke and fire 205

206 Man-made Thunder

This is the part of the job that Tony Stewart could live without – dealing with the motorsports media on a regular basis. Here Stewart is surrounded by journalists during the 2007 Charlotte Media Tour.

never ask anybody to lie for me or cover up anything I do. If I did something stupid, say I did it. But you don't have to write that I did something stupid for the next eight months. It happens one time and it is over with until I do the next stupid one. Once you write about it one time, be done with it. That's the one thing that disappointed me about what you say or what you do because nobody will ever leave it alone."

It's a subject with which he's always been well familiar, so he continued. "I am a human being just like everybody else. We all make mistakes. The problem is a lot of the media won't let it go and let it go on. And that's the thing that keeps people from being able to speak their minds and be open about their thoughts. We know you guys are doing your jobs, and that sells papers. You have to make your mind up. If you want us to speak our minds, fine. But be fair with us about it. If you are going to crucify us, well, listen, we have to do what we have to do as drivers to protect our race teams and sponsors to where we get by and we give you the same – I got my set of cookie cutters sitting on my shelf; I can pull them out at any time.

"If I did something stupid, say I did it. But you don't have to write that I did something stupid for the next eight months"

I mean, if I feel I have to do that, that's what we do. You guys are the ones that actually give us the feel on what we are able to do and not do. If we are getting crucified for every little topic that's out there in the garage area, then it makes us all pull back. All of us drivers do that. I am probably the one guy that's probably not as scared of you guys as most, but even I'm getting paranoid now."

Go to the Internet and find any racing chat site after an event in which Stewart played a prominent role, and you can see both sides of the Stewart contingency: The outpouring of support from his people, as well as the vitriol spewed by those who don't care for his on-track/off-track antics, which often include run-ins with their own favorite drivers.

Tires, for obvious reasons, are important to NASCAR racing. In the early years of stock-car racing, tires were supplied by Firestone and Goodyear. Firestone dropped out of racing in 1974, leaving Goodyear as the lone supplier. Hoosier Tire got into the sport in 1988, sparking a crazy tire war. Hoosier got out of NASCAR after the 1994 season. Soon after, NASCAR signed Goodyear as the exclusive tire supplier to its top three racing divisions.

"If I were Goodyear, I'd be very embarrassed about the tire they brought this weekend"

Some think Stewart is crude, arrogant, immature, selfish, boorish, undisciplined, rakish, loathing, beastly, garish, unkempt and, on the track, downright dangerous at times. Many of those people don't understand the entire Tony Stewart package.

Stewart has stayed true to the fire of his short-track roots while others around him have gone totally corporate and remain within the boundaries of political correctness. Stewart went over that barbed wire many, many years ago. When Stewart goes over the top, he flies in with both feet: Damn the consequences. In 2008, he called out tire giant Goodyear after the first Cup race at Atlanta Motor Speedway. "If I were Goodyear, I'd be very embarrassed about the tire they brought this weekend," said Stewart after the race, where he finished second. "It was ridiculous. If they can't do better than that, pull out of the sport. I guarantee you that Hoosier or Firestone could do a better job than that."

The day after the race, Stewart remained critical during his weekly radio show on *Sirius Satellite*. "We've complained for years on numerous occasions behind closed doors to Goodyear and the problem doesn't get solved," he said. "So maybe this was one of these cases where maybe finally something good will come out of this. And if it sounds like we're whining about it, it's because we're trying to get their attention. For Goodyear to say that they were satisfied with that, if they truly believe that they were satisfied with the way the race went yesterday, I'm more disappointed than ever. And I can't believe that NASCAR, at the end of the day, is truly, honestly, happy with the results."

Stewart invited Goodyear to participate on his show. They declined. NASCAR president Mike Helton, however, came on to give the sanctioning body's point of view, at one point, scolding the two-time NASCAR champ.

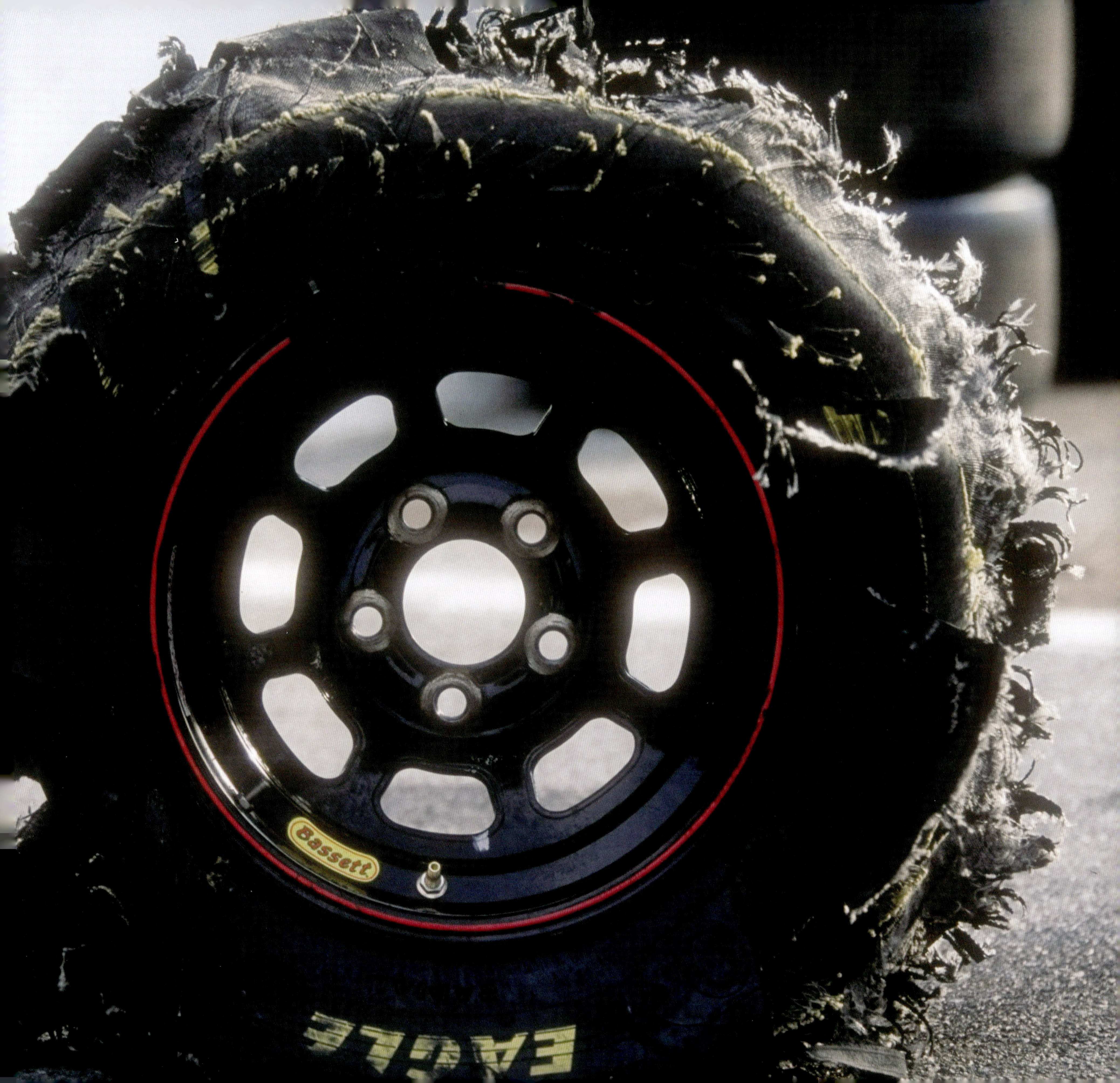
Bassett
EAGLE

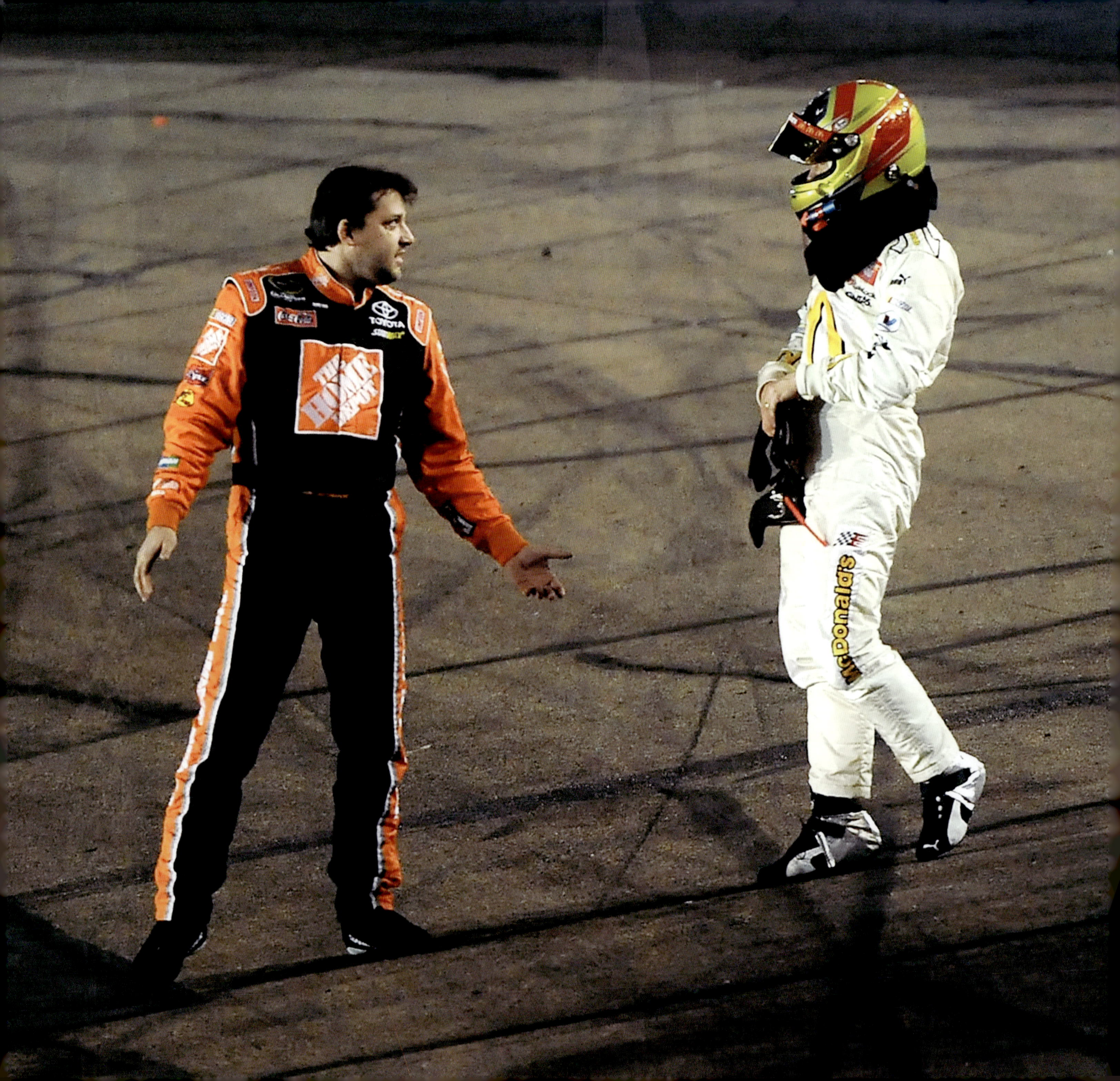
TOYOTA
McDonald's

Left Tony Stewart shows his displeasure with driver AJ Allmendinger after the two crashed during the Checker O'Reilly Auto Parts 500 at Phoenix International Raceway in 2008. Stewart's body language suggests he's ready to rumble.

Right When stock cars are racing this close for a long stretch of laps, tension, anxiety and pressure mounts and tempers can flare if there's some sort of racing incident.

"Tony, we're all well aware of your opinion and your right to express your opinion, albeit, I think maybe a little bit too strong in this case," Helton said, later adding, " I think it is a little bit too much to blame whatever your opinion on Sunday was completely on Goodyear, because we're all in this thing together . . ."

Another example: In 2006, following the Budweiser Shootout, Stewart emerged from his No. 20 Joe Gibbs Racing Chevrolet and said if bump-drafting was going to be allowed, NASCAR would have to carry a dead driver out of Daytona by the end of Speedweeks. Bump-drafting is the term used to describe when a trailing stock car actually makes contact with the car just ahead to increase the speed of both vehicles – preferably only on a straightaway area of the racetrack. It can wreck a car in the high-speed turns. "Yeah, we're going to kill somebody," Stewart said. "Somebody else is going to die at Daytona or Talladega with what we're doing right here. I hope I'm not around when it happens." Stewart, the defending series champion, forced NASCAR's hand, which designated

> *"Tony, we're all well aware of your opinion and your right to express your opinion, albeit, I think maybe a little bit too strong in this case"*

no-bump zones at certain parts of the 2.5-mile tri-oval course and said it would penalize aggressive driving.

Ironically, a week later, Stewart was slapped down by NASCAR. He got an in-race penalty for knocking the shoe-shine off of Matt Kenseth's No. 17 Ford. "I felt like it was an intentional cheap shot," Kenseth said. "I would never do that to him, intentionally put somebody in harm's way at a racetrack like this." Stewart's response? Stewart said Kenseth crowded him earlier in the race, and the nudge that sent Kenseth's car spinning into the infield grass in Turn 3, was a payback. "He should have been smart enough to know not to be tuckin' down our doors in the first 20 laps

Smoke and fire 211

212 Man-made Thunder

Drivers say this is the worst feeling in the world, looking out the windshield and either seeing clouds and sky or pavement and grass. In this sequence, during the 2006 NASCAR Busch Series race at Talladega Superspeedway, Tony Stewart goes sideways, air gets under his No. 33 Chevrolet and the car flips completely over. Stewart was racing for Kevin Harvick Inc. in that event. When Stewart left Joe Gibbs Racing after the 2008 season, he signed Old Spice as a major sponsor.

Smoke and fire 213

of a 200-lap race at Daytona," Stewart groused. "He has no room to complain. He started the whole thing and I finished it."

Where there is "Smoke," there is fire. Since Joe Gibbs Racing snatched Stewart from the IndyCar Series ranks for good in 1999 (Stewart drove a Gibbs' Busch Series car in 1997–98 on a part-time basis), the driver has compiled quite a racing rap sheet. There is a countless list of bad-behavior episodes, such as temper tantrums, tirades, snubs, expletives, punches, pushes, threats and finger gestures, mostly done in the heat of the moment after a race or practice session. He even got a fine outside of NASCAR in 2008. He was at a USAC event, standing on pit road as team owner, and got into an altercation with an official. It cost him $10,000. The media, for the most part, are not around when Stewart is dining with friends at the neighborhood Burger King (he just signed a sponsorship deal), or sharing a case of Schlitz beer (needs to sign a deal), or playing Texas Hold 'Em poker (he's pretty good), or chasing women (he's an old-school racer, so he's had his successes).

"Once he takes his helmet off, he's a completely different person . . . You're able to talk to him and be receptive of him . . ."

Not many see the private side of Stewart, probably because that door is normally closed.

There are two Tony Stewarts, the renowned track bully, and the relatively easy-going guy when away from his chosen arena; a man who once owned a pet monkey and takes his Chihuahua with him on the road. More than one of his peers has observed and noted this intriguing personality split. "Once he takes his helmet off, he's a completely different person," driver Kyle Busch said in 2006. "You're able to talk to him and be receptive of him. It's good to be able to have that relationship off the racetrack, I guess." Stewart said this all goes back to media, who wrongly use his heat-of-the-moment actions when they focus on his personality.

Before Tony Stewart became a NASCAR star, he was top driver in the IndyCar and United States Auto Club series (opposite). In 1995, for instance, he swept championships in USAC Midget, Sprint Car and Silver Crown. Two years later, he captured the IndyCar Series championship. He was an IndyCar Series regular from 1996 to 1998, scoring three victories. It was during this time that he tried his hand in the NASCAR Busch Series, making nine starts in '96, then signed a contract with Joe Gibbs Racing with the intention of leaving open-wheel racing to jump into the Winston Cup Series. Stewart ran for Winston Cup Rookie of the Year honors in 1999, winning three races and finishing fourth in overall points. Mark Dismore, who mentored Stewart when the two-time NASCAR champion raced go-karts, called Stewart "God's gift to the steering wheel." In the photo on the right, Stewart climbs the fence at Martinsville Speedway after winning the 2006 DirecTV 500. After a string of victory celebration climbs in 2005, race fans expected Stewart to scale chain-link fence after every win.

Smoke and fire 215

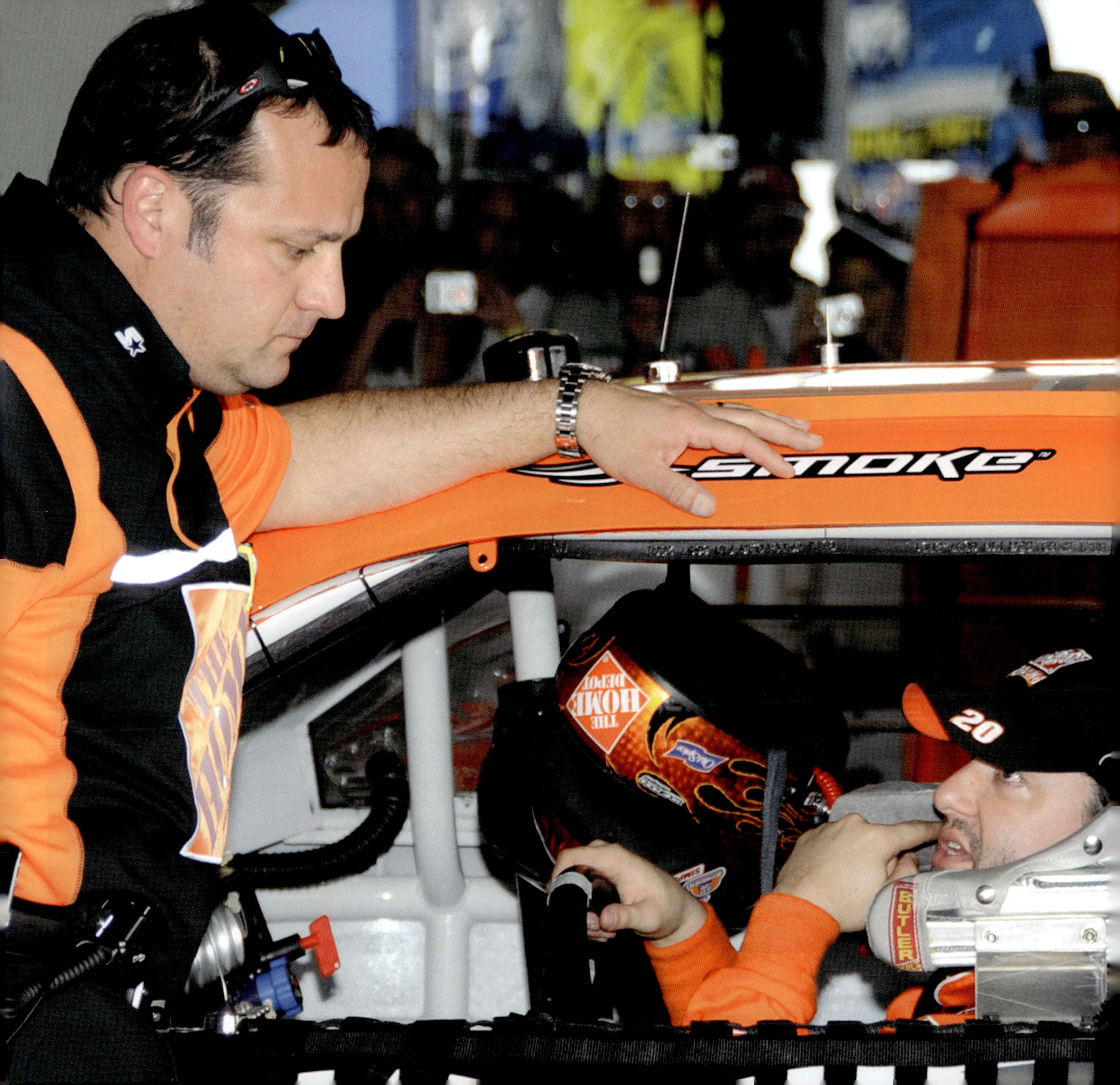
SMOKE
THE HOME DEPOT
20
BUTLER

For 10 years, Tony Stewart had one success after another in NASCAR Sprint Cup Series racing. Here Stewart talks to the man behind the machine, crew chief Greg Zipadelli, who helped navigate his driver through turbulent times. Asked about the secret to their success, Zipadelli said: "I don't know if there's any secret. It's kind of hard-working honesty. We go and do what we're supposed to do. We're friends, but first and foremost I think we work at racing. We work at our jobs."

Trying to keep track of Tony Stewart's personality is like playing Three Card Monte against a street hustler.

He once told the *Performance Racing Network*, "When we talk after the race, you guys [the media] have the luxury of being there right after the race so the emotion is there, you say things that by the time [I] get home that night [I'm] like, 'Nah, it wasn't a big deal. I know who he is, I know him as a person, I know it wasn't intentional,' and [I] discard it." But the media, Stewart says, keeps poking at the hornets' nest. "That's what ticks me off more than anything in this sport, it's what I absolutely hate about it, is the fact that people are trying to make something out of nothing and that's what's frustrating."

Trying to keep track of Tony Stewart's personality is like playing Three Card Monte against a street hustler. You can't keep up. Stewart could be raising thousands of dollars for charity one day, then punching Brian Vickers in the chest the next (it happened at Infineon Speedway in 2004 – Vickers: "I was still strapped in my car with my helmet off. He reached for me and knocked the breath out of me").

Stewart can knock the bejeezus out of you on the track (Chicagoland Speedway, 2004, car owner Ray Evernham, after Stewart crashed his driver Kasey Kahne: "He should have his backside beat. That's the problem with him. Nobody has ever grabbed him and given him a good beating") then rescue a pack of greyhounds which were about to be euthanized. Good Tony has helped Habitat For Humanity build homes and lent his time and sweat to build inner-city parks. Bad Tony got into a scuffle with Robby Gordon in the Daytona garage area, and had a few unseemly shouting matches with Jeff Gordon.

The all-time strangest good-bad comparison came at Daytona, in two races the same year. In the 2007 Daytona 500, he got wrecked from behind by Kurt Busch while leading the race, and sounded as calm and

Tony Stewart left Joe Gibbs Racing at the end of 2008 to take a 50-percent stake in Stewart-Haas Racing in 2009. SHR has a close affiliation with Hendrick Motorsports – so close, that Rick Hendrick asked Stewart to drive one of his Nationwide Series races in the '09 season opener at Daytona International Speedway. To no one's surprise, Stewart won that day, here, celebrating in Victory Lane.

NASCAR Sprint Cup Series drivers must be able to tackle a variety of track configurations, from the never-let-off-the-gas races at Talladega Superspeedway, to the road course at Infineon Raceway in Sonoma, California. Here Tony Stewart is racing his former car, the No. 20 Joe Gibbs Racing Chevrolet, during the Dodge/SaveMart 350 at Infineon. Up to the start of the 2009 season, Stewart had six victories on Sprint Cup road course tracks. The other is Watkins Glen International in New York State. Sprint Cup races only twice a year on road courses. The other 34 events are on oval-type tracks.

Tony Stewart is a racer's racer. All he cares about is racing (and assorted benefits that come with it, of course).

collected as a Key West bartender. Again, he was leading the 500 and got knocked out of the race. "Not completely sure what happened out there," he said back in the garage area. "All of a sudden, it took off on me. I haven't seen it on film, so I am not sure what happened. Pretty impressive to go all the way to the back and come up all the way to front of the field like that. I was really happy about that." He was smiling throughout the short interview.

Five months later, a similar accident during the Pepsi 400 at Daytona . . . only this time Stewart knocks into the rear of race leader Denny Hamlin, blames it all on his teammate and cries foul to the media. "The No. 11 [Hamlin] just stopped for no reason, right in the middle of Turn 4," Stewart said in a rage. "I'm sure he was getting tight because for three laps in a row we were catching him through the center and the exit of the corner. All of a sudden he just stops on the exit of [Turn] 4 in front of 42 cars and I guess expects all of us to drive around him. I don't know. It's tore up two really good race cars. He tried to crash us on Friday in practice and didn't get it done so he finished it off today."

There's an easy explanation for this. Tony Stewart is a racer's racer. All he cares about is racing (and assorted benefits that come with it, of course). As for everything else that comes with performing on the big stage, after all these years in the spotlight he's still squinting at the bulb. "Once I won that first race in the Cup Series, my life was basically turned upside down," he said. "I'm not one of those guys, I don't particularly care for all the attention. I mean, I'm not a guy that wants to be a superstar or media personality or racing personality or anything like that. I just like being a race car driver. I enjoy driving race cars." ∎

Smoke and fire 219

The guiding force

Tony Stewart admits that A.J. Foyt is his personal hero, and he has patterned his career after "Super Tex," who won in all forms of motorcar racing, from midgets on dirt to four Indianapolis 500 victories.

Left A.J. Foyt is relaxed and ready to go stock-car racing in this photo from the 1968 season. Foyt was one of the few drivers who were successful in Indy-type cars and in NASCAR, where he scored seven career victories, including the 1972 Daytona 500.

Right Cars prepare to dart down pit road at Darlington Raceway for service. Foyt made only one start at Darlington, in the 1985 Southern 500, where he finished 25th at the age of 50.

And what's more, "Smoke" and A.J. share waistlines and many personality traits.

Foyt, who always raced with passion and desire and emotion, is one of racing's most heavily decorated drivers, only one of two men to win both the Indy and Daytona 500s. He won the 1972 Daytona 500 driving for legendary Wood Brothers Racing.

In 128 career starts in what is now the NASCAR Sprint Cup Series, Foyt scored seven victories, including three at Daytona International Speedway. He won back-to-back Firecracker 400s in 1964–65. His stock-car career spanned from 1963 to 1994, when at the age of 59, he competed in the inaugural Brickyard 400, the first stock-car race at his beloved Indianapolis Motor Speedway.

Foyt was, and to this day as a car owner remains, cantankerous and feisty, not afraid to speak his mind or openly show his anger to his team and other competitors. In 1997, after an Indy Racing League event at Texas Motor Speedway, Foyt's entry, driven by Billy Boat, was declared the winner, prompting a protest by driver Arie Luyendyk.

Unfortunately for Luyendyk, he went to complain to IRL officials in Victory Lane, which sent Foyt into a rage. Foyt grabbed Luyendyk by the neck and tossed him to the ground. USAC officials, who were the IRL's official scoring and time keepers, later gave the win to Luyendyk.

"The Luyendyk deal, I still got the trophy because I won the race," Foyt explains today. "It's very simple. I haven't been no angel, but I've never went to somebody's Victory Circle . . ."

Does that sound like anybody in the world of today's racers? Some think Stewart was born in the wrong racing era; that he would have felt a bit more comfortable racing 40 years ago, chasing Foyt around an oval. To this day, Stewart sometimes leaves his private jet parked at the airport and just hangs out with his boys at the short track.

"I went and raced the dirt late-model two nights, and I didn't fly to the tracks and get out, I rode in the truck with the team," Stewart said. "We rode in a motor home together. The whole

Smoke and fire 221

entire race team; we were all sitting there working together, riding together. We were telling stories about races five or six years ago.

"Yeah, it makes you appreciate those times. I mean, a lot's changed in racing, not necessarily all of them are for the better. They all have happened for a reason. With that, it's fun to remember those times. I may not have been in the era with A.J. and those guys that I respect the most, but still I still have a lot of good stories and a lot of good things to talk about with friends."

Foyt, who has survived numerous brushes with death (bee stings, a lion attack and near drownings in addition to several nasty racing accidents), says of all the race drivers out there

"I tease him all the time he's not that good in IndyCars"

today, Tony Stewart is the guy he relates to the most, because he's not fancy, mannered or an aristocrat. Stewart, born and raised in Indiana, is nearly a Foyt clone.

"There are a lot of good boys out there," said Foyt, who lives in Houston. "The one probably closest to me today would be Tony Stewart. Regardless of what you put him in, he wins. You put him in midgets, he wins there. He can win in sprint cars and he wins in stock cars. I tease him all the time he's not that good in IndyCars.

I give him a bad time, but we're pretty good friends."

During his extended victory celebration after winning the 2005 Allstate 400 at the Brickyard, Stewart found the time to call Foyt, who was recovering from an African killer bee attack, which happened while clearing brush on his Texas property. He was stung more than 200 times in the face.

"He called me about those damn bees," Foyt said. "I said, 'Big boy, let them get on your butt and see how good you are.' I was probably the most scared in my life. I was like, 'Just finish it off.' It was like somebody beating on you with a stick." Tough and talented. Two men, two of a kind. ∎

Left A.J. Foyt celebrates his 1972 Daytona 500 with Wood Brothers Racing in Victory Lane at Daytona International Speedway. Of Foyt's seven career NASCAR victories, three were at Daytona. During the 1964–65 seasons, he won back-to-back Firecracker 400s for two different car owners.

Right Bobby Isaac, driving the No. 71 Dodge owned by Nord Krauskopf, leads the 40-car field to the green flag for the start of the 1972 Daytona 500. Foyt was right next to Isaac at the start and dominated the race, leading 167 of 200 laps, including the last 120. He won by more than a lap.

Smoke and fire 223

Custer's last stand

The question put forth to Joe Custer went something like this: Are you crazy, man?

Left One of the great dreads of die-hard race fans is when their favorite driver changes teams or sponsors. Why? Because they must have the gear that identifies them with their driver. For instance, when Tony Stewart left Joe Gibbs Racing for Stewart-Haas Racing, he not only changed car manufacturers (Toyota to Chevy), but his car number (20 to 14) and sponsors (Home Depot to Office Depot/Old Spice). His biggest fans were out in force at his collectibles trailer buying up new Stewart stuff for the '09 season. Collectibles are a major revenue stream not only for drivers, but for race teams.

Right Ready, willing and able. Race fans gather on the "football field" in the Daytona International Speedway tri-oval before the start of the 2009 Daytona 500. Nearly 200,000 race fans crammed into the Speedway to watch the "Great American Race."

After all, it was Custer, general manager at Haas-CNC Racing, who helped broker the deal to give Tony Stewart a half stake in the racing operation beginning in 2009. Stewart not only drives the No. 14 Stewart-Haas Racing Chevrolet, but owns 50 percent of the team. So now, "Tony the Tiger," the fiery, sometimes wild-eyed driver, who won two NASCAR Sprint Cup Series championships in a 10-year run in the No. 20 Joe Gibbs Racing entry . . . that guy is a team owner and Custer's boss.

Why did Custer pursue the deal to bring Stewart, a well-chronicled hot-head, into the fold? Precisely for that reason, for the energy, the passion and the flame. You need a strong spark to make a 700-horsepower engine run at

You need a strong spark to make a 700-horsepower engine run at maximum strength.

maximum strength. Tony Stewart is the spark plug that Custer and team owner Gene Haas (actually, his company, Haas Automation, owns 50 percent of the team) needed to turn this stock-car pussycat into a raging tiger. From 2002 to 2008, Haas drivers logged 284 starts and scored one, count it, one, top-five finish – Johnny Sauter, a fifth-place at Richmond in 2007.

Knowing that Stewart wasn't completely happy with Gibbs Racing switching from Chevrolet to Toyota in 2008, Custer was instructed to bird-dog the driver until an agreement could be reached. It was a long, complicated process that took months and months of meetings, agreements, phone calls, e-mails, text messaging and understandings.

"It was very complex," Custer said. "I mean, when I say complex, there were so many issues that happened during this process. You know, we essentially were looking for talent. We felt we had all the resources and infrastructure and equipment, wherewithal, but the people piece was missing. So we got into discussions with Tony, to put together a partnership that could be profitable, but first and foremost, successful on the track. Because we didn't really come here to make money; we came here to win races and not to lose a lot of money."

Custer calls Stewart a rare "franchise player" in the NASCAR industry, the kind of personality that can attract top-notch mechanical-engineering talent and sponsorship funding. Plus there's his undisputed driving ability. There are but a handful of drivers who fit the description of a franchise player, who bring something special to the table. When Stewart signed on, Custer was inundated with phone calls and feelers from the top professionals in the sport who wanted to join the party.

"The people that we've interviewed and the people that have sent resumes, these are

"Be who you are. Demand what you demand, and let the people around you do their job"

high-end people that want to be part of the program because Tony has become involved," Custer said with a gleam in his eyes. "They know his heart's in it. He's not going to be an absentee owner. They feel it's going to be something special. You can feel that in our organization right now, that next year is going to be special. You can't measure that. You can't buy that. It's just somebody that's unique.

"We felt that Tony could drive sponsorship desire through not just his team but other teams, and people, not just his direct people, but other people in [the company]. The last thing is just sheer performance; just Tony getting it done. That is something that I completely believe in. I completely believe in his talent, that he is a premier driver in our sport and will deliver trophies."

Yeah, but what about, you know, "Evil Tony?" The guy who is not afraid to raise his voice, curse on television, challenge authority or punch another driver. The Tony Stewart who stirs the emotional pot, folds his red cape and runs toward the bull, never backs down from a fight? Isn't there some extra baggage there you

Man-made Thunder

Tony Stewart stretches his racing legs in his new stock car, the No. 14 Stewart-Haas Racing Chevrolet, during the 2009 Daytona 500. Stewart finished eighth in his debut run with the new team.

They call 2009 Sprint Cup rookie driver Joey Logano "Sliced Bread" based on the old saying, "the greatest thing since sliced bread." When he made his debut in the No. 20 Joe Gibbs Racing Toyota at the start of the 2009 season, he was young, just 18, and had some big shoes to fill as Tony Stewart's replacement. Crew chief Greg Zipadelli went from trying to win a championship to teaching this talented kid racer the ins and outs of Sprint Cup racing.

may not want to bring into the House of Haas? Some of Stewart's harshest critics have called his trackside behavior unacceptable.

Haas, Custer and the long-suffering Haas-CNC Racing operation see Stewart, his ability and what he brings to the table, through a different lens. They see the man who will lead them to stock-car glory, by God.

"I completely support however he chooses to vocalize himself, and I don't think it will be detrimental," Custer said. "The history I have seen with him, the things he's done in the sport and the way he's conducted himself when something is not right, I haven't been offended by the way. Am I saying every single thing he's done is right or wrong? I'm not going to evaluate that. But the way he's handled himself, he's never tore down his team or his sponsors. Some people might say he's made mistakes, and some people might say he's passionate. I'm not going to judge that.

"But I know in my opinion, I would support the way he's conducted himself. So however he chooses to react to issues that we come up against, I can't see anything in his past that I would be nervous about. I mean, I'll tell you one thing, I'm more nervous that he wouldn't be; that he would maybe dilute himself a little bit, like, 'Oh, I'm an owner and don't want to ruffle any feathers or p*** one of the guys off.' I think he's got to be . . . and I would challenge him, to be himself. Be who you are. Demand what you demand, and let the people around you do their job. Don't try to change. Just push us. Push us to the ragged edge.

"If you're not winning, you better not be happy. I don't want to hear about, 'Oh, we finished 20th, but we're getting a little better.' I'm done with 20th. I hate 20th. I don't ever want to see 20th. If we're running 20th, I want to see people with fire in their eye about it; Tony Stewart does not need to be finishing 20th. That's unacceptable." ■

Smoke and fire 227

U.S. ARMY
U.S. ARMY
RACING
PUMA
Mighty
CHAMPION
GOODYEAR
Snap-on
Coca-Cola
Principal
Financial Group
U.S. ARMY
ARMY STRONG
PUMA
U.S. ARMY
CHAMPION
SPARK PLUGS
Coca-Cola
Principal
Financial Group

Gentleman racer

9

Previous page After nearly two decades of service with car owner Jack Roush, Mark Martin followed a strange series of twists and turns to find himself in the No. 8 Dale Earnhardt Inc. Chevrolet in 2008. As a Roush driver, he battled against Dale Earnhardt Sr. several times for the NASCAR Winston Cup Series title.

Although Mark Martin never served in the U.S. armed forces, he has always been a strong supporter of the military and was delighted to represent the U.S. Army over the 2007 and 2008 seasons. Here, Martin is surrounded by members of the military during pre-race ceremonies in 2006, the year before he represented the Army in stock-car racing.

The NASCAR Sprint Cup Series is all-consuming, exemplified by the first two stops on the coast-to-coast tour. Since 1982, the series has launched at Daytona International Speedway with the Speedweeks program – it's a grueling, two-week ordeal that builds to a Daytona 500 crescendo. It is a nail-biting, nerve-racking, anxiety-building sequence of stock-car events that can turn men with steel spines into a mound of emotional mush. There's single-car qualifying, then two 150-mile qualifying races called the Gatorade Duel, and if you make the cut, you get a grid position for the 500.

It took AJ Allmendinger three tries to make his first Daytona 500, the 2009 race. Allmendinger was moved to tears when he qualified the No. 44 Dodge into the show. "I haven't slept well for about a week and a half now," he said. "This year, I felt like I deserved to be in this race. I earned my way in. This whole team deserved it for how hard they've worked the last few weeks after we put this program together. I feel like there was more pressure on my shoulders than there has ever been."

... it's a grueling, two-week ordeal that builds to a Daytona 500 crescendo.

After the Daytona 500, in Daytona Beach, Florida, it's on to the other side of the country, to Fontana, California, where the second race of the season is now positioned on the Sprint Cup schedule. Five days after spending nearly two weeks in Daytona, the teams and drivers report to Auto Club Speedway for another 500-mile event. Drivers just don't sit around the house and watch television between racing events. There are commercials to shoot, sponsor events to attend, media obligations to fulfill, and other assorted duties that come with the title of Sprint Cup race driver. Those poor fellows in the colorful driver suits are pushed, pulled, summoned, tugged and sometimes dragged to a variety of duties that have absolutely nothing to do with race cars, racetracks or racing. It

AAA.com
NEXTEL
PENNZOIL
GOODYEAR
ROUSH
Coca-Cola
MAXWELL HOUSE
AAA

Left Mark Martin has always been a fan favorite, here signing autographs for fans in 1993 at the fence line at Michigan International Speedway. Martin makes a strong connection to his fan base for his family values, his heavy right foot and his reputation as a clean driver.

Right In 2001, car owner Jack Roush inked a groundbreaking deal with Pfizer, which used NASCAR to brand a prescription drug named Viagra that helps men with erectile dysfunction. With the popularity of NASCAR on the rise, Pfizer paid top sponsorship dollar to land the hood of the No. 6 Roush Racing Ford.

is a nonstop grind. NASCAR added more fire to the pressure cooker by introducing the "Chase for the Championship" in 2004, something of a 10-race playoff between 10 (now 12) drivers. After 26 races, the top dozen drivers in points slug it out for the championship.

The pressure and travel is not conducive to family life or anything remotely considered normal by traditional standards. These men, who all get fat paychecks, are like gypsies dressed in Nomex, or carnival people with Learjets, or salesmen with full-faced helmets. They are in constant motion, either making laps or making money by hyping products to appease their wide array of sponsors, or to keep their fan base happy. The sponsor-driver-fan-product connection is even more essential in difficult economic times. The point here is simple: Yes, the money is good and fame is great, but this is a rugged, many times lonely, merry-go-round lifestyle which can become a dulling blur of events. Expect to miss birthdays and anniversaries and baby's first steps if you sign on as a Sprint Cup driver.

Mark Martin made that commitment to racing. He got on one knee and proposed to the sport as a teenager...

Mark Martin made that commitment to racing. He got on one knee and proposed to the sport as a teenager, then took his vows at the altar of speed as a young man with wild ambitions, but low expectations. His was a struggle. He had to prove his worth, validate his credentials, before realizing his dream of becoming a full-time NASCAR driver. Car owner Jack Roush, who was new to the stock-car sport himself, liked Martin's work ethic and resiliency. They joined forces in 1988 and stayed together, through thick and thin, joy and despair, until the conclusion of the 2006 season. Roush talked about the longevity of the partnership, rare in NASCAR Country.

Gentleman racer

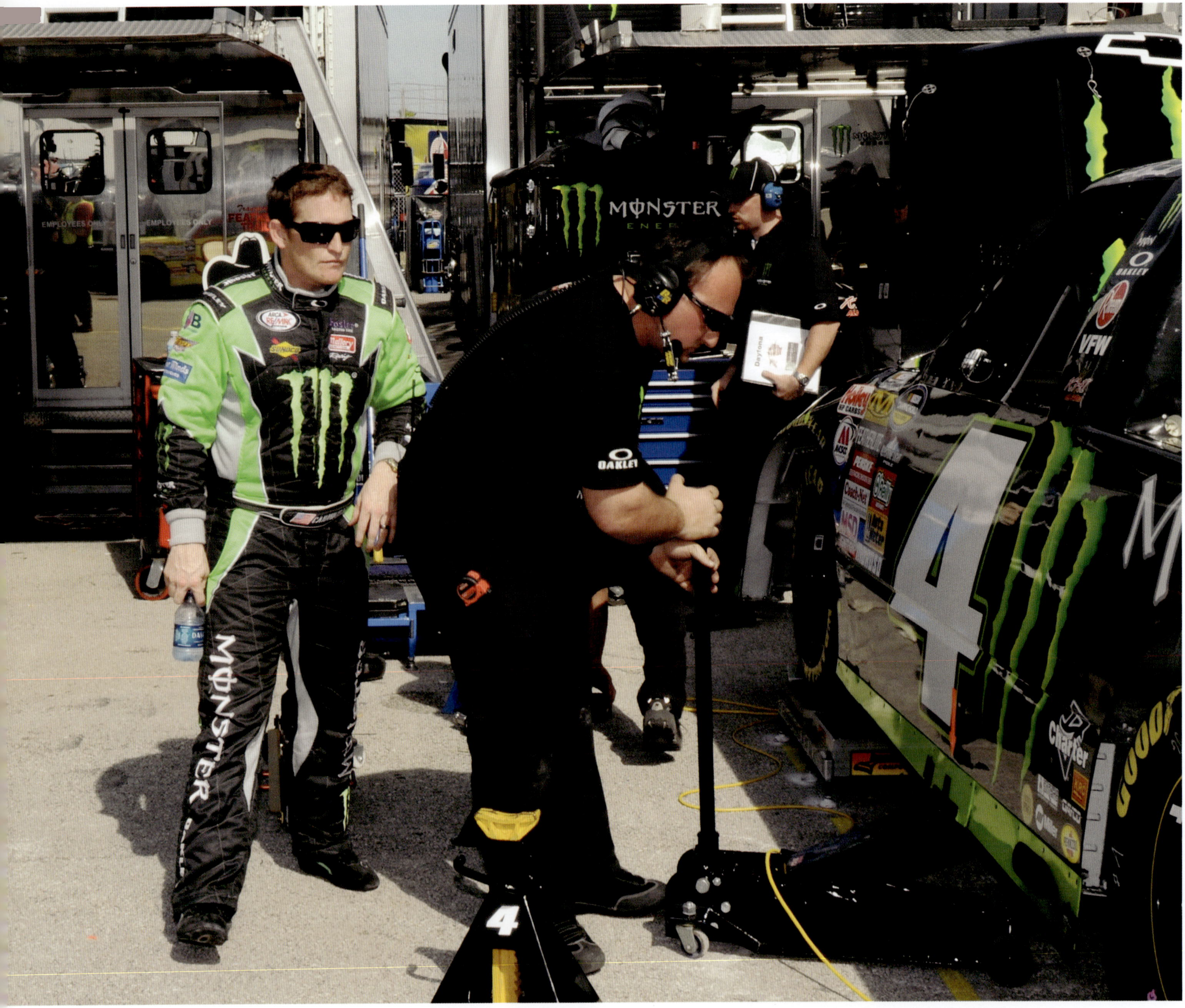
MONSTER
EMPLOYEES ONLY
OAKLEY
VFW
Daytona
4

Left When Ricky Carmichael needed a stock-car tutor, after signing a driver development contract with Nextel Cup Series car owner Bobby Ginn, he turned to Mark Martin for assistance. Carmichael made his first Late Model start in a car owned by Martin and prepared by Martin's mechanics in his Daytona Beach race shop. Carmichael was a multi-time AMA Supercross and Motocross champion, so good that race fans called him the "greatest of all time," or, simply, GOAT.

Right When the Viagra sponsorship contract ran out in 2005, car owner Jack Roush needed to find a replacement, and he asked Mark Martin a big favor – stay one more year in the No. 6 Ford to help land the AAA Auto Club. Martin wanted to do his own thing in 2006, but stayed one more year to seal the AAA sponsorship deal. Here, Martin rests against his AAA-decaled No. 6 car prior to the 2006 fall race at Phoenix International Raceway.

Gentleman racer 235

Left Jack Roush, Mark Martin's former car owner, does a "plug check" on the spark plugs pulled from the No. 6 Ford during Daytona Speedweeks 2006. By checking the plugs, engine experts can determine if the motor is running "too lean" or "too rich."

Right Mark Martin is adept at any NASCAR Sprint Cup Series racetrack. Here he's making a sharp right-hand turn at Infineon Raceway in Sonoma, California. Martin boasts four road-racing victories, including the 1997 Save Mart Supermarkets 300 at Infineon. His other road-racing wins were at Watkins Glen International in New York State.

"I've got one brother, and Mark and I are as close personally as my brother and I," Roush told the *Daytona Beach News-Journal* in 2006. "The fact we've been able to stay in this business for 18 years, and Mark Martin has been willing to drive my car and negotiate for continuation of that relationship, is my proudest accomplishment."

The story went on to explain that Martin was not Roush's first choice for his steering wheel. When Roush first decided to put together a full-time NASCAR team in the late 1980s, he wanted the veteran Bobby Allison. But Allison, late in his career, didn't want to go to a start-up team, and he pointed Roush in the direction of Martin, who had conquered a prominent Midwestern tour called the American Speed Association. "Of the guys I talked to, Mark was the one who was most interested in knowing how often I would test, who would work on and around the car, and how many tires I'd buy," Roush told the newspaper. "We sat down, and in about four hours we talked about the program and how it would work, about my goals and objectives, but never talked about money. We shook hands."

And from that moment until the season finale at Homestead-Miami Speedway in November, 2006, Martin gave Roush his all, every day, 100 percent, nothing left on the table. After almost two decades of making every Sprint Cup race, Martin was mentally exhausted from the wear and tear of the circuit. He wanted out – not outright retirement, but to race on his terms. He didn't want to be chained to the schedule. He left Roush and over the 2007 – 08 seasons, he drove for two teams, starting with car owner Bobby Ginn, who sold his operation to Dale Earnhardt Inc. midway through the '07 campaign. As fate would have it, Dale Earnhardt Jr. left the team started by his father to drive for Hendrick Motorsports in 2008, so DEI put Martin in the celebrated No. 8 Chevrolet. "Those two seasons had major twists and turns," Martin said. "I've always been a straight-and-narrow guy. I stayed the course, man."

With his contract running out at DEI, Martin got an exceptional and unexpected offer from car owner Rick Hendrick, who said, "Come drive my 5 car" for the 2009 Sprint Cup season. There would be no part-time

236 Man-made Thunder

MA
B
AAA
AAA.COM
Ford
FUSION
MOOG
Gatorback
CLEVITE
SUNOCO
WIX
COMP
Edelbrock
GMAC

CRAFTSMAN
23
CERTIFIED
TOYOTA
TUNDRA
22
Checkers
FULLY LOADED FRIES
6
Scotts
MiracleGro.com
14
TOYOTA
TUNDRA

Left Mark Martin has been successful in every form of racing he ever attempted, including the Camping World Truck Series. As something of a lark in 2006, Martin competed in 14 truck races and won six times, including the prestigious opener at Daytona International Speedway. Going into the 2009 season, Martin had 90 NASCAR touring wins: 35 Cup, 48 Nationwide, 7 Truck.

Right The year was 1988 and veteran Bobby Allison had just won the Daytona 500 for third time in his illustrious career and was mugging for the cameras in Victory Lane. Nobody really noticed the No. 6 Roush Racing Ford, making its debut appearance in NASCAR Winston Cup Series racing. Newcomer Mark Martin started 38th and finished 41st that day. He turned only 19 laps because his engine, built by car owner Jack Roush, was hobbled by overheating issues. It would take Martin and Roush almost two seasons to get their first win together.

schedule. Martin would have to work all 36 weekends. He jumped at the opportunity. "Me taking two years of a limited schedule has given me a chance to completely recharge my battery and completely have a different mindset on what's important to me and what I really want to do," he said. The assumption was that Martin, who turned 50 at the start of 2009, came back as a full-time driver to fill the championship void in his long, distinguished racing resume. Martin barks and snarls when you try to connect those dots. "I don't want to hear all that," he groused. "I'm coming back because I want to. I want to race a car that can win. I want to work with Hendrick Motorsports. This is a once-in-a-lifetime opportunity for me before the window closes."

Martin has posted Hall of Fame numbers since giving NASCAR his all in 1988. At the start of the '09 season, he had 35 Sprint Cup Series victories and 12 top-five points finishes, including four times the tour's runner-up. At the NASCAR Nationwide Series level (formerly the Busch Series), he has scored more victories than any driver in history – 48 at last count. He

He occasionally dips his toe into the Camping World Truck Series and boasts seven triumphs.

occasionally dips his toe into the Camping World Truck Series and boasts seven triumphs. And, in International Race of Champions competition, a defunct series better known simply as IROC, Martin scored 13 wins and a record five championships, competing against all of racing's most elite players. The only gap on his long and wide record sheet is the lack of a Cup Series championship. Martin doesn't shy away from the question of "Does that bother you?" – but he is a bit squeamish about patting himself on the back.

"Nah, can't help it," he said, when asked about not winning a championship. "You can say what you want, but I wasn't good enough. If I was better, I would've. The trophy doesn't make the man. Come on,

Gentleman racer 239

Dale Earnhardt goes to Victory Lane to congratulate Mark Martin for winning the fourth and final round of the 1999 International Race of Champions held at Indianapolis Motor Speedway. Earnhardt was hoping for an IROC sweep, since he had won the previous three races that season. Martin got the win that day, while Earnhardt, seen here without his customary mustache, earned the championship.

now. That's not the only measure; that's one measure. That's not the only measure. I've been successful. There are many ways to measure success. I've been successful and I'm very proud of the things I have done and I'm not sore about the things I haven't accomplished."

When it comes to racing, Mark Martin is most concerned about his reputation and the level of respect he receives in the NASCAR garage and on the racetrack. He has developed his own strict code of ethics and conduct and behavior that has become a beacon of white light for others to follow. Of course, many of his peers don't take that high road; it's a trail much less traveled. "Nobody wants to hear a grown man cry," Martin says. "I don't think there's anything wrong with not hiding your passion and the way you feel, but you need to watch out what you say because you'll be sorry; you'll make yourself look bad, too."

Martin says he'll race any driver "like they race me." Meaning, if you want to play nice, Martin will play nice. If you want to play rough . . . well, Martin generally still plays nice. It's in his racing DNA. "I sort of

Of course, many of his peers don't take that high road; it's a trail much less traveled. "Nobody wants to hear a grown man cry"

established a code, through my early experiences on the racetrack," he explains. "Giving some shots, taking some shots . . . and experience in what that felt like, when you didn't really have that coming, and what it felt like giving one to someone that didn't really have it coming. Over time, I just kind of built that. I just really believe that you need to take what you earn and earn what you take."

There isn't one driver out there who thinks poorly of Mark Martin. "I'm very intrigued by the man," Jimmie Johnson said. "I want to understand what he does, how he does it." And this from Carl Edwards: "I think we all marvel at Mark Martin all the time. He's like the fountain of youth. He's tough and driven and competitive." Or this from Jeff Gordon: "He's the

240　Man-made Thunder

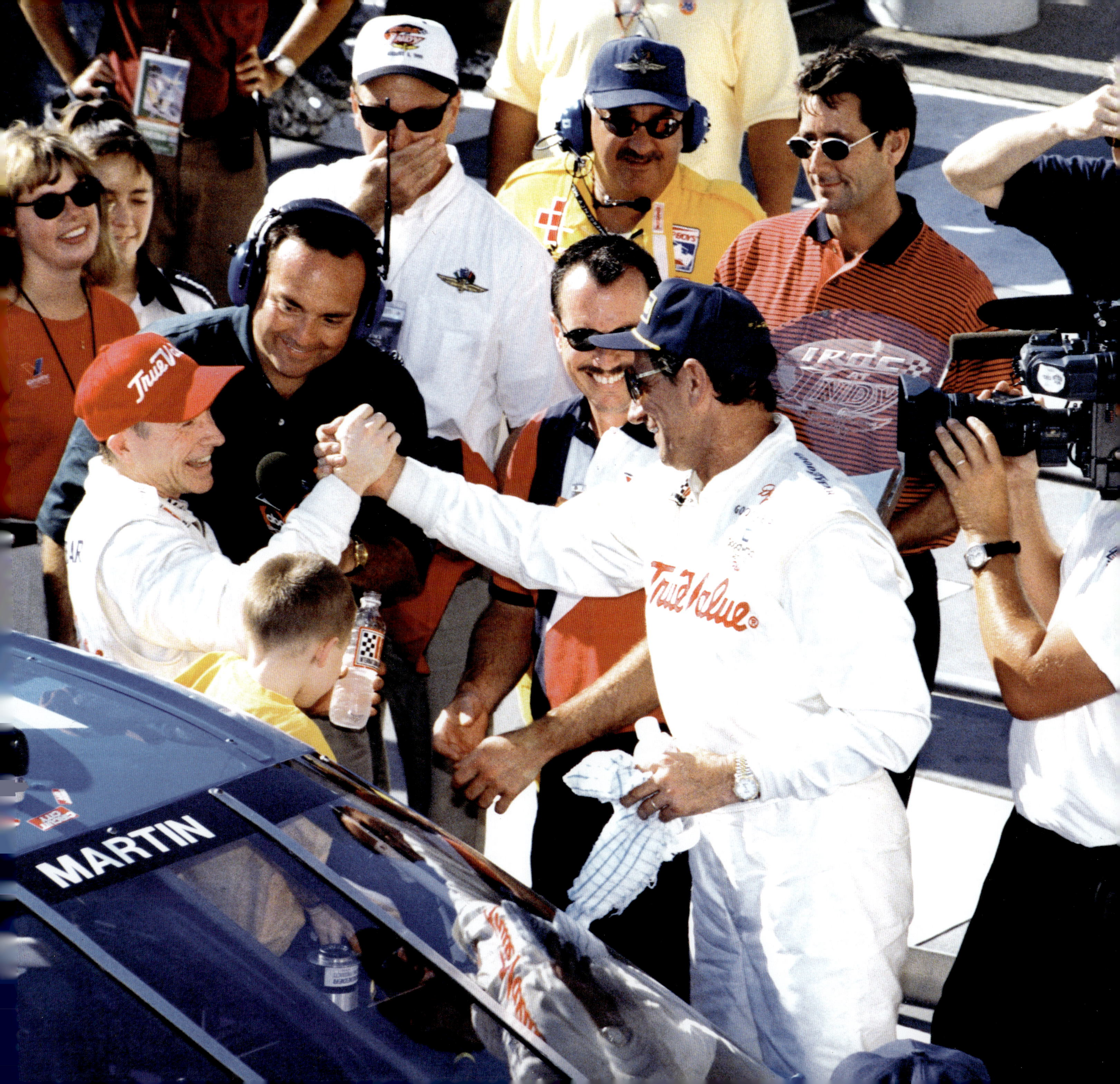
MARTIN
True Value
True Value

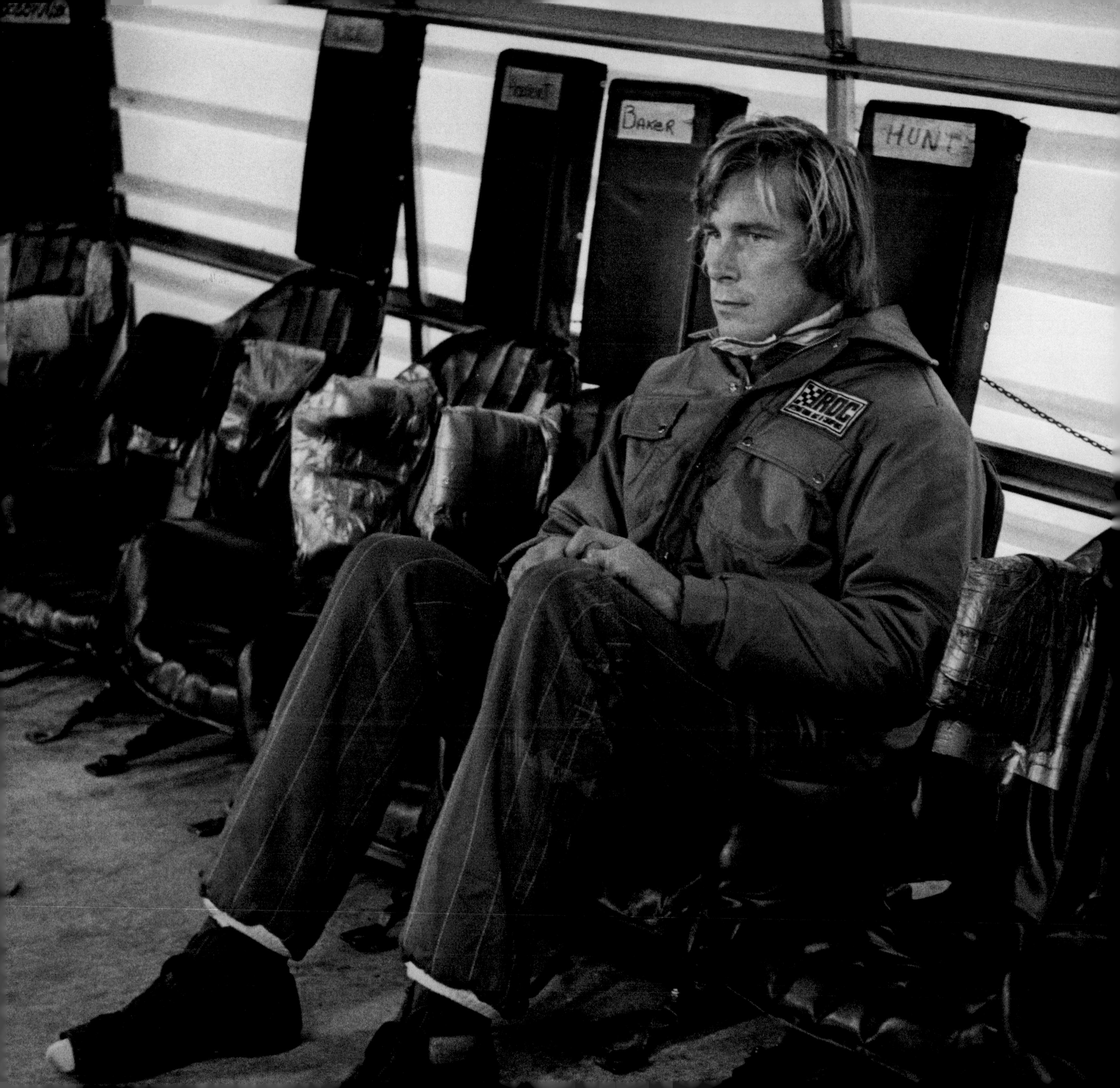
BAKER
HUNT

The year he won the Formula One World Drivers' Championship, James Hunt was invited to participate in the International Race of Champions, which actually began near the end of the 1975 season and finished at Daytona in '76. Hunt's best finish in four career starts – three in 1976 and one in 1977 – was sixth at Riverside International Raceway, a 2.54-mile road course in California. Here, Hunt is getting the feel for his driver's seat in the IROC garage area. The IROC series pitted champions from various professional tours in identically prepared sedans. IROC started in 1974, had a three-year hiatus (1981–83) then returned in 1984 with the advent of in-car technology. The series was discontinued in 2007 for a number of reasons: lack of sponsors, lack of interest and difficulty scheduling races.

most talented race car driver that there is. I mean, the guy is just a natural and he works hard at it, and he keeps himself in great shape. You know, he's just very disciplined and dedicated and driven, a very competitive guy, and you put him in top-notch equipment and there's just no telling what he's capable of doing. I've always been a big fan of his . . . he's just incredible." And this from the up-and-coming David Ragan, who inherited Martin's seat in Roush's No. 6 Ford in 2007: "Mark was just very involved with everything that was going on, and it's great to see a guy like that that's been around for so many years that still has that high level of intensity about his job, and I think that's why he's so successful, and I'm sure as long as he wants to do it and is capable to do it, he'll be fast and he'll be a successful driver."

After hearing those comments, Mark Martin was given to pause, before his response. "Let me tell you, that means more to me than that Cup trophy that you were trying to talk to me about," he said. "That's all good stuff. To me, that stands taller than a Sprint Cup." ∎

Gentleman racer

Racing for wins

...never cared about the title.

The ominous column of smoke at Charlotte Motor Speedway early in the 1964 World 600 was caused by Fireball Roberts' horrifying accident, which burned 80 percent of his body. Friends say he was only weeks away from retiring as a driver to pursue other business opportunities.

The year was 1950 and the final NASCAR Grand National Series race of the season was being held at Occoneechee Speedway, a 1-mile dirt oval in Hillsboro, North Carolina. Edward Glenn Roberts Jr. only had to cruise and finish the 175-lap race to secure the championship. The 21-year-old driver chose to race for the win because the purse paid $1,500 to the victor. According to NASCAR historian Greg Fielden, Roberts could have trotted to a fifth-place finish and won the crown, on the strength of just eight starts that season. Points leader Bill Rexford had made 17 starts. But "stroking," as race drivers called it, was not in Roberts' blood. After all, he was "Fireball" Roberts, the racing kid with nerves of steel, and an extremely heavy

... he was "Fireball" Roberts, the racing kid with nerves of steel, and an extremely heavy right foot.

right foot. His closest friends called him "Balls." In Roberts' mind it was a no-brainer. He could pocket $1,500 for winning the race compared to $1,000 for winning the championship. That $500 was a big difference for a young guy with a wife and newborn baby back home. His wife, Doris, told *Automobile Quarterly* that "Glenn never cared about championships. He went out there to win." He did neither that day. Roberts' engine stopped functioning with about 50 laps left in the race. He finished 21st in the race (won $75) and second to Rexford in the final points standings.

Fireball Roberts, who made his home in Daytona Beach, Florida, would continue racing until his tragic death in 1964, and despite his supreme driving talents, verve, enormous popularity and charisma, he would never win a NASCAR title. Over the 1956–57 Grand National Series seasons, he started 69 percent of the races and won 13 of them, but it wasn't enough to claim championship honors. He finished seventh and sixth in points, respectively, those two seasons. After that, Roberts went to a limited schedule, concentrating on the bigger-paying NASCAR events. The tactic

Gentleman racer 245

worked to his advantage. In 1958, he competed in only 10 of 51 scheduled events, won six times and finished 11th in points. Because of his aggressive driving style – described as "balls out" – his good looks and success at the racetrack, Fireball Roberts became NASCAR's first breakout personality, the first stock-car driver with name recognition beyond the Southern states.

Fielden was one of the first racing historians to realize Roberts' importance to the sport back in those incubation days. In his series of books entitled Forty Years of Stock Car Racing, he writes: "NASCAR badly needed a new star to replace the dozens who had vanished – a fresh face who could draw admiration from the fans and take the sport to a higher plateau. A single creator, it has been said, gives a show its characteristic look, sound and momentum. Edward Glenn 'Fireball' Roberts Jr. was NASCAR's savior in 1958."

As NASCAR transitioned from the tiny, rinky-dink dirt tracks – "bull rings," they're often called – to the super-sized, super-fast, super-sexy, asphalt superspeedways, Roberts led the charge. He was dazzling at the new Daytona International Speedway, opened in 1959. He started a woeful 46th in the inaugural Daytona 500, but sliced through the field to lead 21 laps before a fuel pump ended his spectacular run. He would not be denied in Daytona's Firecracker 250, held on the Fourth of July. He was the fastest qualifier, then led 84 of the 100 laps, en route to a blistering victory. His popularity soared. He was 30 and had the world by the tail. Three years later, he won the 500 in typical Fireball fashion, starting on the pole, then leading 144 of the 200 laps over the taxing 2.5-mile tri-oval course.

In 1964, at the age of 35, Roberts was ready to retire as a race driver. He had plans to become a spokesman for Falstaff Beer, and do some work in electronic media – he would've been the forerunner for all of today's newly retired drivers who slide into comfortable, high-profile jobs. But he never got the chance. On May 24 of that year, his No. 22 Ford spun and went rear-end-first into a concrete wall at Charlotte

Left Sports fans, every one. Some of NASCAR's greats gather around a television to watch the 1963 World Series. Fireball Roberts, who played baseball as a teenager, is standing with his arm around the tent pole. Junior Johnson, fourth from the left on the back row, holding a stick with his left hand, was also a stick-and-ball athlete as a child.

Right Fireball Roberts, in the No. 22 Pontiac owned by Banjo Matthews, leads the field under caution in the 1962 World 600 at Charlotte Motor Speedway. Roberts' car is tilted to the left because of an old stock-car trick called "stagger." Since it was important to get through the sweeping turns as quickly as possible, mechanics would stagger the size of the tires, making the right side larger than the left and jacking the car up on that side, too. While the car looks odd on a straightaway, it would zip through turns faster with this setup.

Motor Speedway. The impact caused his fuel tank to rupture and explode. Roberts suffered second- and third-degree burns over 80 percent of his body. He died on July 2.

With 33 career victories, 32 pole positions and 93 top-five finishes in only 206 career starts, Roberts established himself as NASCAR's first driver with star power. The legend lives on today. Inside the Speedway Club at Lowe's Motor Speedway – the renamed racetrack that took his life – is an oil painting of Fireball Roberts. There is no identification, but everyone who sees the portrait seems to know who they are looking at. "I think we're just going to keep it like that," vowed Humpy Wheeler, the long-time LMS president. ∎

Gentleman racer 247

The best that never was

. . . never got the chance to win one.

Junior Johnson sits in the cockpit as a member of his crew makes an adjustment to his race car. Johnson was a temendous race driver, winning 50 times in what is now the NASCAR Sprint Cup Series, but he never captured a title. Johnson found his true calling in the sport when he became a car owner, winning six championships and 132 races.

After his driver Cale Yarborough won the Southern 500 at Darlington Raceway, car owner Junior Johnson waits for the celebrations to end while trying to stay cool with a wet towel on his head in the blazing hot Labor Day sun.

Some will argue, and forcibly so (depending on whether the debate is taking place at an uptown cocktail lounge or backwoods roadhouse), that Robert Glen Johnson Jr. is, without question, the finest NASCAR stock-car race driver never to win a championship. Of the 17 men who top NASCAR's all-time victory list, Junior Johnson is the only race driver that didn't win the coveted championship trophy. His 50 wins as a driver has him tied for 10th place on the list with Ned Jarrett, a two-time national champion. There are 18 drivers below him on the all-time win list with championships.

Johnson's highest championship points finish was sixth, achieved in 1955 and again in '61. In his best season as a driver – 1965, 13

The under-funded, overachieving duo entered 33 races and won seven times.

wins in 36 starts – he finished a distant 12th in points. Those long of memory claim Johnson's 1963 season was his best because he won races in a Chevrolet that raced for pennies, compared to big-dollar factory efforts of Ford and Dodge. Master engine builder Ray Fox, who owned a race shop in Daytona Beach, Florida, and Johnson, a moonshiner turned chicken farmer from Wilkes County, North Carolina, joined forces to battle the bullies from Detroit. The under-funded, overachieving

duo entered 33 races and won seven times. It was a remarkable feat chronicled in a groundbreaking feature story by Tom Wolfe for *Esquire* magazine published in March, 1965. The article was entitled, "The Last American Hero Is Junior Johnson. Yes!"

Wolfe writes: "...the Junior Johnson they like to remember is the Junior Johnson of 1963, who took on the whole field of NASCAR Grand National racing with a Chevrolet. All the other drivers, the drivers driving Fords, Mercurys, Plymouths, Dodges, had millions, literally millions when it is all added up, millions of dollars in backing from the Ford and Chrysler Corporations. Junior Johnson took them all on in a Chevrolet without one cent of backing from

Gentleman racer 249

Junior Johnson is a man of many talents. He was a gifted race driver. He was well-decorated as a car owner. He was one of the fastest bootleggers in the South. And, he's an accomplished farmer, raising crops, chickens, hogs and cattle. He still gets up before sunrise to start his chores around his farm property in Yadkin County, North Carolina. Johnson never let stock-car stardom run or ruin his life.

Detroit. Chevrolet has pulled out of stock-car racing. Yet every race it was the same. It was never a question of whether anybody was going to outrun Junior Johnson. It was just a question of whether he was going to win or his car was going to break down, since, for one thing, half the time he had to make his own racing parts. God! Junior Johnson was like Robin Hood or Jesse James or Little David or something.

"Every time that Chevrolet, No. 3, appeared on the track, these wild curdled yells, 'Rebel' yells, they still have those, would rise up. At Daytona, at Atlanta, at Charlotte, at Darlington, South Carolina; Bristol, Tennessee; Martinsville, Virginia – Junior Johnson!"

Johnson learned to race in the most unorthodox way – running from the law as a moonshine bootlegger through the hills of western North Carolina. As a young man, he would traverse the region at night, his souped-up passenger car weighted down by "a load," but able to outrun any car with police lights and a siren. "The moonshine business is what made me a race driver," Johnson once told Newsday. "I was not someone who learned to drive a race car. When I went into racing, I was already schooled in high-speed driving. My education came with bootlegging. I attribute a lot of my success to that. It was dangerous. But if you did it the way you were supposed to, the only time it was dangerous was when the officers or the highway patrol got after you. We had fast cars and they didn't, so it wasn't much of a contest. We had race cars and they had cars you'd see on the street. The best race drivers that I've seen were the ones who hauled whiskey before they got into racing."

A year after Wolfe's story ran in *Esquire*, Johnson left the sport as a driver to concentrate his efforts as a car owner, where he made up that championship gap on his racing resume. From his position in the pits, Johnson, the car owner, won 132 races and six Winston Cup Series championships with an all-star roster of drivers, including stallions Cale Yarborough and Darrell Waltrip. Each won three NASCAR crowns for Johnson. "I did not like to lose," Johnson said. ∎

Junior Johnson catches a nap on the trunk of his ride at Charlotte Motor Speedway in 1960. The No. 27 Chevrolet was owned by John Masoni, an Ohio businessman who managed the dog track in Daytona Beach. The car was prepped by master mechanic Ray Fox, whose race shop was also in Daytona.

Mark Martin
Questions & Answers

Inquiring minds want to know if Martin enjoys NASCAR's continuing soap opera dramas.

Left Mark Martin waves at cheering race fans prior to the 2006 Allstate 400 at the Brickyard at Indianapolis Motor Speedway.

Right Mark Martin, in the No. 5 Hendrick Motorsports Chevrolet, dices with Brian Vickers, in the No. 83 Red Bull Racing Toyota, in the second Gatorade Duel qualifying race at Daytona International Speedway during 2009 Speedweeks.

"**Q:** Do you pay any attention to this interaction between your fellow competitors?

Mark Martin: You know, yeah. It's embarrassing to admit, but it is true. There is a bigger story than what goes on on the racetrack a lot of times. The conflict; the personal conflict; arguments; fights; pushing; scuffling; what have you. The fight at the end of the Daytona 500 in '79, nobody remembers anything much about the race. But I remember vividly the aftermath. As embarrassing as it is, that stuff gets people's blood pumping. A good race will, too, don't get me wrong. But it will get – a good race will get enthusiasts' blood pumping. A good fight will get just about everybody's – whether you care about racing or not. You know what I mean? So I'm just trying tell you that, yeah, I pay more attention to that than I would a pass out on the racetrack, for sure.

Q: Would you agree that somewhere in the late 1980s to early 1990s the NASCAR Sprint Cup Series went from performance-based to personality-based and people started paying more attention to the interaction between drivers?

Mark Martin: Yeah. Well, it's a lot more than cars going around, and that brings a lot more of that to it. That's why the race fans are the way they are. They attach themselves to a personality rather than to a car. And that's where the passion comes from. I think that's part of what really makes it interesting, is the personalities, and our sport always allowed itself, its personalities, to be closer to the fans than most professional sports."

Gentleman racer 253

29
Goodwrench
GP
OFFICIAL FUEL
OFFICIAL
Goodwrench
KREUTER

A call to duty

10

Previous page Kevin Harvick's pit crew swarms over his No.29 Richard Childress Racing Chevrolet for a service call during the 2005 MBNA Race Points 400 at Dover International Speedway. Harvick started seventh that day but could only muster a 25th-place finsh at the track nicknamed the "Monster Mile".

Kevin Harvick, thrust into the stock car made popular by Dale Earnhardt, won the first two Winston Cup Series races held at Chicagoland Speedway, in 2001 and 2002. Here he holds the Tropicana 400 winner's trophy aloft for all to see. Said driver Bill Elliott of the new track in Joliet, Illinois: "There's only one way in and no way out."

It would be hard to call the Kevin Harvick-Carl Edwards confrontation a fight. No punches were thrown, no blood was spilled, no teeth were lost, and nobody's snout got busted at Lowe's Motor Speedway in the fall of 2008. It was more like a 20-second clip from a Greco-Roman wrestling match. Edwards grabbed Harvick by the shoulder and they grappled for a short while before one of Harvick's boys got Edwards in a headlock and pulled him away. A camera-for-hire photographer caught a few images of the two men in the brief engagement and at first refused to make the shots available to the media. Several days later, after some severe arm-twisting and media politicking, the series of photos was made public, two guys in a hand-to-hand struggle.

This battle started with a war of words – verbal and written – after Edwards caused an accident earlier in the week at Talladega Superspeedway. After lagging back most of the day, Edwards was charging through the field late in the race, made contact with Roush Racing teammate Greg Biffle, and ignited a chain-reaction accident that knocked six stock cars completely out of the race. Harvick was swept into the wreck but was able to finish the race, thanks to repairs done on his No. 29 Richard Childress Racing Chevrolet. Still, he finished 11 laps down to race winner Tony Stewart. "It looked like the No. 99 [Edwards] made a mistake and tore up most of the field," Harvick said, adding later, "I know that his fans won't be very proud of him sitting back there riding around like a pansy. But when he got up there and decided to start racing, it caused a big wreck. So, it was one of those deals."

When Edwards heard the "pansy" comments, he was furious and left a note in Harvick's private airplane at the Talladega airport before heading home. The note read: "I was really trying to screw up everyone's day. Love, Carl." Four days later, in the Nationwide Series garage at Lowe's Motor Speedway, the two drivers faced off and exchanged verbal "pleasantries," which soon escalated into hand-to-hand combat. It's not the first time two drivers have gone toe-to-toe in a garage. Back in the day, it was a common, post-race experience. But this was different. Upon closer inspection

256 Man-made Thunder

A call to duty 257

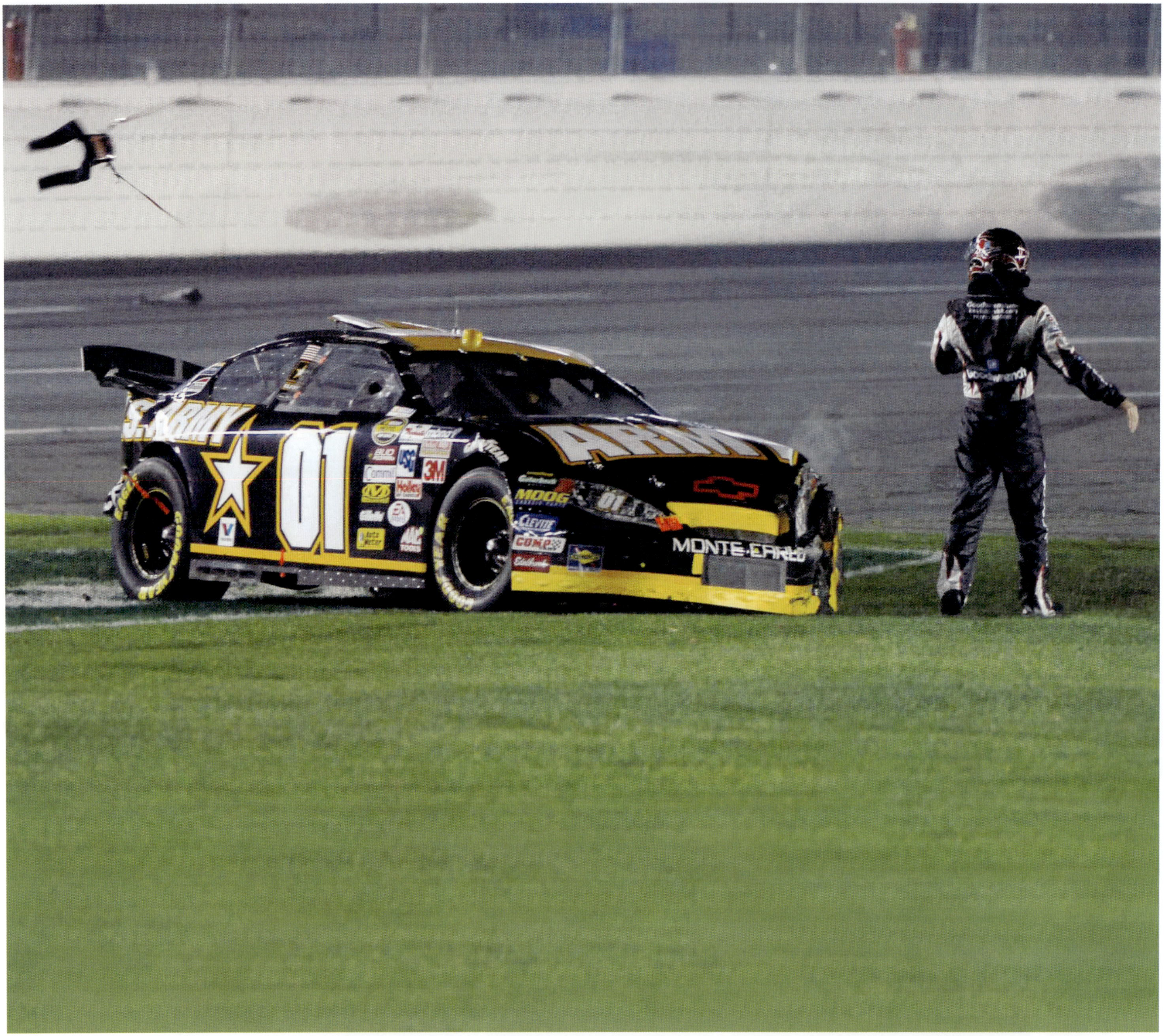
ARMY
01
MONTE CARLO
3M
MOOG
COMP

Angry that he got tangled up in a multi-car wreck not of his making, Kevin Harvick flips his HANS device in the direction of Joe Nemechek in the No. 01 Chevrolet during the 2005 NASCAR Nextel All Star Challenge. The melee on Lap 36 involved seven race cars – all went to the garage for the night.

Carl Edwards led the 2008 NASCAR Sprint Cup Series in victories, but has yet to build a giant, rabid fan base. Here, Edwards waits to take his No. 99 Roush Fenway Racing Ford to the course at Lowe's Motor Speedway for practice.

of the photos, people noticed the look on Harvick's face during the altercation – he had no expression whatsoever. It might be the look you have as you open a jar of peanut butter, or toss clothes into the washing machine, or sweep out the garage. Harvick's face is completely void of emotion. In one frame, there's even a hint of a smile. "Just protecting our turf," was what Harvick told reporters after the scuffle.

The incident and photographic evidence point to one conclusion – Kevin Harvick is hands down, no argument required, NASCAR's most bad-ass driver – or at least, that's the perception. He's the last guy you want to rile. It would be like kicking a slumbering grizzly bear in the head. Harvick even admits to being "two people." "I think it's the competitor on the racetrack – that you don't really give a rat's ass about anybody else who's around you or what you gotta do," he said.

"I guess . . . I'm so easy-going off the racetrack, that sometimes you take it so seriously in certain situations that you try to be as fair as you can off the racetrack and you try to do things that are good for people,"

he continued. "When they disrespect something that you did for them or they do something that you don't think is fair, then that competitive switch kind of turns back on and you say, 'All right, well, if you're gonna do that to me, then I'm gonna do it to you.' And that competitive spirit comes back in as almost a revenge-type spirit. I guess I have a little bit of revenge-type in me."

It was that competitive spirit, nerves of titanium and aggressive driving talents that moved car owner Richard Childress to sign Harvick to a Busch Series contract after the 1999 racing season. The plan was to run the Bakersfield, California, driver for a couple years in what is now the Nationwide Series, then transition Harvick into the Cup Series. Of course, those plans were scrapped after Dale Earnhardt perished at Daytona in 2001. Childress asked Harvick to take Earnhardt's seat, with the car renumbered from 3 to 29. Harvick, then only 25, showed his racing mettle by scoring two Cup wins and Rookie of the Year honors. Plus he had five Busch Series wins and

A call to duty 259

CUP SERIES

After winning the 2005 Pocono 500 at Pocono Raceway, Carl Edwards does his signature backflip off his No. 99 Roush Racing Ford. Says car owner Jack Roush: "That's his schtick."

Kevin Harvick's No. 29 Richard Childress Racing Chevrolet carries a decal in honor of the late Dale Earnhardt. After Earnhardt died in the 2001 Daytona 500, Harvick was asked to drive the same car, renumbered to 29, from that point forward. Going into the 2009 Sprint Cup Series, Harvick had 11 career victories in the No. 29 Chevy.

claimed that series' overall crown, and he did all that in the most tragic of circumstances.

"Kevin came in the sport and was really put in a tough situation to get in the car that Dale drove," Childress said. "But he went in there and he's one of the reasons that RCR is still here today – because of his efforts and his driving and his passion. He just has a passion for winning and he shows it. We need more personalities like that, people that show their emotions for what they do. He did a great job when he took over that team and we started the 29 team with the same people that was with the 3. He had to go through a [difficult] period because everybody was comparing what he was doing to Dale. That wasn't really fair because he was a rookie when he came in. He did such a great job. That's his place in history. Now that he has Shell and Pennzoil as his sponsors, different sponsors, he has all the right things going for him, you know; he's got his own identity."

After his resounding success in 2001, Harvick soon began to get the reputation of a track bully. In a two-week span during the 2002

Two days after intentionally wrecking Gibbs, Harvick watched Kenny Wallace drive the No. 29 RCR Chevrolet in the Virginia 500 at Martinsville.

season, he had a post-race confrontation with Greg Biffle at Bristol Motor Speedway – a tiny, high-banked arena that stirs the emotional pot – followed by a slamming incident in the Truck Series with Coy Gibbs (son of former NFL coach and team owner Joe Gibbs) at Martinsville Speedway. The Biffle deal got Harvick put on NASCAR probation. The Gibbs episode earned him an extremely rare one-race suspension from NASCAR. Two days after intentionally wrecking Gibbs, Harvick watched Kenny Wallace drive the No. 29 RCR Chevrolet in the Virginia 500 at Martinsville.

A call to duty 263

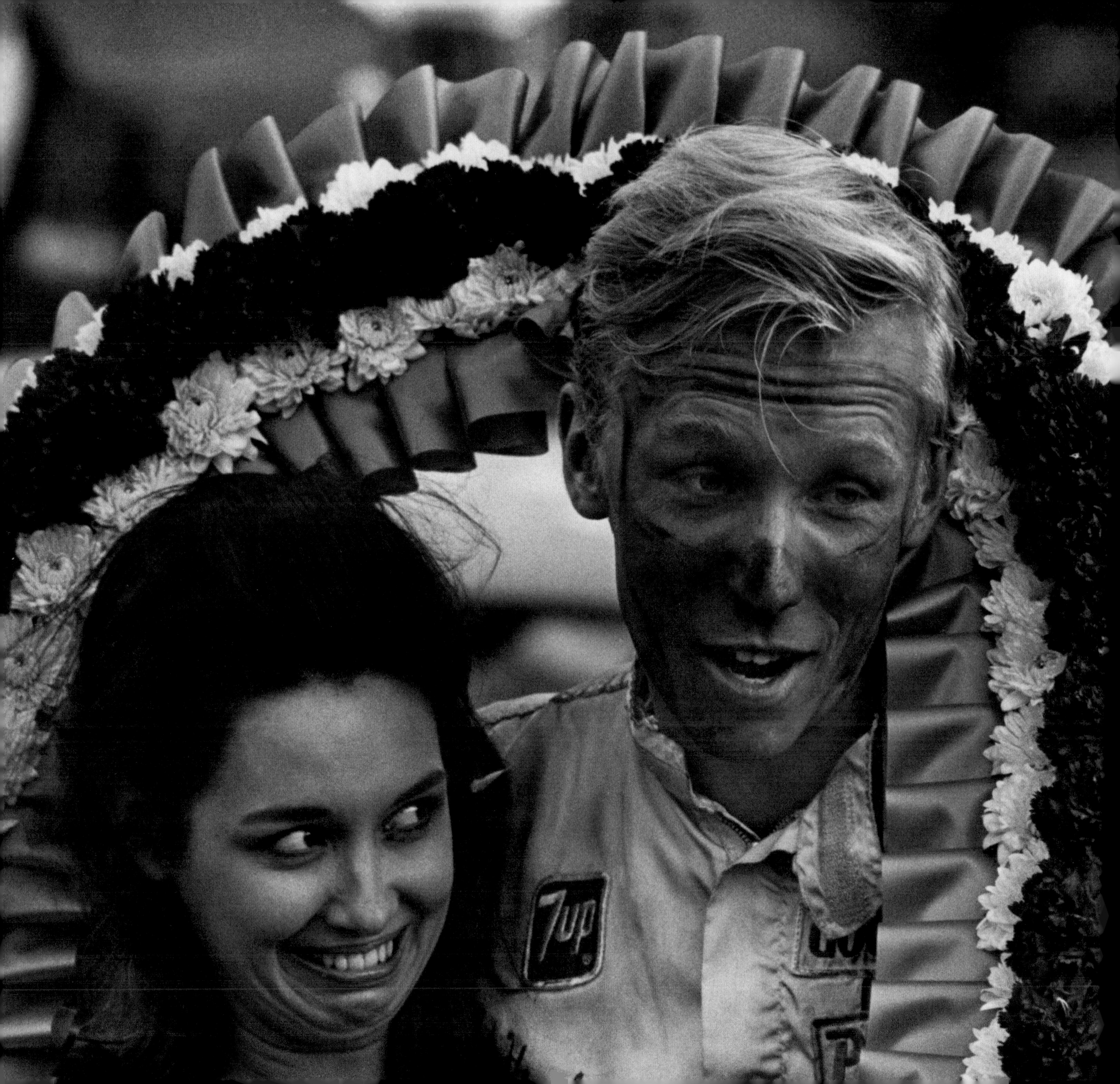
7up

Racing can be a messy business. Back in the day, a driver's face would be covered in oil, dirt and grime after an event. Here's Pete Hamilton, shown in Victory Lane following the 1970 Alabama 500 at Alabama International Motor Speedway. Hamilton's face is so dirty, the trophy girl looks reluctant to kiss the race winner.

Award-winning racing journalist Larry Woody wrote a column for BNET.com about Harvick and his attitude problems soon after the highly publicized suspension. His words captured the moment and the challenges Harvick faced then and now:

The driver was stunned by his suspension: Before his comeback race at Talladega Superspeedway, he sounded neither contrite nor apologetic. Instead, he came across as defensive and defiant. "I don't know that anybody wants or needs an apology," said Harvick, who insisted that the Gibbs incident was blown out of proportion.

But Harvick indicates that he got NASCAR's message. "The most important lesson I learned is that I was not looking at things the same way NASCAR was," he says. "That's something I have to do in order to succeed in this sport. I can win races, but unless I can walk into that NASCAR trailer and have a normal, decent conversation with them, I'm not going to get anywhere, I'm still learning how NASCAR officials work and what is involved in the decisions they make."

Harvick received almost no support from his fellow drivers. "He's lost the respect of a lot of people because of his childish behavior," says Ward Burton. "I'm not going to sit here and say I'm perfect or that I haven't lost my temper, but Harvick loses his every week."

"You gotta draw the line somewhere, and NASCAR finally drew it," says Jimmy Spencer, who has had his own problems controlling his temper. Harvick didn't respond well to his critics. "They're not worth wasting my time on," he says. "I have the support of the people I respect in this sport."

Bobby Hamilton, who had problems with Harvick last season, theorizes that because the youngster was chosen to drive Dale Earnhardt's car, he also tried to assume the late legend's aggressive persona. "He may be driving Earnhardt's car, but he ain't Earnhardt," says Hamilton. "He'd better learn that as quickly as possible."

He did, sort of. Harvick still races with spirit and fire, but he's much more careful about choosing his battles. Edwards, for instance, went to

DeLana and Kevin Harvick share a smile with car owner Richard Childress before the start of the 2007 NASCAR Nextel All Star Challenge at Lowe's Motor Speedway. DeLana Harvick is heavily involved with her husband's racing career. The couple own their own race team that competes in the Camping World Truck Series and the Nationwide Series. DeLana handles many of the management duties at Kevin Harvick Inc.

Bristol Motor Speedway is the ultimate "bull ring" oval in the NASCAR Sprint Cup Series. It measures only 0.533 miles, but the turns in the banking prior to reconfiguration were cocked at 36 degrees. Bristol is truly a speedway stadium, with towering grandstands all the way around the course. It can seat 165,000 spectators, or about double the size of the average NFL stadium.

Harvick's garage stall at Lowe's that day to ignite the flame, but Harvick remained largely cool, though engaged.

Harvick not only has Childress' support, but his blessing, when it comes to matters of competition and emotion. "We've always talked about this," Harvick said. "Richard says, 'Be your own person.' When sponsors don't like something I do, I say, 'I'll do the best I can to try to make that better,' but in the end, I'm not gonna deviate from who I am or what I do because that's just who I am. I'm gonna tell you the truth.

"Sometimes, it's a little too brash for some people, and some sponsors, or some fans don't like it. But I feel like I've been true to myself. I'm not smart enough to try to be somebody else or tell a story that's not true, because sometimes my memory doesn't work long enough for it to all play out. So, I feel fortunate that I have an owner that has let me be how I am. And I think in the end, the people and fans and the sponsors and everybody around me has respected that, because I haven't deviated from that."

NASCAR racing is not for the faint of heart. The really productive drivers are not only fearless, but intelligent. Along the way, they build a reputation. Harvick is in the "black hat" classification, but unlike Dale Earnhardt, who used marketing to promote the "Intimidator" image, Harvick does not have a master plan to sell his personality. "I've never been real big in the self-promoting stuff," he said. "I've always been taught that you live by what you do and who you are. It's always just kind of been who I've been. I don't know about the bad-ass part. I guess that's just the way I was brought up."

Yes, Harvick has been in his share of controversies over the years, but no, Childress has never considered letting him go. Never. "Kevin has his own identity," Childress said. "He speaks what he feels and he don't back down from nobody on the track or off . . . Harvick's edgy, and that's what I like about him. Besides racing the s*** out of a race car, he is edgy."

Harvick has proved that both time and again. ∎

266 Man-made Thunder

Valvoline
AVENGER
DEWALT
Platinum
Energizer
AVENGER
DLP HDTV

Understanding drivers

Richard Childress made his first big-league NASCAR start in 1969 in the inaugural race at Talladega Superspeedway, then known as Alabama International Motor Speedway.

Car owner Richard Childress gave Clint Bowyer an impossible assignment – show a new team at Childress Racing the path to success. Bowyer spent three years with the No. 07 RCR Chevy, winning two races, and now is the driver of Childress' No. 33 Chevy. Bowyer, seen here talking to a crewman, took the challenge to heart. After the first four races of the 2009 season, the team was ranked second in championship points.

Richard Childress, shown here behind the wheel of his No. 3 Chevrolet in 1979. At the urging of friend and mentor Junior Johnson, Childress retired as a full-time driver in 1981 and turned the steering wheel over to Dale Earnhardt at Michigan International Speedway on August 16 of that year. Childress made his final start as a driver at Riverside International Raceway on November 22, 1981, driving a Buick owned by Johnson. Childress turned only five laps before retiring.

Childress raced at the invitation of NASCAR founder and president William H.G. France. Members of the short-lived Professional Drivers Association voted to boycott the inaugural Talladega 500 because of safety issues centered on the speed of Talladega, combined with tires that were deemed less than dependable under such pressure. When the regular drivers packed their gear and headed for the exits, France started calling in favors and making deals so he could put enough cars on the 2.66-mile track to have a race.

One of those guys who benefited from the PDA pullout was Childress, who didn't have a Grand National Series car, but drove his Grand American Series Camaro in the race.

Between his race winnings and appearance money, Childress had enough cash to buy land for a stand-alone race shop. Three years later, Childress returned to the Winston Cup Grand National Series as an owner/driver, making 14 starts. He would become a regular driver over most of the 1970s, but never a winner. Before climbing out of his car to let Dale Earnhardt have the wheel, Childress had made 285 starts and scored 76 top-10 finishes. The closest he ever came to winning a race was a third-place run at Nashville in 1978.

Childress retired as a driver at the age of 35 in the summer of 1981, at the urging of fellow car owner Junior Johnson, who didn't realize at the time that he was creating a stock-car monster of a team. "At that particular time, we weren't set up for two drivers in two different cars," said Johnson. "Richard was having a lot of problems, you know, financially, and [keeping] mechanical people and stuff of that nature. So I asked Earnhardt, I says, 'If I go get Richard to quit driving and put you in his car, will you accept it? And I'll help you.' And that's how the whole thing evolved from that point on. I took Richard and Earnhardt, and we went over to the Hampton Inn and ate lunch. We set around and talked about it and worked the thing out. Richard got out of the car and put Earnhardt in it, and down the road they went.

"Yeah, he got going there, and I'm glad to see what he did over the years," Johnson added. "He

Richard Petty, who was president of the Professional Drivers Association, holds an impromptu news conference with members of the motorsports media to explain why he and the majority of NASCAR's drivers refused to participate in the inaugural Talladega 500 at Alabama International Motor Speedway. Petty told the media that day, "This track is simply not ready to run on. Most of us felt the tires we have are not safe to race on at speeds of around 200 mph. It was just that simple."

was a strong competitor. You know, he beat us a lot, we beat him a lot, but that's racing."

Richard Childress Racing won its first race, the Budweiser 400 at Riverside (California) International Raceway, in 1983 with driver Ricky Rudd at the wheel. They were victorious again at Martinsville, Virginia, before the season ran its course. After the '83 season finished, Bud Moore, who was Earnhardt's car owner in 1982-83, swapped drivers with Childress. Earnhardt said he felt more comfortable in Chevrolets. Moore was strictly a Ford man. Rudd didn't have a manufacturer preference. From the day he signed a contract at RCR until his death, Earnhardt stayed with Childress, and won six NASCAR titles. Earnhardt's championship in 1994 was the last time a single-car team won the crown.

These days, Childress has a four-car team, and his race shop is the size of some college campuses, with a dozen buildings spread over acres and acres of property in a small North Carolina town called Welcome, about an hour north of Charlotte. RCR, which employs about 500 people, quickly outgrew the race shop where Earnhardt's No. 3 was prepared. That building was converted into a Childress-Earnhardt museum.

Why did Earnhardt, who eventually owned his own three-car Winston Cup team, stay with Childress all those years? Simply put, because Childress understands the needs of a race driver, since he logged thousands of race miles behind the wheel of a stock car during his driving career. Childress drivers do not want, because they have. "Richard has done an incredible job of allocating money and spending money," driver Jeff Burton said. "I mean, it's unbelievable. I don't feel like we don't have anything that we need to be successful."

Kevin Harvick may have said it best after winning the 2007 Daytona 500 in Childress' No. 29 Chevrolet. When asked why he didn't pursue a reportedly large offer to drive for Toyota, Harvick responded, "Well, it wasn't all my decision. I mean, it was our decision as a group. We wanted to make sure that we

270 Man-made Thunder

Richard Brickhouse, in the center of the mob dressed in white, celebrates winning the 1969 and inaugural Talladega 500 at Alabama International Motor Speedway, now known as Talladega Superspeedway. Most of NASCAR's regulars, who were members of the short-lived Professional Drivers Association, pulled out of the event for safety reasons. NASCAR founder William H.G. France cobbled together a field of 36 cars, including Richard Childress, who raced his Grand American–legal Chevrolet.

were all on the same page and pulling in the same direction. We wanted to win races. I mean, that's what we wanted to do. That's what I wanted to do, that's what Richard wanted to do.

"You know, you have to follow your heart and let it guide you sometimes and let things happen how they're supposed to happen. I've got a lot of friends and a lot of loyal people that were behind me at RCR and felt like that's what I needed to do, and that's what we did."

"This sport has the highest and lowest [points] of any sport that I've ever known," said Childress, after winning at Indianapolis in 2003. "You know, you can go to the bottom real quick . . . I think that's the thing, is having faith." ∎

A call to duty 271

Richard Childress
First person

Car owner Richard Childress, whose team boasted 89 NASCAR Sprint Cup Series wins and six championships at the start of the 2009 season, discusses a wide range of topics.

Left Richard Childress takes a stroll at Indianapolis Motor Speedway. Childress, who started his race team as an owner/driver out of the garage at his home, now fields four full-time NASCAR Sprint Cup Series teams.

Right Necessity is the mother of invention, so they say. NASCAR race fans have always been creative. These two race buddies built a platform on top of their convertible to get a better view of the inaugural Southern 500 at Darlington Raceway in 1950. Today, hard-core race fans will gut a school bus, dress it in the colors of their favorite driver and take it to the racetrack for a weekend of fun.

On his decision to stop driving his race car, hire a race driver and become a team owner in 1981:

"I didn't want to quit driving. Definitely didn't want to quit driving. I seen what was coming, and I've been fortunate enough to see a few changes in the sport over 40 years. I was a driver in the '70s that had some top-fives and top-10s and was always pretty competitive. I didn't wreck as much, but I had a lot of failures because I didn't have the money to put the parts in it.

"But I could see when car owner Warner Hodgdon come in, probably Hodgdon, M.C. Anderson, Rod Osterlund, J.D. Stacy. I seen that group of people coming in with big money. And as they would add teams, it pushed me back further and further. Next thing I know, it was a struggle to get a top-10 and it was a struggle to be in the top 15. I wasn't enjoying it like I was when I could get up there. My goal was to always be the top independent. Other than Dave Marcis, I was there every week, week in and week out.

"But I seen all this money coming, and I knew I didn't have no money. I knew that if I didn't do something I would be out of business. When the opportunity came along in '81 for Dale Earnhardt to get in the car for those 11 races, I knew I had to take it. It wasn't something I wanted to do. It was something I knew I had to do to survive in the sport."

A call to duty 273

Some argue that Tim Richmond left a void eventually filled by Jeff Gordon. The two drivers shared many of the same attributes: young, Hollywood-handsome, well dressed, polished and talented behind the wheel of a stock car. Each of those drivers played off of Dale Earnhardt's hard-country image. Richmond scored seven wins during the 1986 Winston Cup Series. He died of complications from AIDS in 1989.

On harboring any ill feelings for driver Jeff Gordon, who supplanted Richard Childress Racing's Dale Earnhardt as the sport's top driver in the mid-1990s:

"No. Jeff has his own personality. He's done one hell of a job doing what he's done – he's helped the sport. He brought in different fans and newer fans. I look at Cale Yarborough, David Pearson, Richard Petty, all the greats back in the days. Then you come along with Darrell Waltrip, the Earnhardts, all these guys, Terry Labonte, all these guys that come in, every one of them had their own personality and their own mood.

"When Jeff Gordon came along, he had the clothing, the Hollywood look, the smile. He was so much different than what Earnhardt was, the blue-collar guy, the guy that was out there where the guys were, the working-man's person. Jeff came in with a different polished look and attitude and everything. He brought a lot to our sport. He did a lot for our sport and he'll go down in history as one of the greatest drivers yet.

"I think the sport needed a Jeff Gordon at that time. You know, we had lost Tim Richmond back in the '80s. Tim had a totally different look, smile, and I think the sport needed that side of it to go along with the Dale Earnhardt side of a rough, tough character.

"Dale had a lot of respect for him, and that's just competition. He came in and won the races and won the championship, but I still think for the sport that's what it needed at that time. He was just another team you had to beat. We never focused in on any one person. We raced everybody, and we raced 'em all hard. He just happened to have the talent, the money behind him, the team."

274 Man-made Thunder

Curtis Turner gives a lady friend a quick ride around North Wilkesboro Speedway in 1965 on a scooter. Turner liked to drink liquor, chase women, party until all hours of the night and, of course, race.

On where he first was exposed to the sport of stock-car racing:

"I worked at Bowman Gray Stadium [Winston-Salem, North Carolina] selling peanuts and popcorn from about '62 to '63, somewhere in there. I seen Curtis Turner and the Myers brothers. I used to go to their shops and sit there. And if somebody would say, 'Boy, get me a bottle of that moonshine,' or, 'Boy, hand me a beer over there,' I'd jump up and get one.

"Curtis Turner was my hero. He was a man's man of race drivers. When I was a kid coming up, he was the one I looked at. He was rough and tough, and these guys, they'd party and drink and have their women. I could tell so many stories from sitting around the old big pine tree at Bowman Gray Stadium. Used to be a big pine tree there as you go into Turn 3 sitting next to a big house there.

"Bunch of these old guys would sit out there, or we'd sit outside the house. I'd be a kid. I'd be over there Saturday morning real early watching these guys. They were my heroes. I watched the Pettys. I watched Glen Wood and the old 'Wood Chopper.' There was a lot that didn't make it, you know. I've just watched so many, like Lee Petty, Richard Petty, Junior Johnson. I was only about 12.

"I used to go to all the old shops, all the old guys that was racing back then. One of the craziest sumbitches that ever drove a Modified was a man named Floyd from Virginia. I don't think he ever drove a sober race in his life.

"I look at drivers today, and I'll say, 'Who are the guys that can sit under that pine tree at Bowman Gray Stadium in today's world with those guys that sat under it back in those days?' Some of them never made it, but some of them, they were the real [thing]. I look at today's drivers and the drivers of the day that could sit under that pine tree. Dale Earnhardt could have sat under that tree. Clint Bowyer could've sat under that tree. Tony Stewart could sit under that tree. There's not many out there today that would have been able to sit under that tree and have the fun that they had back in those days."

A call to duty 275

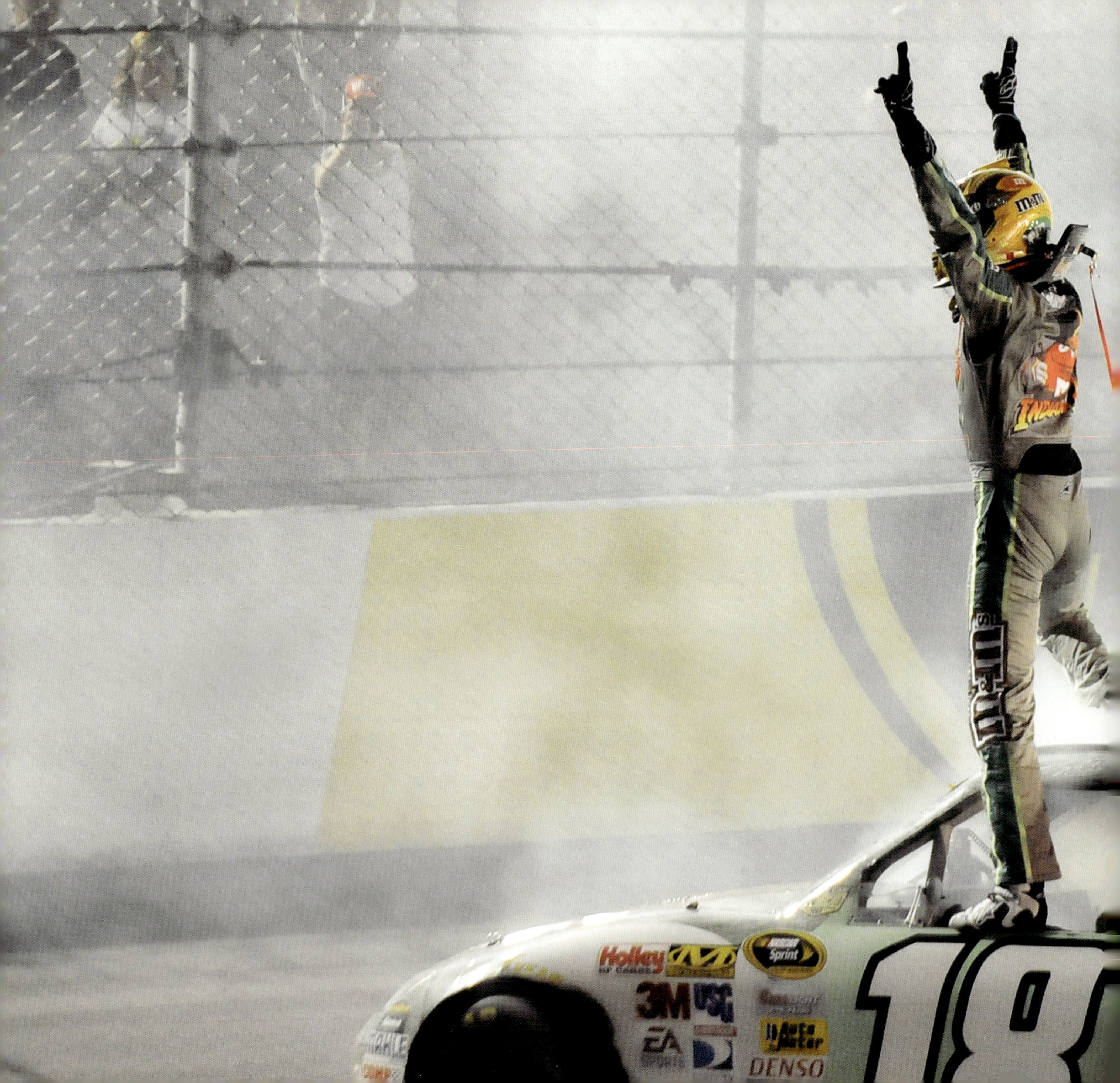
Holley
3M
USG
EA SPORTS
DENSO
18

Young and restless

11

Previous page Kyle Busch performs his patented victory move after winning the 2008 Dodge Avenger 500 at Darlington Raceway. Busch creates a cloud of tire smoke at the finish line, then as the smoke dissipates, he emerges from his No. 18 Joe Gibbs Racing Toyota and bows to spectators in the grandstands. "It is kind of like a Vegas show," says Busch, who grew up in Las Vegas.

Right Kyle Busch, in the No. 18 Toyota, and Dale Earnhardt Jr., in the No. 88 Chevrolet, battle in the 2009 Daytona 500. Earnhardt replaced Busch at Hendrick Motorsports in '08. Busch landed at Joe Gibbs Racing and won eight Sprint Cup Series races.

Far right Sprint Cup spectators saw a lot of this during the 2008 racing season – Kyle Busch in Victory Lane spraying his team with a coat of champagne. Here, Busch is dousing his pit crew at Dover International Speedway after winning the Best Buy 400.

And then there's the curious case of Kyle Busch, the driver it seems everybody loves to hate. The immediate cause of this disgust can be traced back to May 3, 2008, in the closing laps of a 400-mile race at Richmond International Raceway. Everyman's favorite driver, Dale Earnhardt Jr., was leading the event, hoping to snap a losing streak that stretched back into the 2006 season, an agonizing duration of 72 races. When race leader Denny Hamlin had to pit for a tire problem, Earnhardt nabbed the lead on Lap 383 and held it until Lap 397. On the ensuing lap, the trouble started. Busch came up to challenge, they made contact and Earnhardt spun off the three-quarter-mile course. Clint Bowyer slipped by to win. Busch got second place. Earnhardt got diddly-squat.

Afterwards, Busch was serenaded by a chorus of grandstand boo-birds and was called everything from idiot to punk (and much worse). "He's going to need some security," said Earnhardt, after listening to the shouting mob from the stands after the race. "They were going crazy and you see it, but you don't pay attention to it," Busch said. "I don't know why they were telling me I was No. 1 [finger signs], I was in second place. Clint Bowyer got the lead from me – they were all confused I guess, [drank] too many old Budweisers."

Both drivers said it was strictly a racing incident. Nothing more, nothing less. Earnhardt did the old shoulder shrug and said, "It looked like Kyle got loose underneath me. That happens," he said. "We had been racing each other earlier and had no problems. I have done that before." But the Earnhardt Nation had a different view. They thought Busch had done Earnhardt wrong because of what happened in 2007 – when car owner Rick Hendrick released Busch in order to grab Earnhardt, who had declared his free agency from Dale Earnhardt Inc. Busch said there were no hard feelings on his part, even though he was the driver scorned in the transaction. He turned that 2007 pink slip from Hendrick into greenbacks at Joe Gibbs Racing during the 2008 season, by winning an unprecedented 21 NASCAR touring series events. The breakdown: eight Sprint Cup wins, a record-tying 10 Nationwide victories and three truck series triumphs

DLP
INTERSTATE BATTERIES
TOYOTA
m&m
NASCAR
Sprint
CUP SERIES
Combos
NOS
ENERGY DRINK
Pedigree
SNICKERS
m&m's
SIEMENS
GOODYEAR
SUNOCO
Coca-Cola
PION
BEST
BENEFITING
STUDENT

Hendrick
MOTORSPORTS
www.HendrickMotorsports.com
Spectracide
FIRE ANT
KILLER
57
LOWE'S
Improving Home Improvement
GMAC
DELPHI
HITACHI
POWER TOOLS
shop-vac
GOODYEAR
Spectracide
Spectracide
Hendrick
SIMPSON
LOWE'S
MOOG

Left Kyle Busch didn't have ants in his pants when this photo was taken, only on the hood of his NASCAR Busch Series stock car.

Right A skinny Kyle Busch celebrates his record-breaking victory at California Speedway. When Busch captured the 2005 Sony HD 500, he became the youngest driver (20) ever to win a NASCAR Cup Series event.

Far right Kyle Busch is not the only Busch in Sprint Cup Series racing. His older brother Kurt won the 2004 Nextel Cup Series championship. The Penske car in primer paint was Kurt's, during a "Car of Tomorrow" test session in 2006.

(the truck efforts came with Billy Ballew Motorsports, where Busch is known simply as "Rowdy").

The Busch bullet slumped to the ground in 2008 before reaching the ultimate target, the Sprint Cup Series championship. Busch marched into the Chase for the Sprint Cup – the 12-driver, season-ending, 10-race playoffs – with the lead, then to the delight of his detractors, haters, critics and grudge-bearers, the young driver staggered and stumbled and bumbled around in the opening rounds of the title-deciding stretch of events. There was a 34th-place finish at New Hampshire, followed by a last-place showing at Dover, followed by 28th at Kansas. At that point in the tailspin, Busch was last in the Chase standings, more than 300 points behind Jimmie Johnson; his eight Cup wins seemed like a distant memory. Busch capped off the season by attempting a mileage run for the win at Homestead. It backfired. He was glad to be rid of the '08 Chase. "Pretty much as soon as it was over, it was over," he told the media in the days leading up to the '09 season. "I was glad it was over. You know, we even put the exclamation point on the season there at Homestead trying to finish the last fuel run there without stopping, and we let it run out of gas. That just sort of finished it off for us. Went into the off-season, forgetting about everything."

Busch turned 24 in 2009, his fifth full year of Sprint Cup competition, and had already recorded some remarkable numbers: He's driven for three legendary race-team owners (Jack Roush, Rick Hendrick and Joe Gibbs) and holds the all-time record as NASCAR's youngest Cup Series winner. He was a mere child – 20 years, 4 months, 2 days old – when he claimed the second race at Auto Club (California) Speedway in 2005. Then, there's the other side of the coin, such as when he made history by winning NASCAR's first "Car of Tomorrow" race. He emerged as the history-making victor and bad-mouthed the car, which NASCAR engineers had spent six years designing to improve safety for drivers. "I still am not a very big fan of these things," he said on national television

Young and restless 281

Left A flat tire forces Kyle Busch to pit road for service during the 2007 Kobalt Tools 500 at Atlanta Motor Speedway. Pit crews like to have fun, and in this case, it is with the team's pit board, featuring Kyle Broflovski, a cartoon character in the Comedy Central show *South Park*.

Right The crowd and event become one when a grandstand section at Bristol Motor Speedway helped display the American flag. The spectators were asked to hold up pieces of colored cardboard during the national anthem to form the large display.

from Victory Lane after the 2007 Food City 500 at Bristol Motor Speedway. "I can't stand to drive them. They suck."

Less than a month later, Busch had a real boo-boo of a day at Texas Motor Speedway. First, he rammed into the back of Earnhardt Jr.'s No. 8 Chevrolet, then climbed out of his own battered No. 5 Chevy and left the track, thinking the damaged stock car was done for the afternoon. Crew chief Alan Gustafson and his team pieced it back together to run some late laps and maybe gain a handful of championship points. Busch was nowhere to be found, so Rick Pigeon, the jackman for the No. 5 machine, asked Earnhardt if he would drive the car to the checkered flag. "My buddy 'Pig' asked me to do it so I wasn't going to say no," Earnhardt said. A few months later, Earnhardt was in at Hendrick and Busch was out, a free agent for the '08 season. It turned out to be wake-up call for young Kyle Busch, who got several offers before accepting the No. 18 ride from Joe Gibbs Racing, where drivers with talent are embraced, and emotional outbursts, to some degree, are acceptable.

"They got to be careful the way they act," said team president J.D. Gibbs on the day he signed Busch. "How do you balance being careful what you say, the way you act, with really showing who you are? That's a hard thing to figure out. For Kyle, he came in the sport as young as he was, that takes a while. I'm still figuring it out. I'm 38. I think for those guys to really kind of get a feel for how much do I show of my own personality versus how much can I control and be careful what I say, that's hard to do. I do love the fact . . . our guys, we let our guys be yourself. Our guys got neat personalities. Don't try to change the way you are. You might have to be careful what you say. Just 'cause you're thinking it doesn't mean everyone needs to hear it."

After a 10-year run with Tony "The Tiger" Stewart, Busch probably looked more like a nun in church than a problem child. And there's no denying Busch's talent factor, which has trumped most of his boneheaded statements ("I say a lot of things probably I shouldn't say") or ill-advised actions (wrecking older brother Kurt in the 2007 Nextel All Star Challenge). "His attitude and his driving style, his desire to win – he's

282   Man-made Thunder

Young and restless 283

TOYOTA
m&m's
RACING
GOODYEAR
Holley
HP CARBS
3M
18
GOODYEAR
Gatorback
BELTS
MAHLE
COMP CAMS
WIX
FILTERS
Edelbrock
EA SPORTS

Kyle Busch's stock car looks like it is about to eat a mechanic and engine during a motor change during Speedweeks 2008 at Daytona. All things considered, changing engines is relatively routine for a Sprint Cup Series race team. Here, the motor is lowered into place with the help of a hydraulic lift. If a team changes an engine after arriving at the racetrack, the car must start at the rear of the field. Busch won the 2009 Sprint Cup race at Las Vegas from the back row of the grid after a motor swap at the track.

a very, very talented young man," said veteran team owner Richard Childress. "He just drives the wheels off that thing." Indeed. Busch's predominant driving trait is that he constantly hustles his car. If he's running 10th, he wants to be ninth. If he's running second, he wants the lead. He relentlessly tries to improve his position with every lap, which makes for entertaining viewing as he slings his car through turns. "The guy is driving his ass off and there's people that love him and people are booing him," said Ray Evernham, the crew chief that guided an extremely young Jeff Gordon to glory. "You know what, you need to have some guys running side-by-side, bumping and banging. I think that Kyle Busch is that brash young guy that maybe says some things that he'd like to take back once in a while."

Kevin Harvick, who had his own growing pains as he matured in the Sprint Cup division, agreed that Busch is a lightning rod for controversy. "Kind of follows him around," Harvick mused. "And he'll learn how to deal with a lot of that stuff as he goes forward." Harvick said Busch hasn't been around long enough to wear a particular label, such as bad guy or bad-ass or good guy or jackass. Right now, Busch has a foot in black-hat territory, but he really doesn't fit that role. "To me, it don't matter," Busch said. "It's not who I wanted to portray. It's not something I tried to portray. But it's something that happened. People want to throw me under that category; fans want to throw me under that category. So I'll play it that way. And sometimes they may not like it, and that's their fault. They gave it to me."

Busch knows there are drivers he races against who don't like him, but that could have something to do with winning a dozen races in his first four years in Sprint Cup. "You know, you'd like to be friends with all the drivers and get along with all of them," he said. "But I think it's just like the fans; it's hard to get all of them to like you. It's hard to get all of them to appreciate who you are, what you do, and how you do it and how you drive with the different aspects you take out on the racetrack. You know, some guys don't care how aggressive you are; other guys wanna punch you in

More and more NASCAR Sprint Cup Series events start in the late afternoon and finish at night. Here, the sun sets over Darlington Raceway during the 2005 Dodge Charger 500, the first Sprint Cup race staged at night over the quirky race course that opened in 1950.

your face because you're too aggressive. It's just the way some people are." In Busch's "gets-along-with" camp are Hamlin, Stewart, Martin Truex Jr. and others. In his "hard-to-get-along-with" area are Jimmie Johnson, Brian Vickers, Jeff Gordon and Earnhardt. "Jeff Gordon, he sometimes is a little more difficult," Busch said. "It's more of 'his way or the highway' sometimes. I mean, he'll joke around with you and make you think it's OK. But in the back of your mind, you know he means different than what he says. It's just about how well you understand the person and what they are saying."

Understand the person. That's what NASCAR competitors and race fans are trying to do with Kyle Busch right now. He may be perceived as a bratty kid driver or some sort of villain or a guy with a bad attitude, but those personality types would not have thrown a lifeline to a broke, down-on-his-luck, sickly racing legend. When Busch won his 10th Nationwide Series race at Texas Motor Speedway in 2008, he tied Sam Ard's record for season wins, originally set in 1983. When Busch found out that Ard was ill and destitute, he pledged a $100,000 donation to help the former series champion. Busch was reminded that giving money to help someone down on their luck wasn't the best way to nurture a bad-guy image.

"Tying the guy's record meant a lot to me," Busch explained. "That record has been around for however many years. So Harvick came close, and he's been helping out Sam a little bit. I learned through Harvick how Sam was doing and what was going on there. I was thinking about doing just a monetary donation out of the public eye and just trying to help out, like Harvick did. But it came down to winning and tying his record. I was a little too overzealous and threw away a hundred grand. But it's to a good guy and hopefully it will help him out and get him through some rough times."

It may take a few more seasons to get the right handle on this guy, Kyle Busch. "People grow up and get a little bit smarter and learn from lessons and stuff like that," Busch says. ■

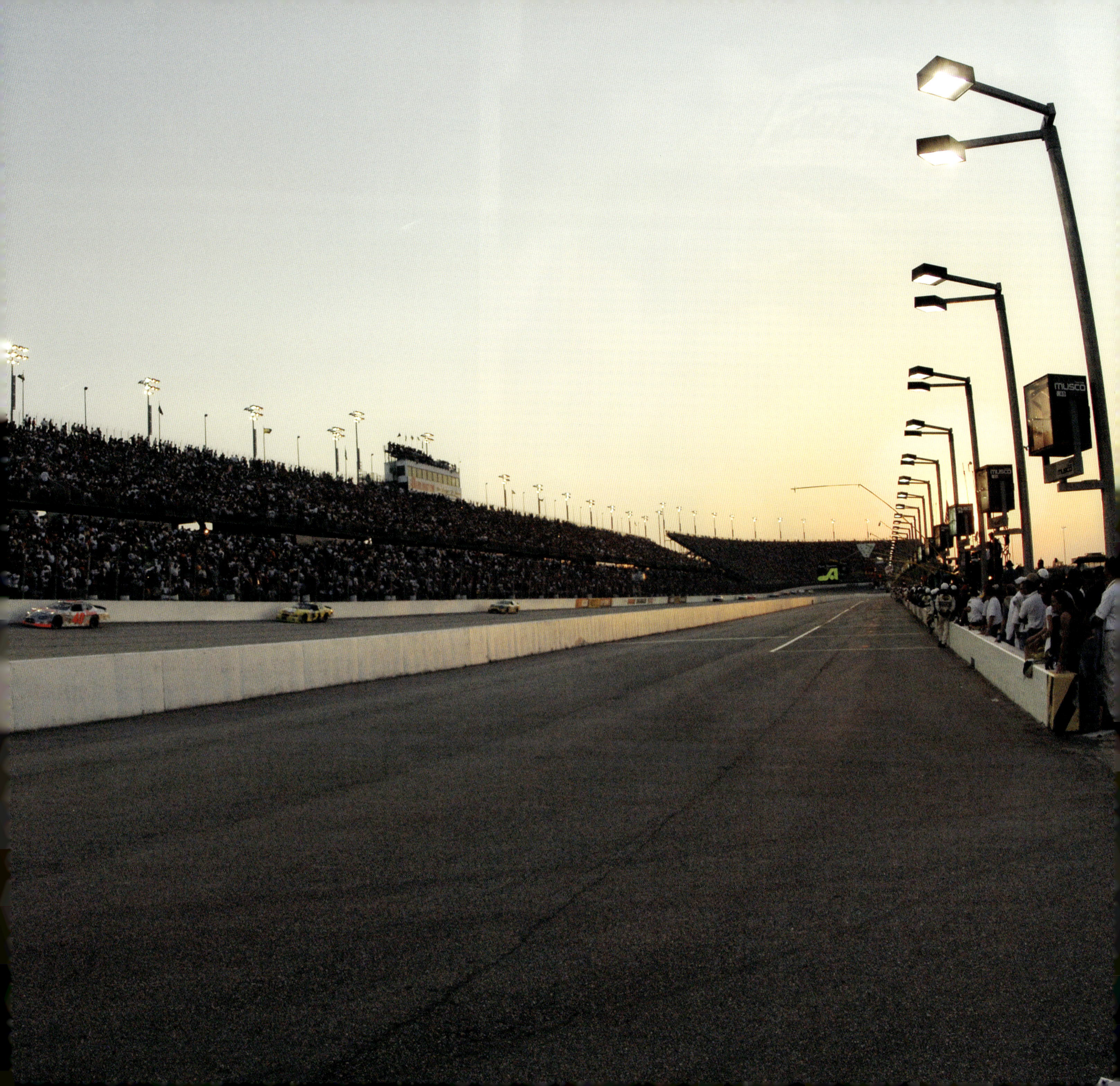
MUSCO

Number-nerd's hero

NASCAR statistical geeks and number nerds love David Pearson because of his percentage figures.

Left NASCAR racing's "Silver Fox," David Pearson, celebrates his one and only Daytona 500 victory in 1976, which some describe as the greatest finish of any stock-car race in history. Richard Petty and Pearson crashed exiting Turn 4 on the final lap. Pearson was able to keep his motor running and limped across the finish line at about 35 mph for the victory.

Right Leonard Wood, co-owner of the famed Wood Brothers Racing No. 21 entry, looks like he is dancing after changing the front right-side tire of David Pearson's stock car during the 1972 American 500 at North Carolina Motor Speedway in Rockingham. The team is credited with developing the modern-day pit stop.

These people have crunched the numbers over and over again, and come up with the same conclusion. The following is an entry made in a comment area on www.racing-reference.info by WillG_46, who, at 11:44 p.m. on August 8, 2008 (or 08-08-08), joined the "Silver Fox" legion of believers.

WillG_46 writes: "Although Richard Petty's numbers are higher, David Pearson had a better win, top-5 and top-10 percentage. On average, he won 1 out of every 5 races he competed in. Running a part-time schedule definitely kept him from winning more championships. David Pearson, The Silver Fox, and IMO (coming from a Petty and Earnhardt fan) the greatest driver ever."

On average, he won 1 out of every 5 races he competed in.

For those not familiar with modern text-messaging shorthand, IMO stands for "in my opinion," and in the opinion of many, Pearson is the ultimate stock-car warrior. He made his first NASCAR Grand National Series appearance in 1960, and as a raw rookie, had three top-five and seven top-10 finishes. And he snagged a pole position at tiny Gamecock Speedway in Sumter, South Carolina, a quarter-mile, dirt oval, which was so rural that it hosted one, and only one, big-league NASCAR event.

Pearson's next big racing moment happened on a much bigger stage, under much brighter lights. The sequence of events reads like a script from a bad Tom Cruise movie. Car owner Ray Fox showed up at Charlotte Motor Speedway for the 1961 World 600, NASCAR's longest race, thinking he had highly respected veteran Darel Dieringer as his driver. One problem. Dieringer had a Goodyear Tire contract and the Fox Pontiac was riding on Firestones. There were more cars than qualified drivers and Fox was desperate. Meanwhile, Pearson, 26, was building a roof on a house in Spartanburg, South Carolina.

"Ray gave me my chance to get into big racing like that," Pearson says in Fox's biography. "He

Young and restless **289**

"The right rear tire blew with about two laps to go and I wasn't about to stop"

came to Charlotte and didn't have nobody to drive for him. They had qualifying races back then and then ran the 600. He had Junior [Johnson] for the qualifying race but didn't have nobody for the 600. So Joe Littlejohn, who was a friend of mine over here in Spartanburg, he talked to Ray and told him he ought to give me a chance to run it. Joe thought I would do a good job. Ray did it. They called me and I went over there to Charlotte to run that car. Heck, I didn't even know Ray. I heard the name, but I didn't know him."

In another interview, with journalist Bob Moore, Pearson said, "Man, was I surprised! I just threw everything down. One of the guys I was working with said, 'What if you win the race?' I said, 'I'll never come back here.'" As it turned out, he never did go back to roofing.

Thanks to a solid qualifying run by Johnson, Pearson started third in the No. 3 Pontiac prepped by Fox. He led 225 of the 400 laps, including the final lap – on three tires. "The right rear tire blew with about two laps to go and I wasn't about to stop," Pearson said in the Fox book. "I didn't know I was so far ahead. When I blow'd that tire, I didn't know I was about seven laps ahead, at least that's what the scorer told me. When it had that one wheel pulling, I couldn't run too fast, maybe 30 miles per hour I guess, with a flat tire. Every time I mashed the gas, it would just spin that wheel."

Fireball Roberts, driving Smokey Yunick's No. 22 Pontiac, passed Pearson at least four times as the race leader limped toward the finish line. Even with the problem, Pearson won by more than two laps over the 1.5-mile superspeedway course. "I just kept going," Pearson says today. He kept going figuratively and literally, as it turned out. In his 574 career starts, Pearson scored 105 wins. He ran a full-time schedule only four times and won three championships. In comparison, Petty had 200 wins in 1,184 starts and seven titles, running the full schedule each season for more than 30 years.

Left Legends go door-to-door at Hickory Speedway in 1966, as Bobby Isaac (No. 26) rubs fenders with David Pearson (No. 6). Pearson would go on to win the race and the NASCAR Grand National Series championship that season. He won three titles over a four-year span.

Right David Pearson, who was in the prime of his racing career driving the Wood Brothers Racing No. 21 Mercury, gets ready to rumble with Bobby Allison's No. 12 Chevrolet at the start of the 1972 World 600 at Charlotte Motor Speedway. It's not where you start, but where you finish in racing. Buddy Baker claimed the checkered flag that day.

Pearson had one last major upset – in 1999. *Sports Illustrated* conducted a poll of racing industry leaders, for NASCAR's 50th anniversary, and Pearson was voted the Driver of the Century, beating Richard Petty one more time. Even Petty acknowledged Pearson's driving ability, telling *SI*, "It never hurt as bad to lose to somebody you knew was better." ∎

Kyle Busch
First person

Kyle Busch on following his older brother Kurt Busch, who won the 2004 Nextel Cup Series championship, into NASCAR racing.

NASCAR's current top brother act features Kyle Busch, left, bowing to the crowd after winning at Bristol Motor Speedway in 2007, and Kurt Busch, right, preparing for a run in his No. 2 Penske Racing Dodge. When Kyle won at their hometown of Las Vegas on March 1, 2009, Kurt visited Victory Lane to give his little brother a big hug.

> I mean, it's both. There's a lot of goods and there's a couple bads. Mainly it's all good. Him coming up through the ranks and learning the different tracks and giving me the advice for the different tracks helped me out; sped up my learning curve somewhat. You know, him coming into the sport before me and doing some of the things he did sort of shed the bad light. That hurt a little bit. But it all wears on over time and you get over it. I mean, Darrell Waltrip went from being one of the least-liked drivers to being one of the favorite drivers. Same with Rusty Wallace, Dale Earnhardt, all those guys. There's spells you go through in this sport.
>
> I wasn't given a fair shake. Yeah, I did some stupid stuff myself. But since it was already done by Kurt . . . It was just because I was his brother . . . I didn't get to work my way down. I started down here and was already thought of as an idiot, I guess. So, I didn't start where everybody else got to start.

Young and restless 293

ENCO
Driver A.J. Foyt
Geo. Bignotti
CHAMPION
PREMIER
BEAR
SUNNEN
PROTO TOOLS
MONROE
PUROLATOR
FILTERS

12

Indianapolis importance

Previous page The supreme crossover driver, A.J. Foyt, the day after winning the 1964 Indianapolis 500 at Indianapolis Motor Speedway. To close out his Indy career, Foyt started the inaugural Brickyard 400 Winston Cup Series race, the first stock-car race at the 2.5-mile track. Foyt made his first Indy 500 start in 1958. He is only one of two drivers to win the Indy 500 and Daytona 500. The other is another racing legend, Mario Andretti.

On June 11, 2003, history was made when Jeff Gordon, representing the NASCAR Winston Cup Series, and Juan Pablo Montoya, from the Formula One circuit, converged on Indianapolis Motor Speedway to swap equipment for a day of fun and, of course, publicity for the track. In this photo, Montoya, then an F1 regular, and Gordon take the wheel of each other's car. "This is a pretty unique situation where we have two young men with very well-achieved racing backgrounds internationally and nationally, and consequently this is a fun day," said USAC racing official Johnny Capels. Montoya left F1 in 2006 and became a NASCAR regular in 2007.

It took decades, but the security force at Indianapolis Motor Speedway built a take-no-crap, be-nasty-as-hell reputation over many, many decades. These burly men in their bright yellow shirts man positions throughout the complex, barking orders and blowing whistles to maintain peace and order among the racing throngs, whose head count on race days numbers in the hundreds of thousands. In recent years, this force has toned down and become more "fan friendly," a popular buzz phrase in the current auto racing lexicon. One can only imagine the invoice Indy received for the anger-management classes. Back when mean and cruel ruled at the stately 2.5-mile course, William H.G. France felt the wrath of the yellow-shirt Safety Patrol. Mechanical genius and racing pioneer Smokey Yunick was witness to the ugly episode. In his autobiography, he gives the perfect description of Indy's old-guard yellow shirts, then tells what happened to NASCAR's founder.

Yunick writes in his book *Best Damn Garage In Town, The World According To Smokey*: "Special world, old traditions, no way to explain Indy without the guards. These are a cadre of older (most cased retired) males (no guns), yellow shirts with lite blue lettering. In most cases really nice retired race fans 60 to 75 years old, many with a history of 'ain't missed a race since nineteen o-s**t.' These guys work on a very small pay scale, they did it partly for money, partly 'cause they were fans and partly to meet and know the players on a first name basis. We had our own post office, and the guards had a communication center and paging system for us to receive phone calls and messages and visitors. So if Keeley Smith called A.J. five times a day we all kinda knew what was going on. If Miss Universe called Peter Revson every hour or so, the guard got it posted on the inner hot line. You know, 'Peter R. is screwing Miss Universe, but don't tell anybody,' or that 'good lookin blonde with the big t**ties from the governor's office is sure chasing Smokey.' (Yup, she caught me.)"

Yunick continues: "Sex was just a li'l part of it. How 'bout parts supplier, bill collectors, wives, news media. What I'm trying to get you to see is the guards got wove into our lives. The guards controlled people motion very

Indianapolis importance 297

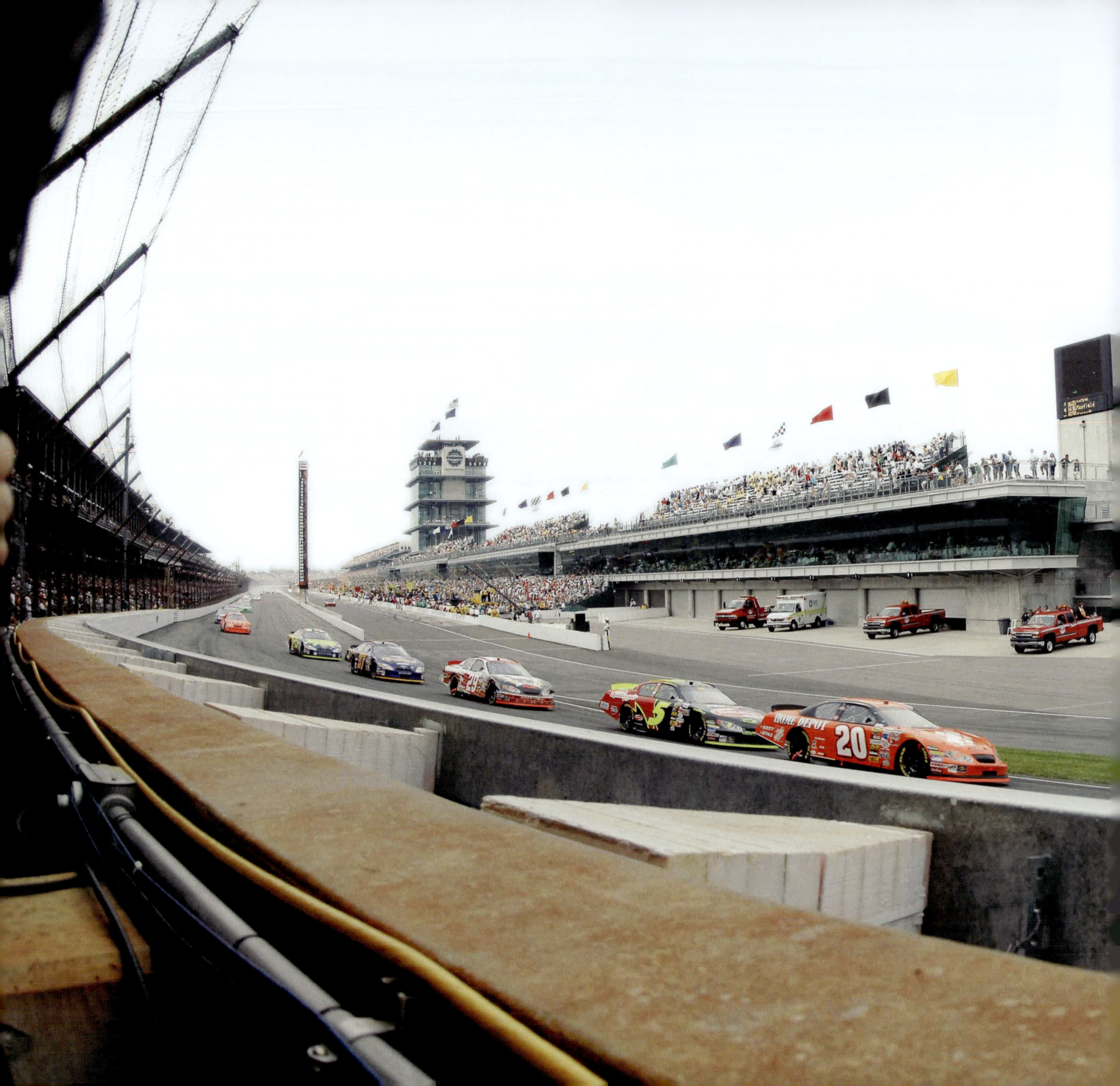
HOME DEPOT
20
5
29

Tony Stewart, driving the No. 20 Joe Gibbs Racing Chevrolet, leads the field into Turn 1 at Indianapolis Motor Speedway in 2005. Kyle Busch, in the No. 5 Hendrick Motorsports Chevrolet, is giving chase. Stewart won the Allstate 400 at the Brickyard that day, a victory that helped launch him to his second NASCAR Cup Series championship.

very efficiently. They were under the control of Harry Quinn and Clarence Cagel. When push came to shove there were certain guards that didn't take any s**t from anybody. I can still see two of 'em picking Bill France up by his ass and arms and flinging him out the back pit gate onto a cinder covered mud hole."

That episode happened in 1958, as NASCAR founder Bill France Sr. was frantically building Daytona International Speedway – the 2.5-mile length is the same as Indy – and the folks at the United States Auto Club (USAC) didn't take kindly to a sanctioning body competitor poking around inside their garage area, better known as "Gasoline Alley." In an interview with the *Daytona Beach News-Journal*, Yunick explained the yellow shirts – France incident in greater detail. "One day he came up to visit me up there," Yunick told the newspaper. "The guards physically picked him up and threw him out on his ass. It tore up his hands and his pants. That was Bill France leaving Indianapolis in '58. In all fairness to Bill, it wasn't Indianapolis that ordered him out. [Indy Speedway owner] Tony

Indianapolis importance 299

At the height of his professional racing career, LeeRoy Yarbrough made three Indianapolis 500 starts. His best finish was 19th in 1970, the year this classic driver-car grid photo was shot. The Jacksonville, Florida driver, who won the 1969 Daytona 500, was one of the few NASCAR drivers able to cross-pollinate to Indy-style racing. Unfortunately, Yarbrough suffered brain damage after crashing several times.

Moments after becoming the first woman to qualify for the Indianapolis 500, Janet Guthrie is interviewed by one of the track announcers at Indianapolis Motor Speedway. Guthrie's gender-breaking run happened in 1977. She qualified 26th but finished 29th when she encountered engine problems. To this day, she's the only female to start the Indy 500 and Daytona 500. She finished 11th in the 1980 Daytona 500 as a quasi-teammate of Dale Earnhardt. At least, they had the same car owner, Rod Osterlund. Earnhardt finished fourth in that 500.

Hulman was a great guy. He had nothing against Bill France. All the crap came from USAC, some old guy that had control of AAA for years, who terrorized all the racers. He's the one that ordered France out." (The AAA, now known as a not-for-profit, national auto club, sanctioned or timed or scored many racing events across the land in the first half of the 20th century.)

For years – for decades – after France was tossed out of "Gasoline Alley" like a rotten sack of apples, there was a frosty chill between the two giants in American racing. France got the last laugh on several fronts. First, he went deep into his shallow pocket to obtain a Federation Internationale de l'Automobile sanction for his two big NASCAR races at Daytona. Why? Because with an FIA sanction, USAC drivers – the big-name guys who raced in the Indianapolis 500 – were allowed to compete in France's stock-car race. Very few NASCAR races to this day carry the FIA sanction. It was a loophole that cost a lot of money, but reaped many benefits. A.J. Foyt said he would have been tossed out of USAC if he ran a race that didn't have the international agency's blessing, which is why he didn't run many NASCAR events during his prime in the 1960s and '70s.

A year before Bill France Sr. died (1992), his oldest son, William C. France, and Hulman's grandson, Tony George, started a serious dialogue about Indianapolis Motor Speedway hosting a NASCAR Winston Cup Series event. John Cooper, the only man to serve as president at Indy and Daytona, was working at NASCAR and acted as the messenger and liaison between the two camps. In June, 1992, NASCAR held a two-day, racing-feasibility test with nine race teams at the Brickyard, which attracted an estimated 50,000 fans to the old track. The highlight of the session was a demonstration race, and the stock-car drivers put on a show, racing two-by-two, exchanging the lead several times. Car owner Richard Childress, who attended with driver Dale Earnhardt, has to hold back the giggles when he talks about the exhibition race. "There was *some* racing going on, and a little bit was staged, too, to put on a show," Childress says. "It wasn't all staged, because, hell, everybody wanted to

300 Man-made Thunder

Indianapolis importance 301

302 Man-made Thunder

A classic look through the "Human Canyon" at Indianapolis Motor Speedway. Marching bands play, the national anthem is sung and balloons are released before America's oldest race.

finish out front at the end. So them last four or five laps did some changing. Hell, Earnhardt and them guys, they wanted to be out front. He wanted to be the lead dog when he came around for that last lap."

Despite the cost of a major upgrade to the retaining walls and catch fences that outlined the track, George put his stamp of approval on hosting the NASCAR event. France and George made a joint announcement on April 14, 1993. The Brickyard 400 Winston Cup Series race was scheduled for August 6, 1994. It was a day that forever changed the face of NASCAR. Many racing graybeards have this event in their top five moments on the NASCAR timeline, those momentous snapshots in time that helped push stock-car racing to a new level of prestige and popularity. These are easy to indentify: the opening of Daytona International Speedway, NASCAR's answer to Indianapolis; Winston becoming title sponsor of the Grand National Series in 1971; the 1979 Daytona 500, as the first NASCAR race carried live by network television (CBS), plus the race-ending fight; the landmark, $2.4 billion TV contract

"Indianapolis was kind of like a shrine, you know... You almost put it up there with the Roman Colosseum"

that started in 2001; and the inaugural 1994 Brickyard 400, won in fairytale fashion by Jeff Gordon, a well-spoken, Hollywood-looks driver who had once called Indiana home.

"Indianapolis was kind of like a shrine, you know," said Rick Hendrick, who owned the No. 24 Chevrolet that took Gordon to victory. "You almost put it up there with the Roman Colosseum – that much of sacred ground. Then as the years went by, I never thought I'd race there and go there. But to be part of that and having Jeff win the inaugural race, I think that was almost like a script. Because here's a guy from Indiana that was gonna go open-wheel racing, that went to NASCAR, young guy, very popular and he

Sam Hornish Jr. worked his way up the IndyCar Series ranks to earn a ride with the tour's top team, Penske Racing. In 2006 Hornish reached the pinnacle of United States open-wheel racing by winning the Indianapolis 500. Soon after that tremendous victory, he started talking about NASCAR racing. In 2008 he left open-wheel racing to drive the No. 77 Dodge owned by Roger Penske. Juan Pablo Montoya used his 2000 Indianapolis 500 victory as a springboard to a Formula One ride. He is the only driver to compete in the three big auto racing events at Indianapolis Motor Speedway – the Indy 500, the F1 United States Grand Prix and Allstate 400 at the Brickyard. The F1 event was staged from 2000 to 2007.

wins the first race there in his home state. So I don't know if there could've been a better script for that."

"It was special to me, I can tell you that," said Ray Evernham, who prepared the stock car that Gordon took to victory in that inaugural race. "The more we look back on it, the more certainly we'll start to realize what impact that was, you know. That was hallowed ground for stock cars. Nothing never run there but the Indy 500 and now they were bringing the NASCAR stock cars in there. At that point, it was probably the biggest crowd we'd ever run in front of. God, there were 350,000 people. So it was big to the sport, certainly, in its growth because a lot of those people who were open-wheel people that really had never looked at the NASCAR took a look at it that day. And probably a lot of them stuck with it. So I think it was big; big to the growth in the sport."

Tony Stewart, a two-time NASCAR winner at Indianapolis, watched the first Brickyard 400 from the grandstands and says he was mesmerized by the sight of 43 stock cars thundering around the track shaped like a

304   Man-made Thunder

1 2 3 4
5 6 7 8
SCOTT SHARP 8 DELPHI FERNANDEZ RACING
HONDA
SIRIUS
United Auto
Mobil 1
BOSS
Marlboro
TEAM PENSKE
Firestone

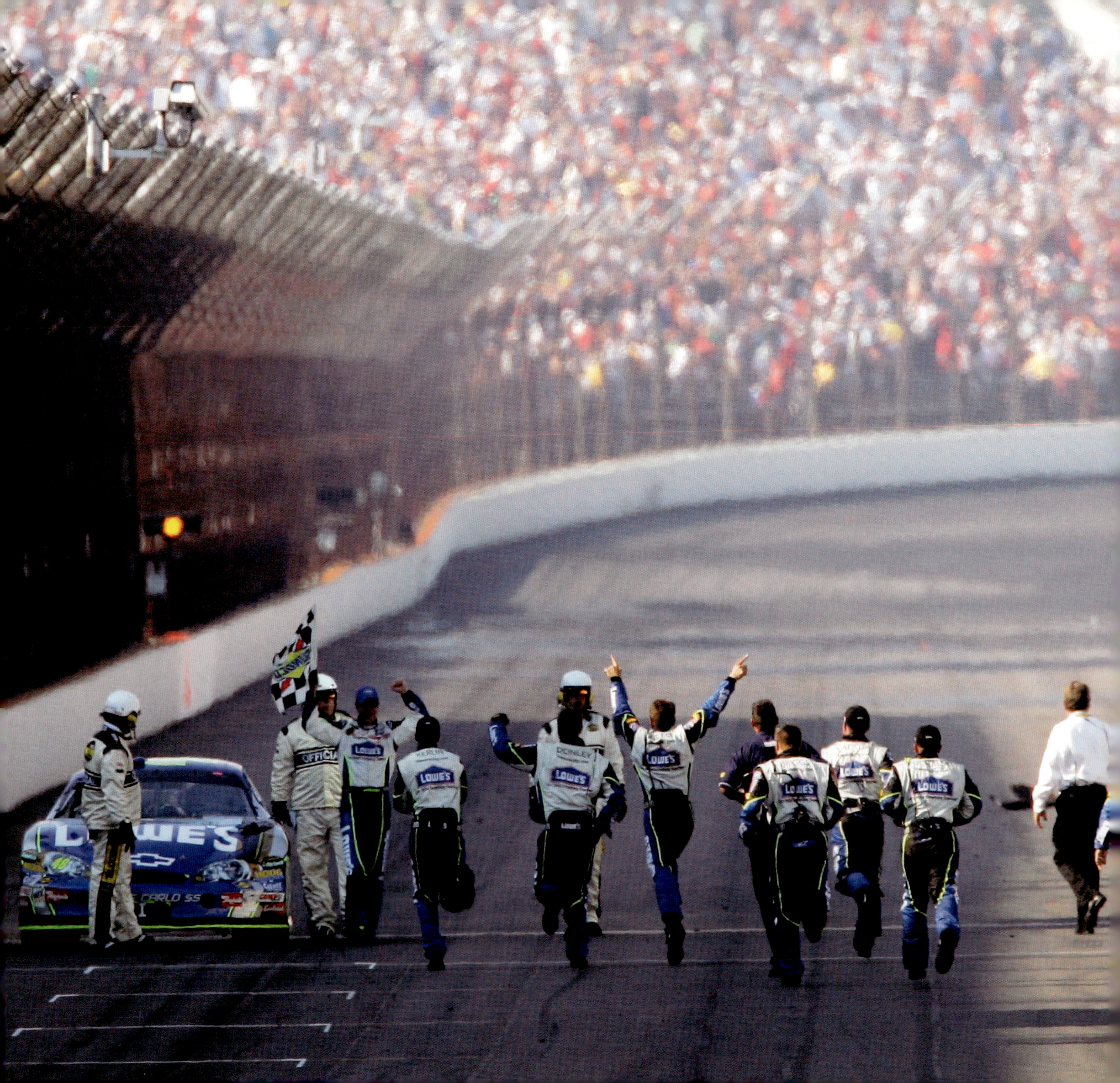
LOWE'S
OFFICIAL
DONLEY
KERLIN

Jimmie Johnson parks at the finish line, exits his No. 48 Hendrick Motorsports Chevrolet and waits to greet his race team after winning the 2006 Allstate 400 at the Brickyard. The stock-car race at Indy has become a launching pad to the Sprint Cup Series championship. Seven times since the first race in 1994, the Brickyard winner has gone on to championship honors. Jeff Gordon (1998, 2001) and Johnson (2006, 2008) have each done it twice.

rectangle. "I mean, it was cool," he said. "I thought it was awesome. I thought it was pretty cool to finally have NASCAR here."

Sensing the magnitude of the moment, Bill France Jr. made a rare appearance at the pre-race driver's meeting ("I don't attend a lot of these meetings, and I speak at even fewer of them") to read his competitors the riot act and act as a cheerleader. "Everyone in the world will be watching us here," he told the assembly of drivers and their crew chiefs. "Let's show the critics we belong here . . . You guys are a part of history. You're carrying the name for NASCAR. I'm proud to know you and I'm proud to be a part of you."

There are several ironies to the NASCAR-Indianapolis union. Soon after the first Brickyard 400, George started his own open-wheel league, a split from the Championship Auto Racing Teams sanctioning body. George founded the Indy Racing League in 1994 and it started racing in 1996. Unlike CART competitors, IRL regulars were guaranteed a starting position in the Indy 500. The split fractured open-wheel racing and set NASCAR's Winston Cup Series on course to become the top racing tour in the United States. Open-wheel, or Indy-type racing, was the dominant motorsports series into the 1980s. The lure of big money and fame in NASCAR lured many IRL candidates, such as Stewart, to stock cars.

In short order, the Brickyard 400, now called the Allstate 400 at the Brickyard, became the No. 2 race on the NASCAR calendar, behind the Daytona 500. Why? Because it became another high-profile arena for driver interaction, for personalities to compete and clash – a magnifying glass for joy and bitter disappointment. And all those people, in the canyon of humanity, watching every twitch on the racetrack. All those people. It's a sight Evernham and anybody else there that day will never forget.

"We pushed that car out on the starting grid, then looked up and saw all those people on the front straightaway and I was like, 'My God. We're at Indianapolis.' That's when it started to hit me."

It hit everybody – that NASCAR had arrived as a major-league sport, and its drivers were bigger than life; truly, man-made thunder. ■

Stealing talent

There was a time in NASCAR — the '60s and '70s, specifically — when you'd occasionally see an Indy-car driver show up at Daytona or Talladega or Charlotte or maybe some other stop along the stock-car trail.

Tony Stewart, who grew up near Indianapolis, was one of the top names when the Indy Racing League was formed in the mid-1990s, winning the series championship in 1997. Here, Stewart prepares to make a qualifying run at Texas Motor Speedway in 1997. The IRL lost its fiery, young star to NASCAR in 1999 when Stewart signed a contract with Joe Gibbs Racing. He won three Winston Cup Series races that season en route to the Rookie of the Year Award.

Casey Mears was another driver from an IndyCar Series family that left open-wheel racing for a steady paycheck in NASCAR. The nephew of four-time Indianapolis 500 winner Rick Mears, Casey is shown here exiting his race car after crashing at Bristol Motor Speedway in 2005. Mears now drives the No. 07 Chevrolet for car owner Richard Childress.

You'd see A.J. Foyt here and there, Mario Andretti on rare occasions, maybe a little look-see from Johnny Rutherford and Gordon Johncock; and at the road courses any number of open-wheelers (and international sportscar racers) would show up. But usually they'd load the hauler afterwards and head back to their own racing world, which basically revolved around Indianapolis, Indiana.

Of course, back then, the Indy-car circuit was thriving – it was mainly sanctioned by the United States Auto Club (USAC) and, eventually, at its highest level, the Championship Auto Racing Teams (CART). The annual Indianapolis 500, held each Memorial Day weekend at the Indianapolis Motor Speedway, was easily the world's biggest single-day motorsports event. The Daytona 500 was huge in its own way and in its own "neighborhood" down South, but on the North American racing landscape, it was no better than second fiddle to Indy.

In the 1980s, things began changing. CART's IndyCar Series – where the Unsers (Bobby, Al, Little Al) battled with Foyt and Andretti and Danny Sullivan and Arie Luyendyk and others – was becoming more and more of a road-course series. Also, as the '90s approached, young American-born drivers were becoming fewer and fewer in number. One of those potential racing Yanks was born in California, but raised in the small Indiana town of Pittsboro. He was young, attractive and, as the amazing record confirms, incredibly talented in the cockpit of an open-wheel race car. As he reached his upper teens, he began looking for open seats, or simple opportunities, within the IndyCar Series, the upper rung of his chosen form of racing. No one wanted the little transplanted Hoosier, despite his record.

That's how Jeff Gordon ended up in NASCAR. Nearly a decade before Gordon's 1991 full-time jump to NASCAR racing, Tim Richmond left the Midwestern open-wheel world for stock-car racing. About five years before Gordon, Ken Schrader did the same thing. But only Gordon clearly carried the type of pedigree that seemed destined for Indy-style greatness. Only after he became a legitimate challenger to Dale

Kasey Kahne was a United States Auto Club sensation, winning the USAC Midget championship plus the USAC Silver Bullet Series Rookie of the Year title in 2000. Soon after making a name for himself in open-wheel racing, he sought out a NASCAR ride, and ended up replacing Bill Elliott in the No. 9 Evernham Motorsports Dodge in 2004. Here he's being interviewed in the garage area by SPEED.

Earnhardt for king of the NASCAR mountain, did the Indy world begin lamenting the "one that got away." Along with everything else Gordon has accomplished on NASCAR tracks, he should also be remembered for igniting a trend. Nothing gathers imitators like success, and after team owner Bill Davis nurtured Gordon in his formative years, and after Rick Hendrick made him a superstar, other owners began copying their move.

As Indy-car racing became ravaged by "civil war" – the mid-'90s split between CART and the upstart Indy Racing League – and NASCAR continued its explosive growth, stock cars became more and more attractive to open-wheel racers at precisely the same time open-wheel racers became more attractive to NASCAR owners.

A look at some of the open-wheel racers who made the NASCAR jump after Gordon's success:

Kenny Irwin Jr. – Showed some flashes, but generally fell short of expectations, then died trying.

Ryan Newman – Became a big winner at Penske Racing, then slumped before winning the 2008 Daytona 500.

Tony Stewart – His love remains the Indianapolis 500, but his success in NASCAR (he's a two-time champ) is evidence he made the right choice.

Dave Blaney – Was a short-track god on the USAC short tracks, but largely fell flat in NASCAR.

Scott Pruett – Only got a short look in NASCAR before returning to his pre-Indy vocation, sportscars.

Steve Kinser – Didn't try NASCAR until in his 40s, and lasted just five races before returning to the World of Outlaws racing that made him a legend.

Kasey Kahne – Has had mixed results, but is generally considered a modern-day star, and has the big-league sponsor (Budweiser) to take advantage of that star power.

Casey Mears – Moved from one high-profile team (Hendrick Motorsports) to another

Casey Mears prepares for an important practice session in the days leading up to the 2009 Daytona 500. After two years in the Hendrick Motorsports camp, Mears was hired to drive the No. 07 Chevrolet owned by Richard Childress.

(Childress Racing) in 2009, with hopes of fulfilling his potential.

In recent years, others have "gone NASCAR." Juan Pablo Montoya, former Indy-car star, left Formula One for NASCAR. Jacques Villeneuve tried to do the same, but ran into sponsorship issues. Sam Hornish Jr. was the Indy Racing League's biggest star when he jumped at team owner Roger Penske's offer to try NASCAR in 2008. Dario Franchitti gave it a try in 2008, but sponsorship issues also forced his early exit. Scott Speed (who was groomed for Formula One) and AJ Allmendinger are two others for whom the jury is still out. ∎

All in the family

William C. France had seen this before – the dread, the fear in the eyes of NASCAR competitors.

The transfer of power, and keys. NASCAR founder William H.G. France, a.k.a. "Big Bill," hands the keys of the NASCAR office to his oldest son, William C. France, a.k.a. "Bill Jr.," on January 10, 1972. Bill France Jr. was 38 years old and many of the old-time NASCAR competitors thought he was too young to be put in charge of the sanctioning body. "Bill Jr." served as NASCAR leader for 31 years before handing the family-owned business over to his son, Brian France, in 2003.

Former New York City Mayor Rudolph Giuliani makes the rounds at Daytona International Speedway in the weeks leading up to the Florida presidential Republican primary in January, 2008. Here, he's shaking hands with NASCAR chairman and CEO Brian France. NASCAR racetracks attract conservative candidates because of the "NASCAR Dad" demographic, which is politically right-leaning men with children.

It happened, in January, 1972, when his dad, William H.G. France, handed him the keys to the NASCAR kingdom. "Bill Jr." was now in charge. The old-time stock-car legion was sure this handoff of power would lead to stock-car Armageddon. After all, "Big Bill" France had founded the sport, and his 38-year-old son had seemingly no management experience, and therefore little ability to rule stock-car racing like his big, gregarious father. But a funny thing happened on the way to that predicted collapse: NASCAR grew and flourished and modernized, and became second only to the NFL in national popularity.

Bill France Jr., who had fought a variety of illnesses since 1997, knew what to expect when he named his son, Brian Z. France, as NASCAR chairman and CEO. He realized the skeptics would whine and fuss and gripe that Brian didn't have enough experience to lead the NASCAR Nation. So far, the NASCAR chief has done a pretty good job with the baton in his hand. Under his watch, NASCAR has stressed diversity; developed the driver-safe "Car of Tomorrow"; signed a second, multi-billion-dollar TV deal; successfully found new title sponsors for all national series; and introduced the Chase for the Sprint Cup, which puts more emphasis on the championship late in the season.

It wasn't easy for Bill France Jr. to get his son focused on the family business. It took countless hours of tutoring and mentoring.

So far the NASCAR chief has done a pretty good job with the baton in his hand.

On September 13, 2003, the family-owned company was put in the hands of Brian, during a ceremony in the lobby area of NASCAR headquarters in Daytona Beach, Florida, that was short on pomp and circumstance.

"Brian is well prepared to lead this sport and this company into the future," Bill Jr. said. "I am confident that the future of NASCAR is in very capable hands. NASCAR is my life's work, and my father's before me; this

Indianapolis importance 313

Fans pack the grandstands preparing to watch the first 500-mile race on a paved superspeedway at the inaugural running of the 1950 Southern 500 at Darlington Raceway. If you look closely, you'll notice there is no pit wall to protect pit crews from cars on the track. And, there are very few women in the grandstand area. The track chewed up race tires, so pit crews "borrowed" tires from spectators' cars parked in the infield area.

decision is probably one of the most important ones I've made at NASCAR – and I know it's the right decision."

Like his father before him, Bill Jr. never retired, and kept an eye on his son from an office on the other side of the NASCAR complex. The elder France created a NASCAR board of directors and installed himself and younger brother Jim France as vice-chairmen, a role Jim continues to play today. Bill France Jr. died in the summer of 2007, knowing he had accomplished his mission to move the sport forward, through his only son.

Sprint Cup Series car owner Felix Sabates was one of France's pallbearers, and before laying his good friend to rest, explained his

"I think we're a better sport today because Bill Jr. believed in his son"

utmost achievement. "Bill's greatest legacy is that he never gave up on Brian," Sabates told the assembled media, as he recalled the days when Brian was shuttled to Tucson, Arizona, to oversee the operation of a short track owned by the France family. "I told Brian, 'When they put you in Arizona, I thought they were gonna keep sending you farther and farther until you ended up in Mexico and we'd never see you again.' But Bill had a plan for Brian. These last four or

five years, a lot of this sport's growth can be attributed to Brian. I think we're a better sport today because Bill Jr. believed in his son."

Bill France Jr. believed in his only daughter, too. Lesa France Kennedy came up through the ranks of the France family's other business, International Speedway Corporation, where she now serves as president. She was named to the position in 2003. Together, Brian France and his sister Lesa are continuing the work of their father, pushing stock-car racing to be bigger and better. ■

Right Kevin Harvick's No. 29 Richard Childress Racing Chevrolet looks like a dragon as it spits fire and belches smoke during a practice session for the 2008 Sprint All Star Challenge at Lowe's Motor Speedway.

Next page Moments after being declared winner of the rain-shortened 2009 Daytona 500, Matt Kenseth celebrates the triumph by standing on his No. 17 Roush Fenway Racing Ford in Victory Lane. Said Kenseth: "It's pretty unbelievable to be able to actually be in the Daytona 500, much less win one. It's just a dream come true."

Indianapolis importance 315

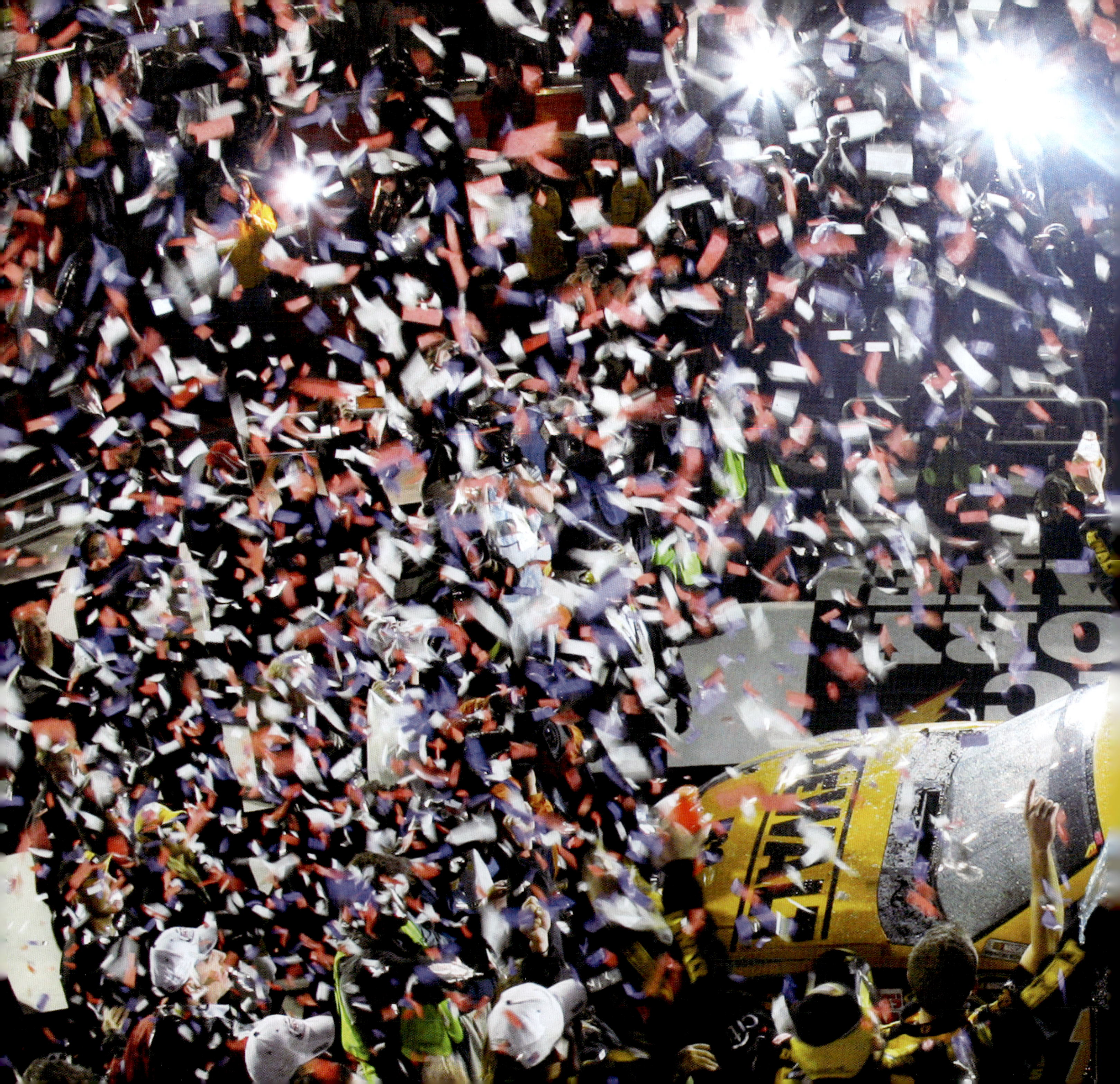

Index

A

AAA Auto Club, 235, 300
"Alabama Gang", 116, 169
Alabama International Motor Speedway *see* Talladega Superspeedway (formerly Alabama International Motor Speedway)
All Star Challenge, 100, 115, 118–19, 170, 177, 258–9, 266, 282, 315
Allison family (Bobby, Donnie, Davey), 33, 42, 82, 86, 116, 168–9, 170, 236, 239, 291
Allmendinger, AJ, 124, 210, 230, 311
Allstate 400 (formerly Brickyard 400), 8, 14–15, 122, 129, 134, 144–5, 179, 202–3, 221, 222, 296, 303–7
Andretti, Mario, 296, 309
Ard, Sam, 286
Asheville-Weaverville Speedway, 57, 61, 62, 139
Atlanta International Raceway, 41, 43, 70, 166
Atlanta Motor Speedway, 86, 114, 120, 135, 148, 166, 208, 282
Auto Club (California) Speedway, 230, 281

B

Baker family (Buck, Buddy), 110–11, 116, 139, 165, 169, 291
Bodine brothers, 82, 116–17, 117, 139
Bonneville Salt Flats (Utah), 22–3
Bowman Gray Stadium, 275
Bowyer, Clint, 195, 268–9, 275, 278
Brickhouse, Richard, 41, 271
Brickyard *see* Indianapolis Motor Speedway (the Brickyard)
Brickyard 400 race (now Allstate 400) *see* Allstate 400 (formerly Brickyard 400)
Bristol Motor Speedway, 43, 61, 76, 80–1, 160–1, 186, 262, 266–7, 282, 283, 292
Budweiser, 94, 97, 109, 176, 270, 310
Budweiser Shootout, 44–5, 48, 76–7, 178–9, 204, 211
bump-drafting, 211
burnouts, celebration, 158, 178–9
Busch, Kurt, 114, 117, 159, 169, 170, 204, 217, 281, 282, 292–3
Busch, Kyle, 114, 117, 159, 276–86, 292–3
Busch Series (now Nationwide Series), 120, 135, 149–50, 173, 176, 179, 212–14, 215, 259, 262, 280–1
Byron, Red, 40, 46, 49, 61, 169

C

California Speedway, 230, 281
Campbell, Sir Malcolm, 24–9
Camping World Truck Series, 238–9, 262, 266, 278–81
"Car of Tomorrow" (COT), 43, 196, 197, 281–2, 313
Carmichael, Ricky, 234–5
Championship Auto Racing Teams (CART), 307, 309, 310
Charlotte Motor Speedway (now Lowe's Motor Speedway), 41, 47, 61, 70, 76–7, 97–100, 115, 129, 140, 251, 289–91
Charlotte Speedway (dirt track), 40, 50, 61–3, 115, 140
Chase format (introduced 2004), 43, 170, 281
Chevrolet, 21, 44–5, 97, 120, 123, 249–50, 251
 cars, 12, 108, 125, 178–9, 225, 226, 251, 253, 258–9, 278, 282, 291, 311
 No. 2 car, 92–3, 96, 108, 269
 No. 20 car, 183, 211, 219
 No. 24 car, 34–5, 123, 151, 303
 No. 29 car, 254–5, 256, 259, 262, 263, 270, 315
 No. 3 car, 188–9, 190–3, 250, 269
 No. 33 car, 212–13, 269
 No. 48 car, 147, 150, 151, 153, 163, 173, 306–7
 No. 8 car, 109, 176, 177, 179, 183, 186, 230, 236
Chicagoland Speedway, 149, 217, 256–7
Childress, Richard, 97, 103, 109, 136, 137, 179, 262, 266, 268–75, 285, 300–3
 see also Richard Childress Racing
Chrysler, 50, 76, 110–11, 140
Convertible Series, 52–3, 63, 64
Cope, Derrike, 103
crashes and accidents, 19, 38, 42, 48, 57, 149, 195, 197, 212–13, 256, 278
 Jimmie Johnson and, 144–5, 149, 163
 Richard Petty and, 83, 86, 108, 289
 see also deaths of drivers
Custer, Joe, 224–7

D

Dale Earnhardt Inc., 140, 176, 177, 189, 228–9, 236
 Chevrolet No. 8 car, 109, 176, 177, 179, 183, 186, 230, 236
Darlington Raceway, 36, 40, 50, 54–5, 70, 101, 180–1, 221, 249, 273, 276–7, 287, 314
 crashes at, 19, 56, 149
Davis, Bill, 120, 310
Davis, W.R. 'Slick', 49
 death of Fireball Roberts (1964), 41, 73, 244–5, 246–7
Daytona 500 race, 6–17, 21, 115–16, 225, 226, 230, 239, 270, 278, 288–9, 309, 310, 316–17
 crashes and accidents, 43, 83, 86, 109, 179, 191–3, 195, 196–9, 217–18, 259, 262–3
 Dale Jr. and, 116, 181, 182, 183
 Dale Earnhardt and, 43, 103–9, 113, 116, 183, 188–93, 195
 father-son winners, 70, 116, 183
 fight after (1979), 42, 86, 253, 303
 A.J. Foyt and, 221, 222–3
 Jeff Gordon and, 126, 133
 Janet Guthrie and, 132–3, 300
 inaugural running (1959), 90–1, 246
 Jimmie Johnson and, 173
 Richard Petty and, 70, 76, 83, 86, 112
 television coverage, 42, 43
Daytona Beach, 18–21, 29, 38, 46, 49, 88, 89, 91
Daytona International Speedway, 6–17, 44–5, 46, 102, 103, 166, 178, 218, 221, 238, 246, 300
 Firecracker races, 42, 221, 223, 246
 William H.G. France and, 38, 41, 89–91
 Gatorade Duel, 197, 230, 253
 lighting at, 61, 91, 102
 opening of (1959), 38, 41, 70, 90–1, 303
 Speedweeks, 172–3, 204, 211, 230, 253
deaths of drivers, 41, 49, 56, 73, 195
 Dale Earnhardt (2001), 43, 109, 179, 190–3, 195, 196–9, 259, 262–3
 Fireball Roberts (1964), 41, 73, 244–5, 246–7
Detroit motor industry, 50–3, 56–9, 249–50
Dieringer, Darel, 47, 289
dirt tracks, 25, 32, 37, 38, 40, 49, 60–3, 140, 165, 245, 246, 289
Dodge, 43, 124, 129, 143, 170, 230, 310
Dover International Speedway, 10, 26–7, 76, 279
drivers
 all-time best lists/polls, 113, 291
 bloodlines and, 70, 114–17, 183
 celebrity status, 12, 82, 129–33
 cross-over (Indy/stock car), 109, 214, 296, 300, 301, 308–11
 deaths of *see* deaths of drivers
 female, 132–3, 300–1
 fights between, 42, 86, 217, 253, 256–9, 303
 Jeff Gordon and, 126, 133
 Janet Guthrie and, 132–3, 300
 inaugural running (1959), 90–1, 246
 Jimmie Johnson and, 173
 Richard Petty and, 70, 76, 83, 86, 112
 television coverage, 42, 43
Dunnaway, Glenn, 62–3

E

Earnhardt, Dale, 92–109, 120, 140, 146, 165, 169, 176, 241, 269–70, 273–5, 310
 Daytona 500 and, 43, 103–9, 113, 116, 183, 188–93, 195
 death of (2001), 43, 109, 179–80, 190–3, 195, 196–9, 259, 262–3
 Jeff Gordon and, 135–7, 143
Earnhardt, Ralph Dale (Dale Jr.), 20, 26–7, 109, 117, 174–87, 189, 190, 194, 200–1, 278
 Daytona 500 and, 116, 181, 182, 183
 Hendrick Motorsports and, 138, 141, 181, 187, 236, 282
Earnhardt, Ralph Lee, 110–13
Earnhardt family, 97, 102, 103, 117, 180, 184–7, 189
Economaki, Chris, 53, 123
Edwards, Carl, 240, 256–9, 260–1, 265–6
Edwards, Norman, 166
Elliott, Bill, 42, 100, 170, 256
engines, 11, 51, 76, 127, 139, 284
Esquire magazine, 50, 73, 249–50
Eury, Tony, 179, 182
Evernham, Ray, 126, 129, 130, 135–6, 142–3, 217, 285, 304, 307, 310

F

Fan Clubs, 82
Federation Internationale de l'Automobile (FIA), 300
female drivers, 132–3, 300–1
Fielden, Greg, 245, 246
Flock brothers, 25, 56, 61, 117, 139
Ford, 21, 46, 50, 113, 120, 123, 139
 cars, 62–3, 97, 110–11, 120, 125, 166, 246–7, 259, 260–1, 316–17
 No. 6 car, 232, 233, 235, 236, 237, 239, 243
Formula One, 296–7, 304–5, 311
Fox, Ray, 249, 251, 289–90
Foyt, A.J., 16, 113, 129, 220–3, 294–5, 296, 300, 309
France, Brian Z., 43, 65, 313–14
France, William C. (Bill Jr.), 42, 43, 65, 66, 88–9, 90, 106, 109, 300, 307, 313–14
France, William H.G., 17, 29–32, 41, 65, 269, 271, 300, 311–12
 Daytona International Speedway and, 38, 41, 88–91
 eviction from "Gasoline Alley" (1958), 17, 296, 299–300
 formative years of NASCAR, 18, 46–50, 53, 61, 63
 founding of NASCAR (Dec. 14, 1947), 32, 40, 46

G

Gamecock Speedway (Sumter, North Carolina), 289
Gazaway, Bill, 63
General Motors, 50–3, 59, 97, 100
George, Tony, 300, 303, 307
Gibbs, Coy, 262, 265
Ginn, Bobby, 236, 239
Giuliani, Rudolph, 313
Goldsmith, Paul, 56
Gordon, Jeff, 118–30, 146, 165, 169, 198, 217, 240–3, 286, 297, 309–10
 Brickyard/Allstate 400 and, 122, 129, 134, 303–4, 307
 Daytona 500 and, 126, 133, 189
 Dale Earnhardt and, 135–7, 143, 274, 310
 first race (1992), 43, 86
 Hendrick Motorsports and, 34–5, 120–3, 134, 138–40, 150–6, 310
 Jimmie Johnson and, 149, 150–6
 personal life, 18, 130–3
Grand National Series (1950–70), 25, 40, 50, 62, 63, 70, 76, 79, 245
grandstands and spectator areas, 10, 11, 12, 70, 80–1, 266–7, 283

H

Gustafson, Alan, 282
Guthrie, Janet, 132–3, 300–1

Haas, Gene, 225–7
Hamilton, Bobby, 265
Hamilton, Pete, 264–5
Hamlin, Denny, 218, 278
HANS safety device, 194, 195
Harroun, Ray, 21
Harvick, Kevin, 213, 254–5, 256–67, 270–1, 285, 286, 315
haulers, race, 32, 204
helmets, 20, 86, 195, 198–9
Helton, Mike, 193, 199, 209–11
Hendrick, Rick, 109, 120–3, 135–6, 138–41, 150, 153, 157, 166, 187, 278, 303–4, 310
Hendrick Motorsports, 135–6, 139–41, 149, 150–7, 178–9, 218, 236–9, 278, 282, 311
 Chevrolet cars, 36, 123, 151, 178–9, 253, 278, 282, 306–7
 Dale Jr. and, 138, 141, 181, 187, 236, 282
 Jeff Gordon and, 34–5, 120–3, 134, 138–40, 150–6, 310
Hickory Speedway, 110–11, 290
Holman, John, 50, 89, 113, 139
Homestead-Miami Speedway, 205, 236, 281
Hornish Jr., Sam, 304–5, 311
Howard, Frank, 165–6
Hulman, Tony, 299–300
Hunt, James, 242–3
Hutcherson, Dick, 113

I

Indianapolis 500 race, 17–18, 21, 133, 221, 294–5, 300, 301, 302, 304–5, 309
Indianapolis Motor Speedway (the Brickyard), 8–18, 98–9, 294–5, 296–303, 297, 298, 304
 Bill France's eviction from "Gasoline Alley" (1958), 17, 296, 299–300
 inaugural Brickyard 400 (1994), 122, 129, 134, 221, 296, 303–7
 NASCAR and, 17, 38, 43, 296, 300–7

318 Man-made thunder

Indy-type (open-wheel) racing, 17–18, 38, 109, 214, 215, 221, 222, 307, 308–11
Infineon Speedway, 217, 219, 236–7
International Race of Champions (IROC), 239, 241, 242–3
International Speedway Corporation, 61, 65, 90, 314
Irwin Jr., Kenny, 195, 310
Isaac, Bobby, 22–3, 169, 223, 290

J
Jarrett family (Ned and Dale), 112, 113, 115–16, 169, 170, 249
Joe Gibbs Racing, 14–15, 140, 169, 211, 219, 227, 276–7, 278, 282
   Tony Stewart and, 140, 211, 213, 214, 215, 219, 225
Johnson, Jimmie, 126, 138–9, 140, 144–63, 166, 169, 172–3, 240, 281, 306–7
   three-peat (2006–08), 146–9, 153, 165
Johnson, Junior (Robert Glen Johnson Jr.), 56, 73, 100, 113, 126, 246–7, 248–51, 290
   Junior Johnson Racing, 51, 66, 94–7, 146, 165, 166, 171, 250, 269–70
Jones, Hank, 100

K
Kahne, Kasey, 143, 217, 310
Kenseth, Matt, 124–5, 166, 169–70, 173, 184, 211–14, 315–17
Kiekhaefer, Carl, 111, 139, 140
Kite, Harold, 41
Knaus, Chad, 126, 152–3, 156
Kulwicki, Alan, 170

L
Labonte brothers (Bobby, Terry), 117, 136, 139–40, 169, 189, 274
Land Speed Record site (Daytona Beach), 21–9, 91
Langhorne Speedway, 41
Las Vegas Motor Speedway, 143, 285, 293
Leake, Harry, 52
Logano, Joey, 227
Lorenzen, Fred, 113

Lowe's Motor Speedway (formerly Charlotte Motor Speedway), 100, 118–19, 177, 183, 187, 193, 199, 247, 254–6, 259, 266, 315
Luyendyk, Arie, 221, 309

M
Mann, Larry, 41
Marlin, Sterling, 189, 190
Martin, Mark, 138–9, 228–9, 231, 232, 233–43, 252–3
Martinsville Speedway, 108, 149, 157, 158, 215, 262, 270
Mears, Casey, 309, 311
mechanics, 32, 51, 58, 59, 126, 129, 179
Melvin, Dr. John, 196–9
Michigan International Speedway, 117, 137, 142, 183, 194–5, 232, 269
Midget championship, USAC, 215, 310
Modifieds, 38, 46, 48–9, 50, 61, 63, 88, 166, 275
Montoya, Juan Pablo, 124–5, 296–7, 311
Moody, Ralph, 50, 113, 139
moonshine alcohol, 53–6, 249, 250
Moore, Bud, 97, 270
multi-driver team concept, 139–40, 270
Murchison, Clint, 89–90
museum, Childress-Earnhardt, 270
Myers, Bobby, 56, 275

N
Nab, Herb, 51
NASCAR
   advertising and publicity, 46–9, 65–7
   founding of (Dec. 14, 1947), 32, 40, 46
   history of, 18, 32–8, 40–3
   Most Popular Driver Award, 179, 201
   records *see* records, NASCAR
   rival sanctioning bodies, 61
   Southern fan base, 18, 29, 32, 49–50, 65, 86, 130, 176–9, 309
   national anthem, 8–9, 11, 29, 109, 282–3, 303
Nationwide Series (formerly Busch Series), 120, 218, 239, 256, 259, 266, 278, 286
Nelson, Gary, 126
Nemecheck, Joe, 258–9
Newman, Ryan, 184, 310
Nextel Cup Series (2004–07), 40, 43
night races and lighting, 54–5, 61, 91, 102, 287
North Carolina Motor Speedway, 103, 171, 289
North Wilkesboro Speedway, 275
numerology, 173

O
Occoneechee Speedway (Hillsboro, North Carolina), 63, 245
Oldfield, Barney, 24
Oldsmobiles, 21, 49, 56, 116
Ormond Challenge Cup sprint race, 21–4
Osterlund, Rod, 94, 97, 273, 300

P
pace laps, 130–1
Pagan, Eddie, 18–19
painters and paint schemes, 16–17, 187, 198
parade or victory lap (New York), 154–5
Pardue, Jimmy, 41, 73
Park, Steve, 189
Parks, Raymond, 46
Parsons, Benny, 42, 169
Pearson, David, 82, 139, 165, 169, 274, 288–91
Penske Racing, 170, 281, 293, 310, 311
Petty, Kyle, 82, 115
Petty, Lee, 41, 62, 70, 73, 76, 115, 116, 117, 165, 169
Petty, Richard, 42, 68–72, 73–87, 91, 114–17, 127, 146, 165, 169, 270
   crashes and accidents, 83, 86, 108, 289
   Daytona 500 and, 70, 76, 83, 86, 112, 116
   Dale Earnhardt and, 43, 108, 109, 135
   David Pearson and, 289, 290, 291
   retirement of (1992), 43, 86

Petty Enterprises Inc., 63, 72, 73–6, 79, 82, 86, 127, 169
Petty family, 63, 72, 195
Phoenix International Raceway, 210, 235
Pigeon, Rick, 282
pit crews/roads, 8–9, 11, 13, 34–5, 84, 86, 96, 97, 133, 148, 152, 254–5, 282, 314
Pitt, Blackie, 57
Pocono Raceway, 128, 260–1
Pontiac, 17, 56, 59, 70, 86, 115, 189, 190, 247, 290
prayer, pre-race, 29, 91
Professional Drivers Association (PDA), 41, 89, 269, 270, 271

R
radio, two-way, 11, 162, 189
Ragan, David, 243
rain, 12
Reagan, Ronald, 42
records, NASCAR, 42, 43, 135, 146, 165, 166, 239, 278, 281, 286
   most titles, 103, 169
   speed records, 21–9, 42, 116
Red Bull Racing, 63, 124–5, 253
Reese, Charlie, 29
Research and Development Center, NASCAR, 196
restrictor-plates, 24, 42, 63
Rexford, Bill, 169, 245
Rich, Mike, 148
Richard Childress Racing, 94, 97, 135, 140, 179, 259, 269–71
   Chevrolet cars, 188–9, 190–3, 269, 311
   Chevrolet No. 29 car, 254–5, 256, 259, 262, 263, 270, 315
Richert, Doug, 97
Richmond, Tim, 109, 139, 143, 274, 309
Richmond International Raceway, 13, 225, 278
Riverside (California) International Raceway, 73, 243, 269, 270
R.J. Reynolds Tobacco Co. (RJR), 42, 65–6, 85, 97, 103, 126, 262, 303
Roberts, Edward Glenn 'Fireball', 17, 41, 59, 61, 62, 70–3, 244–7, 290

Roper, Jim, 40, 50, 62–3
Roper, Tony, 195
Roush (Fenway) Racing, 232, 233, 235, 236, 237, 239, 243, 256, 259, 260–1, 316–17
Roush, Jack, 230, 232, 233–6, 239
Rudd, Ricky, 139, 270

S
Sabates, Felix, 314
safety, 19, 41, 48, 57, 160–1, 194–9, 269, 270, 271, 314
Sauter, Johnny, 225
Schrader, Ken, 99, 139, 190–1, 309
Shore, Barney, 52
Skeen, Buren, 41
Skinner, Mike, 189, 195
Smith, Jack, 70
Smith, Bruton, 61, 63, 66
South, American, 18, 29, 32, 49–50, 65, 86, 130, 176–9, 309
Southern 500 race, 18–19, 36–7, 56, 221, 249, 273, 314
   spectators, 8–17, 39, 57, 79–82, 90, 104–5, 128, 192–3, 201, 215, 314
   flags, signs and clothing, 85, 90, 95, 100, 103, 167, 192
   infield activities, 36, 37, 225, 273
   merchandise and collectibles, 138–9, 201, 224–5
   Southern fan base, 18, 29, 32, 49–50, 65, 86, 130, 176–9, 309
Speed, Scott, 63, 124–5, 311
Spencer, Jimmy, 265
sponsorship, corporate, 37, 38, 42, 94, 120, 123–5, 156, 204, 213, 233, 235, 262
   art work/logos/colors, 12, 20, 64–5, 187
   Richard Petty and, 82, 85–6
   see also Budweiser; R.J. Reynolds Tobacco Co. (RJR)
Sportsman cars, 49, 111, 112–13
spotters, 160–1
Sprint Cup Series champions, 164–70
   name progression (1949–2009), 40

   number of races in, 42, 49, 50
Sprint Cup Series (from 2008), 6–7, 8–14, 39, 40, 43
Stacy, Nelson, 166
Stewart, Tony, 14–15, 159, 183, 189, 195, 202–22, 275, 304–6, 307, 308–9, 310
   Joe Gibbs Racing and, 140, 211, 213, 214, 215, 219, 225
   Stewart-Haas Racing, 218, 225–7
Strictly Stock Series (1949), 32–7, 40, 46, 49–50, 61–3, 115, 140, 169
superspeedways, 38, 40, 60, 70, 246, 314

T
Talladega Superspeedway (formerly Alabama International Motor Speedway), 33, 63, 133, 140–1, 153, 166, 184–5, 189, 256, 264, 265
   crashes and accidents, 42, 212–13, 256
   PDA boycott of first race (1969), 41, 89, 268–70, 271
   speed records at, 24, 42
teams, 50, 138–41, 270
television coverage, 38, 39, 41, 42, 43, 65, 86, 120, 130, 185, 303
Texas Motor Speedway, 29, 32, 166, 221, 282, 286
Thomas, Herb, 56, 61, 169
Thomas, Horace, 21
Thompson, Speedy, 111, 184
Time magazine, 109, 193
tires, 12, 41, 74–5, 208–11, 289
Toyota, 63, 124, 227, 253, 276–7, 278
track surfaces, 25, 32, 37, 38, 40, 49, 60–3, 76–7, 140, 165, 245, 246, 289
Truex Jr., Martin, 12, 286
Turner, Curtis, 58, 61, 70, 113, 275

U
United States Auto Club (USAC), 214, 215, 221, 296, 299–300, 309
Unsers, the (Bobby, Al, Little Al), 309

V
Vickers, Brian, 140, 217, 253, 286
Villeneuve, Jacques, 311

W
Wade, Billy, 41, 73
Waldorf-Astoria hotel (Manhattan), 103, 137, 155
Wallace brothers, 24, 116, 170, 262, 293
Walt Disney World Speedway, 308–9
Waltrip, Darrell, 116, 139, 146, 165, 169, 170, 171, 190–3, 250, 274
Waltrip, Michael, 116, 159–62, 189, 190
Warren, Dan, 89, 91
Watkins Glen International, 149, 218, 236
"The Wave" at Bristol Motor Speedway, 80–1
Weatherly, Joe, 41, 73, 165
Westmoreland, Hubert, 62–3
Wheeler, H.A. "Humpy", 61, 100, 183–4, 187, 193, 247
White, Rex, 169
Wilson, Waddell, 139
Winston Cup Grand National Series (1971–85), 40, 42, 85, 146, 303
Winston Cup Series (1986–2003), 40, 42, 43, 66, 86, 103, 115, 130, 135, 156, 205, 269
Winton, Alexander, 21
Wood, Glen, 275
Wood Brothers Racing, 166, 221, 222–3, 289, 291
Woody, Larry, 265
World 600 race, 47, 70, 76–7, 244–5, 247, 289–90, 291

Y
Yarborough, Cale, 42, 47, 82, 86, 113, 164–7, 169, 249, 250
   three-peat (1976–8), 146–9, 165
Yarborough, LeeRoy, 300
Yunick, Smokey, 17, 37, 58, 59, 70–3, 126, 169, 290, 296–300

Z
Zipadelli, Greg, 216–17, 227

319

Photocredits

Don Hunter Collection/Smyle Media: 16–17, 22–25, 33, 36–38, 47–52, 56–62, 63(r), 65(r), 68–72, 76–78, 83–89, 92–97, 101–02, 103(r), 108, 109(l), 110–13, 115–17, 121, 127, 129, 132, 139–40, 164–68, 171, 180, 220, 222–23, 239, 242–51, 264, 269–71, 273–75, 288–91, 302, 314

Don Smyle Racing Archives: 66–67

Getty Images: 106-07 (George Tiedemann), 209 (Jamie Squire), 210 (Robert Laberge), 304–05 (Darrell Ingham), 306 (Ezra Shaw), 312 (Racing One)

SPEED TV/John Kringas: 39, 172, 310

Mark Rebilas: 6–7, 44–45

PA/AP Photos: 9 (Darron Cummings), 20 (Jeff Siner), 32 (Jed Leicester), 80–81 (John Russell), 144–45 (Scott Anderson), 191 (Glenn Smith), 308 (L.M. Otero)

Phil Ryder: 120, 214(r)

Rachel Tinney & Shaun Osbon: 109(r), 158, 201, 283,

Reuters: 154–55 (Jacob Silberberg), 173 (Mark Wallheiser), 313 (Mark Wallheiser), 316–17 (Matthew Stockman)

Russ Lake: 30–31, 46, 90–91, 98–99, 124–25, 131, 138, 142, 163, 194, 197, 206, 214(l), 216–18, 224–26, 232–34, 238, 241, 280, 281(r), 293–97, 300–01

Sam Sharpe/www.TheSharpeImage.com: 10–15, 21, 26–28, 34–35, 54–55, 63(l), 64, 65(l), 74–75, 80–81, 103(l), 104–05, 114, 117(r), 118–119, 122, 128, 133–37, 141, 143, 147–52, 157, 160–61, 169–70, 174–79, 181–89, 192–93, 195, 198, 200, 202–05, 211–13, 215, 219, 221, 227–31, 235–37, 252–63, 266–68, 272, 276–79, 281(l), 282, 284–87, 292, 298–99, 309, 311, 315

Tom Kirkland Archive/Smyle Media: 19

First published 2009
Copyright © dakini Ventures Ltd

dakini ventures

All rights reserved. No part of this publication may be reproduced, stored or transmitted, in any form or by any means, without the prior permission of dakini Ventures Ltd.

Production by dakini books NP

dakini is an award-winning and innovative London-based publisher specializing in books of exceptional quality on sport, the environment, popular culture and design. The products we create in partnership with companies, international institutions, governments and individuals are critically acclaimed and generate a great deal of publicity. Our celebrated title, *Speed Addicts: Grand Prix Racing* is also available to purchase through SPEEDtv.com

211–212 Piccadilly
London W1J 9HG

T +44 (0) 20 7830 9692
F +44 (0) 20 7830 9693

www.dakinibooks.com

Publisher
Lucky Dissanayake

Author
Godwin Kelly

Sub-Editor
Ken Willis

Project Co-ordinator
Jo Grummitt

Research Support
Julia Zumstein & Gemma Grass-Orkin

Design
Mark Jones, mj@poisedesign.co.uk

Reproduction
Richard Deal at dpm

Advisory Board
Gregg Leary, Don Smyle, Buz McKim, Larry Bradley, Bob Reuschle

With special thanks to Hunter Nickell

SPEED and the SPEED logo are trademarks of Speed Channel, Inc

All rights reserved

A CIP catalogue record of this book is available from the British Library

ISBN 978 0 9552615 1 0

Printed and bound in the UK by Butler Tanner & Dennis

FSC Mixed Sources
Product group from well-managed forests and other controlled sources
www.fsc.org Cert no. SGS-COC-005091
© 1996 Forest Stewardship Council

Printed on Fedrigoni Freelife Satin paper

The carbon emitted during the production of this book has been offset